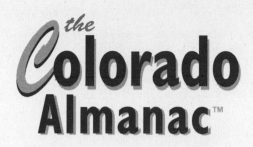
the
Colorado
Almanac™

Facts About Colorado

1st Edition

Thomas J. Noel

WestWinds Press®

✳

First edition published 2001

ISBN 0-55868-598-7
ISSN 1534-9462

Key title: The Colorado Almanac

✳

WestWinds Press®
An imprint of Graphic Arts Center Publishing Company
P.O. Box 10306, Portland, Oregon 97296-0306, 503-226-2402; www.gacpc.com

President/Publisher: Charles M. Hopkins
Associate Publisher: Douglas A. Pfeiffer
Editorial staff: Timothy W. Frew, Ellen Harkins Wheat, Tricia Brown, Jean Andrews, Kathy
    Matthews, Jean Bond-Slaughter
Production staff: Richard L. Owsiany, Susan Dupere
Editor: Don Graydon
Cover designer: Paulette Livers Lambert
Page Composition: William H. Brunson Typography Services
Maps: Gray Mouse Graphics

Printed in the United States of America

To Our Readers

WestWinds Press® is proud to release the first edition of The Colorado Almanac™, another in a series of state fact almanacs by WestWinds Press® and its sister imprint, Alaska Northwest Books™. Look for our other almanacs covering everything you need to know about Alaska, Arizona, Oregon and Washington. The Colorado Almanac™ was written by Thomas J. Noel, a.k.a. Dr. Colorado, a welcome addition to our stable of expert writers and editors. With 25 other books on Colorado to his name, Tom Noel is a respected historian and professor who leavens the facts with wit and humor. ✳

Contents

Acknowledgments

Fernie Baca and the University of Colorado at Denver contributed financial aid and staff support, as did Chair Myra Rich and my colleagues in the history department.

Thanks also to Bill Bessesen, Hugh Bingham, Judge Larry Bohning, lobbyist Leo Boyle, Eileen Sullivan Brozna, Chuck Cannon and Denver International Airport, Colorado Ski Country USA, Bill Coors and the brewery crew, Alan Culpin, Dennis Gallagher, Steven Hall and Colorado State Parks, Andrew Hudson and John Gray of the Denver Mayor's Office, Cameron Lewis and the Colorado Department of Wildlife, and Martin Lockley and CU-Denver's Dinosaur Museum.

Also my appreciation to Tom Hembourg and the Colorado Geological Survey staff, Don Koch, Terry Kettelsen and the Colorado State Archives, Jim Krebs of Krebs Uptown Photography, and manager Jim Kroll and the people at Denver Public Library's Western History Department, especially Bruce Hansen, Phil Panum, Lori Swingle, Jennifer Tom and Barbara Walton.

Another tip of the hat to the Colorado Historical Society, especially Dale Heckendorn, Debbie Neiswonger, Eric Paddock and Mark Wolf. Thanks also to Steve Leonard, Jack Murphy and the Denver Museum of Nature and Science, Grace Noel, Julia Noel, Max Noel, Vi Noel, Duane A. Smith, Ryan Struthers, Wayne Sundberg, Thomas E. Ward, and James Whiteside. Thanks, too, to Graphic Arts' Tricia Brown, Ellen Wheat, editor Don Graydon and the Graphic Arts team who turned all this data into a book.

Special thanks to my CU-Denver students who teach me and generously helped research, write and edit this book: Gail Beazon, Jamie Field, Barbara Gibson, Steve Hart, Pam Holtman, Natalie Hook, Ann Jones, Suzie Morton, Don Walker, and chief collaborator Chuck Hanson. Finally, thanks to you, dear reader. Please let us know how we can improve the next edition.

Colorado. Rare Colorado. Yonder she rests:
Her head of gold pillowed on the Rocky Mountains,
Her breast a shield of silver, her feet in the brown grass,
The boundless plains for a playground.
She is set on a hill before the world.
The air is very clear, that you may see her well.
She is naked as a newborn babe; naked but not ashamed.

—Joaquin Miller

Fast Facts About Colorado

Entered the Union: *Aug. 1, 1876 (38th state).*

Nickname: *Centennial State, because it was admitted to the Union during the centennial year of the Declaration of Independence. (Also often called the Highest State, a term currently out of favor because of an association with drugs and alcohol.)*

Native nickname: *The Utes called it "the land of the long look."*

Motto: Nil Sine Numine *(Nothing without Providence).*

Capital: *Denver.*

Size: *104,247 square miles (eighth-largest state); 276 miles north to south and 387 miles east to west.*

Population: *4.3 million.*

Ethnic makeup: *White 76.7 percent; Hispanic 17.1 percent; African American 3.8 percent; Asian and Pacific Islander 2.3 percent; Native American 1 percent.*

Population growth: *Third-fastest-growing state in the 1990s (after Nevada and Arizona).*

Fastest growing county: *Douglas County; from 60,391 residents in 1990 to 175,766 in 2000.*

Fastest growing town: *Superior; from 276 residents in 1990 to 7,399 in 2000.*

Largest city in population: *Denver, 554,636.*

Smallest town in population: *Lakeside, 11.*

Largest county in population: *Denver County; 554,636.*

Smallest county in population: *San Juan; 558.*

Largest county in area: *Las Animas; 4,798 square miles.*

Smallest county in area: *Gilpin; 149 square miles.*

Oldest town: *San Luis (1851).*

Newest town: *Centennial (2001).*

Personal income: *Per capita (1999), $30,947.*

Inventions: *The cheeseburger (by Louis Ballast, Humpty Dumpty Drive In, Denver, 1931); the Denver Boot (to immobilize a car until a parking fine is paid).*

Highest temperature: *118°F at Bennett, Adams County, on July 11, 1888.*

Lowest temperature: *−61°F at Maybell, Moffat County, on Feb. 2, 1985.*

Highest 24-hour precipitation in Denver: *6.5 inches of rain, May 22, 1876.*

Highest one-year precipitation in Denver: *23 inches (1908 and 1974).*

Lowest one-year precipitation in Denver: *6 inches (1955).*

Highest snowfall: *838 inches at Wolf Creek Pass (winter of 1978–1979).*

Highest point: *Mount Elbert, at 14,433 feet.*

Lowest point: *The town of Holly, at 3,397 feet.*

Mean elevation: *6,800 feet.*

Nation's highest paved road: *Mount Evans, 14,264 feet.*

Nation's highest yacht club: *Lake Dillon, 9,017 feet.*

Nation's highest community: *Alma, 10,355 feet.*

Nation's highest incorporated city: *Leadville, 10,152 feet.*

Nation's highest suspension bridge: *Royal Gorge Bridge, 1,053 feet above the Arkansas River.*

North America's most popular ski area: *Vail.*

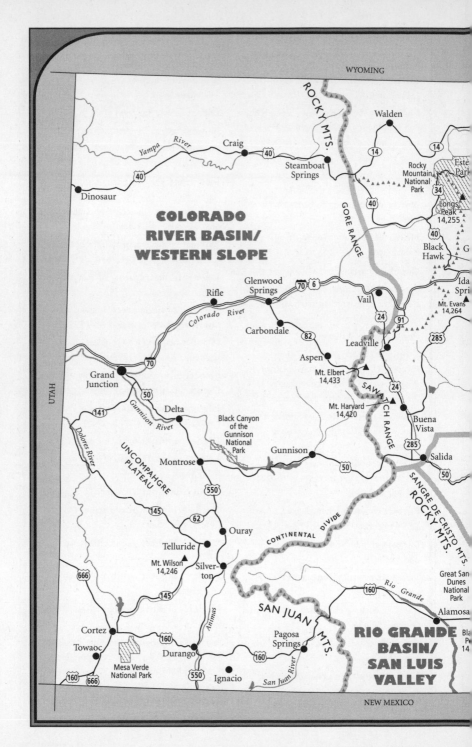

COLORADO RIVER BASIN/ WESTERN SLOPE

RIO GRANDE BASIN/ SAN LUIS VALLEY

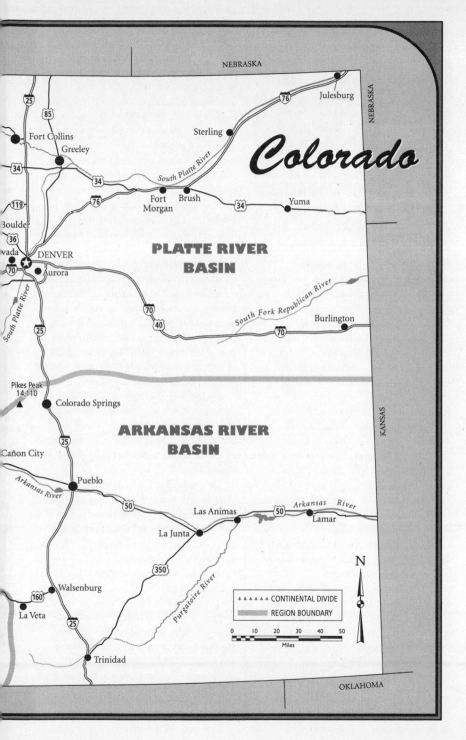

Colorado

NEBRASKA

NEBRASKA

KANSAS

OKLAHOMA

Julesburg

Sterling

Fort Collins

Greeley

Fort Morgan

Brush

Yuma

Boulder

vada

DENVER

Aurora

PLATTE RIVER BASIN

South Platte River

South Fork Republican River

Burlington

South Platte River

Pikes Peak 14,110

Colorado Springs

ARKANSAS RIVER BASIN

Cañon City

Pueblo

Arkansas River

Las Animas

La Junta

Arkansas River

Lamar

Walsenburg

La Veta

Purgatoire River

Trinidad

N

▲▲▲▲▲▲ CONTINENTAL DIVIDE
▬▬▬▬ REGION BOUNDARY

0   10   20   30   40   50
Miles

Wellington Webb is Denver's first African American mayor. Denver Mayor's Office.

African Americans

(SEE ALSO BROWN, AUNT CLARA; FORD, BARNEY; FORD, JUSTINA) African Americans have played active roles and achieved prominence in Colorado. James P. Beckwourth, a mulatto mountain man prominent in pioneer Pueblo and Denver, tried to prevent the slaughter of his Indian friends at the Sand Creek Massacre (see entry) in 1864. African American males arrived in Colorado Territory as miners, cowboys, railroad workers and U.S. Army "buffalo soldiers," as Indians called blacks after examining their thick, curly hair.

Frederick Douglass Jr., son of the famed abolitionist, along with Barney Ford and others, helped delay federal approval of Colorado statehood until after black male suffrage became Colorado law in 1867. Colorado's relatively small, prosperous and articulate black community also fought for integrated schools, which were guaranteed by the 1876 state constitution.

Colorado's black population grew from fewer than 500 in 1870 to some 12,000 by 1890. That year Denver had three African American churches, various businesses (including a black newspaper, *The Denver Star*) and, according to the *Denver Republican* of March 17, 1890, "proportionately more colored home owners than any other northern city."

A national trend toward ghettoizing blacks led to greater discrimination against these Coloradans in the early 1900s. Property deeds in Denver and elsewhere began to prohibit the sale or lease of homes in many neighborhoods to "persons of color." In one of the worst instances of violence against blacks, John Preston Porter Jr. was burned to death Nov. 16, 1900, at Lake Station near Limon. The state's only antiblack race riot occurred in Denver in August of 1932, when civil rights activists, including 150 blacks, tried to integrate the bathing beach at Washington Park. Whites drove the demonstrators away with sticks and stones, beating some. The police arrested 17 people—10 blacks, and 7 whites who had encouraged blacks to assert their rights.

While most Colorado blacks lived in Denver, Colorado Springs or Pueblo, a few bold and enterprising individuals lived in smaller communities. Dearfield, 27 miles east of Greeley in Weld County, was created in 1911 as Colorado's only African American colony. Founder Oliver T. Jackson's niece, Jennie Jackson, operated the lunch counter there until 1953, when she became the last colonist to leave. Like many farming communities, Dearfield failed in the face of the economic realities of high-plains agriculture.

Colorado's black population of 39,992 in 1960 lived primarily in black neighborhoods. With the civil rights movement and federal laws of the 1960s, many blacks were able to move out of such prescribed neighborhoods as Denver's Five Points.

Although Colorado schools had initially been integrated, the federal courts held that the Denver Public Schools were pursuing a de facto segregation policy and ordered busing to achieve racial balance in 1969. Despite much ill will, minor scuffles and an exodus of many white families with children to suburbs, busing helped to integrate schools until federal courts allowed Denver to drop this plan in 1998.

Denver's blacks provided statewide leadership, including George Brown, whose 1978 election as lieutenant governor made him the first black to be elected statewide. In 1991, Wellington Edward Webb became Denver's first black mayor and was twice reelected by large margins in a city where only one resident in seven is African American. In 1999, Coloradans elected Joe Rogers, a black attorney, as lieutenant governor.

Colorado's black population is better educated, paid and housed than that of many states. Prominent black leaders have gained respect and often equality, thus attracting new black residents. Between 1980 and 2000, the number of blacks in Colorado grew from about 102,000 to 165,000, up from 3.5 percent to 3.8 percent of the total state population. Denver, which long was home to two-thirds of the state's blacks, now has less than half of a much more widely distributed African American population.

Agriculture (See also

Economy) Colorado ranks 18th in the nation among all states in total agricultural sales, including both crops and livestock. It leads the nation in millet production; ranks third in carrots, lettuce, and market sheep and lambs; fourth in dry beans, onions, spinach and sunflowers; and fifth in potatoes, cattle, winter wheat and wool. Two-thirds of Colorado's $800 million annual net return in agricultural sales is for livestock, the other third for crops.

Livestock. The presence of vast bison herds convinced pioneer settlers that Colorado could be a haven for grazing animals. Hispanic settlers successfully raised horses, cattle, sheep, hogs and chickens in the San Luis Valley of southern Colorado. With the mass migration of the gold rush, livestock became a large industry.

Some pioneer Euro-Americans, lacking barns and hay, left their cattle and horses outdoors in winter. The animals grew fat on the grama and buffalo grasses. This natural winter pasture led many to take up ranching, and they found ready markets among the hordes of hungry miners and railroad workers.

Rancher John Wesley Iliff built a huge cattle kingdom on the South Platte River during the 1870s, while John W. Prowers became a cattle baron in the Arkansas River Valley. Iliff got his start buying footsore and crippled cattle from immigrants. He later bought wild longhorns driven up from Texas by cattlemen such as Charles Goodnight, who in 1868, along with his partner Oliver Loving, established the Goodnight-Loving Cattle Trail along the Front Range, roughly parallel to today's Interstate 25.

The Colorado Stock Growers Association, formed in 1867 to register brands and control rustling, established the Denver Union Stockyards in 1886. At the stockyards, huge packing houses prepared Colorado beef for transport in refrigerated railcars to markets nationwide. Fresh, inexpensive beef changed the American diet to steak and hamburgers.

Cattlemen dominated the Colorado plains until the 1880s when farmers began moving in and opposing open-range cattle drives because the cattle ate and trampled their crops. An 1885 federal law and farmers' barbed wire fences forced cattlemen to settle down on ranches, but many continued to drive herds to high-country pasture every summer. To celebrate the livestock industry, and to

provide an auction, exhibitions, rodeo and trade show, Denver inaugurated its annual National Western Stock Show in 1905.

After blizzards in 1885–1886 decimated the cattle industry, sheep became more important. Between 1900 and 1950, Colorado had more sheep than cattle. By 2000, 3.2 million cattle far outnumbered the 440,000 sheep, but 4.5 million chickens outnumbered all other Colorado livestock, with 910,000 hogs and pigs holding third place.

Low cattle prices in the 1990s led many ranchers to sell out to developers or to gentleman farmers seeking rural retreats and tax breaks. In today's depressed livestock markets, one of the few bright spots is the emergence of the huge hog farms that are economically reviving several Colorado plains towns such as Yuma.

Crops. Crops have been grown in Colorado since Native Americans began cultivating corn, squash and beans some 2,000 years ago. Not only the Anasazi in southwestern Colorado, but also the Apache on the Arkansas River in southeastern Colorado, established prosperous, long-lived agricultural villages.

With the 1858–1859 gold rush, the tremendous expense of importing food inspired crop-raising in the area that explorer Stephen H. Long had branded the "Great American Desert." In the San Luis Valley of southern Colorado, Mexican Americans used irrigation to grow lettuce, potatoes, peas, onions, wheat and other crops. During the 1850s, grain mills in the San Luis Valley provided wheat and corn meal to the mining regions. During the gold rush, farmers like Denver's Rufus "Potato" Clark and Pueblo's Joe Doyle capitalized on tremendously inflated food prices.

Wheat proved difficult to grow in Colorado as drought and hail often devastated the crop. Farmers learned to cultivate winter wheat, allowing snows to nourish plants harvested in early summer before drought time.

Settlers needing nourishment for their livestock promoted a large feed-grain industry. Hay, grown throughout Colorado, became the most common crop by 1900. Other livestock feed included alfalfa, barley, corn, oats and rye. Hay, be it clover, field peas, grasses, timothy or wild hay, cures quickly in Colorado's dry climate. Many ranchers got their start by providing hay for livestock in cities and mining towns. Potatoes, a mainstay in the San Luis Valley and other higher, cooler regions, became a major crop by 1900.

Colorado's most important crop during much of the 1900s was sugar beets. Three giant firms—Great Western, Holly and National—transformed the South Platte and Arkansas Valleys into beet kingdoms. During the 1920s, sugar beets replaced wheat as Colorado's No. 1 crop. Colorado led the nation in beet-sugar production until the industry turned sour in the 1960s.

Other Colorado specialty crops include asparagus, barley, beans, carrots, celery, corn, lettuce, mushrooms, onions,

Six tons of hay are delivered by Longmont farmer David Boswick, in this photo from the old days of Colorado agriculture. Longmont Museum.

pinto beans, squash and tomatoes. Fruit growers produce apples, cherries, peaches, pears, plums, strawberries and raspberries. Fruit growing has been most productive in the Colorado River Valley around Grand Junction, Fruita and Palisade. The Arkansas Valley is famous for its cantaloupes and honeydew melons.

Firms such as D. V. Burrell Seed Co., founded in Rocky Ford in the 1860s, made the Arkansas Valley a major source of flower and fruit seeds. Colorado floriculturists, specializing in carnations and roses, thrived after World War II, but have faded in recent decades due to foreign competition and the high cost of heating greenhouses.

Colorado's Top Agricultural Products (2000)

Cattle and calves	3.2 million head
Corn, grain	159 million bushels
Wheat	107 million bushels
Dairy	1.7 billion pounds
Hay	4.6 million tons
Greenhouse/nursery	(not available)
Hogs	910,000 head
Chickens	4.5 million animals
Potatoes	28 million pounds
Sheep	440,000 head

Source: Colorado Department of Agricultural Statistics; www.nass.usda.gov/co.

Irrigated farming greatly expanded agricultural production. Dryland farming also flourished, especially on the eastern plains. Between 1890 and 1917, cultivated acres grew from 4.6 million to 23.7 million. After slumping during the Depression and dust storms of the 1930s, farm acreage climbed to 40 million during the 1950s. Recent development of high-volume pumps and center-pivot irrigation have triggered a new boom in irrigated farming. Yet the collapse of sugar beet farming and low prices for wheat have kept those two once-leading industries in decline.

To learn more
Colorado Department of Agricultural Statistics, 645 Parfet St., Lakewood 80215; (800) 392-3202, (303) 236-2300; www.nass.usda.gov/co.

Agricultural history exhibits are offered at the Plains Conservation Center (in Aurora), Littleton History Museum (Littleton), Cross Orchards (Grand Junction) and Pioneer Town (Cedaredge).

Air Force Academy

(SEE ALSO MILITARY) On a scenic 18,500-acre site 9 miles north of Colorado Springs sits the national college for the U.S. Air Force. Congress created this counterpart of West Point and Annapolis in 1954; Colorado Springs captured it by offering a spectacular site blending rolling prairie with ponderosa-clad foothills. Skidmore, Owings and Merrill, the Chicago firm noted for skyscrapers, won the design competition, beating out rivals such as Frank Lloyd Wright, who called Skidmore's stark, angular steel, aluminum and glass campus a "factory for birdmen."

Cadets at Attention

The Air Force Academy is a child of the Cold War with its glass and aluminum-clad rectangles connected by vast expanses of concrete. The Spartan box buildings include windowless classrooms with desks designed to force cadets to sit alertly on the front edge, maintaining perfect posture.

Landscape architect Dan Kiley designed an Air Garden for the terrazzo-level plaza and parade grounds, but the Air Force ripped out the trees and shrubs and cemented over the water ponds. That soft, peaceful, green refuge just did not fit in with this hard-edged military school. However, native evergreens, shrubs and grasses do provide natural landscaping. ✤

The campus opened in 1958 to train cadets, later including growing numbers of women, as future Air Force officers. From the Barry Goldwater Visitor Center (1961), a half-mile nature trail leads to the soaring Academy Chapel, whose shape has been compared to folded wings or praying fingers. The chapel's 17 spires consist of tetrahedral frames made of aluminum-clad steel pipe and fitted with stained-glass panels. It's Colorado's most visited church. The Academy also welcomes visitors to its 150-seat planetarium. However, much of the campus is off-limits.

To learn more: Free tours daily, 9 A.M.–5 P.M., start at the Goldwater Visitor Center, 2346 Academy Drive via North Entrance Road, I-25 exit 156. USAF Academy 80840; (719) 333-9400.

Airports (SEE ALSO AVIATION AND AEROSPACE; DENVER INTERNATIONAL AIRPORT)

Coloradans welcomed aviation early in the 20th century as a fast, direct way to conquer the many geographical obstacles in the mountain state. Communities endeavored to construct airports just as they had once built depots to capture railroad service.

Denver's first "aerodrome" opened in 1910. Eleven years later, the Curtis-Humphreys Airplane Co. launched Colorado's first commercial passenger service from its Denver aerodrome to Cheyenne, Wyoming, Estes Park, and the Broadmoor Hotel in Colorado Springs. Denver had at least nine different private airports before Denver Municipal Airport opened in 1929 to consolidate most air activity.

By 1930, Colorado had 27 airfields and landing strips, ranging from the American Legion field in Akron to the original Lowry Army Air Corps Field in Denver. Following World War II, Colorado Springs, Pueblo and La Junta bought local army air bases, which they converted to municipal airports. By 1960, 12 cities offered regularly scheduled public flights, and 32 others provided on-call private aviation.

During the 1980s, when the Federal Aviation Administration deregulated airlines, carriers abandoned less-profitable rural routes. Although commuter airlines picked up some of the routes, regularly scheduled passenger service was abandoned to Cañon City, Craig, Delta, Glenwood Springs, Grand Lake, Greeley, Fort Collins,

La Junta, Leadville, Salida and Trinidad. Many small airports deteriorated and some closed, while bigger cities such as Denver, Durango, Fort Collins–Loveland, and Grand Junction improved or built new airports.

Denver renamed its municipal airport in 1944 for its promoter, Mayor Benjamin Franklin Stapleton. By the 1980s, Stapleton International had become the world's fifth-busiest airport and Denver began building a new airport, which opened in 1995. Denver International Airport, with its 53-square-mile site, is the nation's largest airport in terms of area.

Amache Japanese Relocation Camp

After the Japanese attacked Pearl Harbor on Dec. 7, 1941, the U.S. government interned all Japanese living in California, Oregon and Washington, although many were U.S. citizens. Between 1942 and 1945, a total of 7,657 Japanese Americans from those three states were held at the Amache camp.

Named for a Cheyenne woman who married cattle baron John W. Prowers, the camp lay one mile southwest of Granada in southeastern Colorado's Arkansas River Valley. The camp sprang up in 1942 and quickly became the tenth-largest community in Colorado. The self-sufficient camp produced a surplus of crops and livestock. Internees also worked in factories and on farms, and some joined the U.S. military to help win the war. A Japanese volunteer battalion with members from Amache saw heavy combat and many fatalities in Italy.

The government closed Amache after the war ended in 1945. Only a few concrete foundations survive along with a cemetery, a Buddhist shrine and a historical marker. President Clinton introduced legislation in 2000 to designate Amache and other internment camps as National Historic Sites.

Anglo Americans

During the 19th century, English-born immigrants made up Colorado's second-largest foreign-born group, after the Germans. Railroads began crossing Colorado with considerable financial support from Britain. Dr. William A. Bell, a London society doctor, invested in the Denver & Rio Grande Railroad and promoted it among his patients. His son, Dr. William A. Bell Jr., became so intrigued with this narrow gauge "toy" railroad that he came to America, where he became the railroad's vice-president.

Bell and the English-backed D&RG made Colorado Springs (see entry) a favorite haven for British tourists and immigrants. "Little London," as locals dubbed the city 60 miles south of Denver, boasted cricket and polo games, clubs and pubs and Anglican churches, as well as Tudor Style mansions such as Briarhurst and Glen Eyrie. Residents sipped tea, enjoyed crumpets and marmalade and strolled about with umbrellas. The Broadmoor Hotel's Golden Bee Pub, a transplanted 19th-century haven, remains the finest of Colorado's English-style pubs.

Colorado ranching also appealed to the English, who had no trouble imagining the rewards of roast beef, milk and fresh cream. The Scottish investor James Duff steered English investors into the Colorado Ranch Co. and other agricultural schemes.

By the 1880s, the St. George's Association and the Albion Club were

Looking Back

June 24, 1870

A train of the Denver Pacific Railway became the first in history to chug into Denver.

organizing cricket matches in Denver. Englishmen also belonged to the Denver Club, the Denver Athletic Club, the University Club and the Denver Country Club—all exclusive enclaves imitative of Britain's private clubs.

Although Englishman G. W. Stevens pronounced the Queen City of the Plains "more plain than queenly," he and his countrymen did much to transform the raw western crossroads of Denver into a handsome and prosperous metropolis with solid Victorian churches, office buildings, hotels, clubs, and mansions. Unlike Colorado Springs, Denver did not call itself Little London. Yet visitors staying at the Brown Palace, Oxford and Windsor hotels, admiring St. John's Episcopal Cathedral and touring Capitol Hill's elegant English-style mansions might conclude that the English set Colorado's standards.

The English connection remains strong today. Establishment of an English consulate in Denver and direct Denver-to-London British Airway flights in 1998 further cemented Colorado's ties with the Brits.

Animals Colorado's wide variety

of terrain and vast amount of unsettled land make it a haven for animals and animal watchers. The total of more than 900 animal species in the state makes it possible to spot wild creatures even in urban environments, with their growing coyote, fox, elk, deer, wildcat and raptor populations.

See the following separate entries in this book: Antelope; Bears; Bighorn Mountain Sheep; Buffalo; Burros; Cats; Coyotes; Dinosaurs; Eagles; Elk; Fish; Jackalopes; Jackrabbits; Lark Bunting; Magpies; Marmots; Mule Deer; Mules; Pikas; Prairie Chickens; Prairie Dogs; Ptarmigan.

Antelope At a top speed of

70 mph, antelope (*Antilocapra americana*)

Pronghorn. From *The Great Rocky Mountain Nature Factbook;* illustration by Marjorie C. Leggitt.

are the fastest Colorado land animal. Properly called pronghorn, these reddish brown to tan, gazelle-like creatures have short, sharp, pronged horns and white markings, especially on the rump. Adult pronghorn stand about three feet high at the shoulder. Males weigh up to 150 pounds, females up to 100 pounds. Pronghorn generally travel in herds, grazing on prairie grasses and other plants on the high plains, the central mountain parks, and the canyonlands of western Colorado.

Pronghorn are noted for their keen eyesight and preference for open spaces with broad visibility, yet they possess a curiosity that hunters use to lure them to their deaths. The estimated two million antelope that inhabited Colorado in 1800 were hunted almost to extinction. Protected from 1905 to 1945, they are once again fair game in 34 of Colorado's 63 counties. Predators, besides humans, include coyotes, bobcats, bald eagles and golden eagles, giving pronghorn a life expectancy of less than 10 years.

Archaeology (SEE ALSO

HISTORY; NATIONAL PARKS; ROCK ART) Colorado's well-documented human prehistory begins with the Clovis Culture (about 11,000–9,000 B.C.), named for projectile points discovered in 1936 near Clovis, N.M.

George McJunkin, an African American cowboy, made another key discovery during the 1920s while working on a ranch just south of the Colorado border near Folsom, N.M. The prehistoric bison bones that McJunkin unearthed prompted an investigation by Jesse D. Figgins, director of the Colorado Museum of Natural History (now Denver Museum of Nature and Science). Figgins found stone projectile points embedded between the bison ribs, evidence that Folsom People hunted in the area around 9,000–8,000 B.C.

Jesuit priest Conrad Bilgery and some of his Regis College students made a major discovery at Dent, Colo., in 1932. Assisted by Figgins, Father Bilgery found Clovis projectile points amid bones of mammoths.

Lindenmeier Ranch, Colorado's most important Folsom site, was a camp and kill site in Larimer County, unearthed in 1924. Archaeological teams from the Smithsonian Institution and the Colorado Museum of Natural History found stone scrapers, knives and projectile points as well as bone needles, beads and engraved bones possibly used as gambling devices or jewelry.

Among Colorado's places of archaeological interest are:

Anasazi Heritage Center. This Bureau of Land Management museum houses two million records and artifacts and offers tours of the 12th-century Dominguez and Escalante sites. Open 9 A.M.–4 P.M. daily; $2. 27501 Highway 184, Dolores 81323; (970) 259-2402; www.co.blm.gov/ahc.

Chapin Mesa Archaeological Museum, Mesa Verde National Park. Open daily 8 A.M.–5 P.M.; $10 per car. Milepost 20, Ruins Road; (970) 529-4465; www.nps.gov/meve.

Chimney Rock Archaeological Area. U.S. Forest Service rangers lead tours of the site that was home to as many as 2,000 Anasazi Indians, who left a 35-room great house, great kiva and some 200 structures. Open daily 9 A.M.–4 P.M. May 15–Sept. 30; tours $2–$5. 3179 Highway 151, 17 miles west of Pagosa Springs; (970) 264-2268; www.chimneyrockco.org.

The Cortez Center, University of Colorado. Open Mon.–Sat., 10 A.M.–10 P.M. summer, 10 A.M.–5 P.M. winter; free admission. 25 N. Market St., Cortez 81321; (970) 565-1151.

Crow Canyon Archaeological Center. Offers courses and other chances to dig archaeology. 23390 County Road K, Cortez 81321; (800) 422-8975, (970) 565-8975; www.crowcanyon.org

Ute Mountain Ute Tribal Park. Ute Indians conduct tours of historic and prehistoric sites. Towaoc 81334; (970) 565-3751, (970) 565-4684.

To learn more

The state archaeologist tracks more than 67,000 recorded archaeological finds in Colorado. Colorado History Museum, 1300 Broadway, Denver 80202; (303) 866-3682.

Colorado Archaeological Society sponsors lectures and tours and publishes *Southwestern Lore* magazine; (970) 407-1927; www.coloradoarchaeology.org.

Architecture (SEE ALSO

HISTORICAL PRESERVATION) The greatest surviving Native American architectural

Frank Edbrooke, Colorado's leading 19th-century architect. 1907 illustration by Dr. Bird Finch. Tom Noel Collection.

achievements in the United States are the prehistoric cliff dwellings, pueblos and pit houses at Mesa Verde National Park.

Historic Colorado Indians, such as the Arapaho, Cheyenne and Utes, left less to inspect—caves, rock shelters, pit houses, earth lodges, eagle traps and fortifications. These tribes often used a portable architecture of buffalo hides and pine poles. Only a few tipi rings—either functional or ceremonial—survive as stone circles in remote sites near Cowdrey in Jackson County, Keota in Weld County, Virginia Dale in Larimer County and on upper Dominguez Creek in Mesa County.

During the 1830s and 1840s, the largest and most important edifice in southeastern Colorado was Bent's Fort (see entry) on the Arkansas River, an adobe trading post built by Charles and William Bent, two St. Louis traders operating on the Santa Fe Trail. (The fort was reconstructed by the National Park Service in 1976 with adobe by skilled Hispanic laborers.) Hispanics built adobe towns in the San Luis Valley as early as 1851 that survive yet today. Adobe churches at Conejos and San Acacia also date from the 1850s.

Fortune seekers rushing into Colorado after the 1858–1859 gold strikes tended to build as quickly and cheaply as possible. They used canvas, dirt and logs from cottonwoods, the only common native tree on the eastern plains. Cottonwood log walls were covered with cottonwood ridgepoles and split saplings, and often roofed with sod.

During the flush times between 1870 and the silver crash of 1893, Colorado experienced a rush to respectability. Mining-era structures were replaced by grander edifices in Italianate, Queen Anne, Romanesque and other fashionable modes. Leadville's silver king, Horace A. W. Tabor, brought brothers Willoughby and Frank Edbrooke from Chicago to Denver in 1879 to design the Tabor Grand Opera House (see Opera Houses).

Frank Edbrooke stayed to become Colorado's premier 19th-century architect, leaving such monuments as the state Capitol and the Brown Palace Hotel. Edbrooke and notable architects such as William Lang and Robert Roeschlaub gave Colorado stylish structures of locally manufactured brick and locally quarried sandstone, rhyolite, limestone, marble and granite.

After 1900, the architecture of Native Americans and Hispanics gained greater respectability. Pueblo Revival, Hispanic, Mission, Spanish Colonial and Spanish Territorial styles became the choice for some of the state's finest residential neighborhoods, such as the Broadmoor area in Colorado Springs and Denver's Country Club District.

Coloradans took to indulging tourists with rustic log structures adorned with stone fireplaces and Stick Style trim and furniture. Many fading mining towns and ranches survived by courting tourists and capitalizing on the early 20th-century conservation movement and America's romance with the great outdoors.

Switzerland, the world's 19th-century pacesetter in tourist promotion, became a model. Estes Park and Ouray began puffing themselves as the "Switzerland of America." Shops, hotels, cafes, summer homes and public structures began wearing the Alpine style, with its steep roofs over white stucco and half-timbered walls with window flower boxes. Vail and other mountain resort towns have since moved beyond ersatz Swiss styles to showcase some of Colorado's best modern and postmodern architecture.

Dr. Colorado's List of Impressive Structures

- Cliff Palace, Mesa Verde
- Red Rocks Amphitheater, Morrison
- National Center for Atmospheric Research, Boulder
- Colorado Springs Fine Arts Museum
- Air Force Academy, Colorado Springs
- Mayan Theater, Denver
- Lace House Miners Cabin, Black Hawk
- Denver International Airport
- Denver Public Library
- Coney Island Diner, Conifer

Archives
The Colorado State Archives collects, preserves and makes available records of the state executive, legislative and judicial branches. It is also the depository for many older records from local governments, and contains county, municipal, school district and other governmental documents. Location of the State Archives is 1313 Sherman St., Denver; (303) 866-2055.

A branch of the National Archives and Records Administration is in the Denver Federal Center, Building 48, in Lakewood, a Denver suburb; (303) 236-0801.

The University of Colorado, Colorado State University, the University of Denver and other institutions of higher education house their own archives and special collections.

Area Codes
Colorado uses four telephone area codes. The Denver metropolitan area has two area codes— 303 and 720—that serve the same region, so local calls within that region require the use of 10 numbers. The 719 area code serves southern and eastern Colorado; the 970 area code covers northern and western Colorado.

Art and Music (SEE ALSO CALENDAR OF EVENTS; EVANS, ANNE; OPERA HOUSES; RADIO STATIONS; ROCK ART)
A rich tradition of Native American and Hispanic art has given Colorado a colorful arts scene that has become particularly vibrant since the 1970s. The state of Colorado in 1976 inaugurated an Art in Public Places program requiring that 1 percent of the construction cost of any state-funded building be set aside for permanent art displayed on the site. This funding has allowed more than 350 artworks from some 160 Colorado artists to be installed (at a cost of more than $4 million).

Denver Mayor Wellington E. Webb and his wife, Wilma, made art a major thrust of his administration throughout the 1990s and into the new century. In 1991, Webb created the Mayor's Office of Art, Culture and Film. Denver has installed 87 works of art at a cost of $16 million in the 1 percent for art program enacted in 1991 as one of

Webb's first city ordinances, and more than 140 other public artworks were in progress. The city's cable television channel 8 has become a voice for discussing a full spectrum of artistic endeavors. In 2001, Americans for the Arts named Webb as

The gold-seekers of 1859 came to Colorado to "see the elephant," a slang term of the day for chasing unlikely dreams. They discovered that gold often was as hard to find as elephants.

the U.S. mayor who has done the most to champion the arts.

In 1985, Loveland became the first Colorado city to require that 1 percent of municipal capital construction funds be earmarked for public art. The program has helped this city of more than 50,000 residents transform Benson Park into Colorado's best sculpture garden. Since 1983, Loveland has sponsored "Sculpture in the Park," one of the largest such shows in the nation. The 1972 transformation of an industrial foundry in Loveland into Art Castings of Colorado eventually attracted prominent sculptors to Colorado, including Ed Dwight, George Lundeen, Dan Ostermiller, Susan Grant Raymond, Ed Rose and Fritz White.

Colorado communities such as Arvada, Aurora, Denver, Fort Collins, Greeley and Longmont have adopted similar programs. Boulder boasts one of Colorado's few museums of contemporary art, complete with a performing arts capacity. Delta has made itself the city of murals by encouraging depictions of local history and local products on downtown buildings.

Breckenridge sponsors an international ice sculpture contest. The Art on the Corner program in Grand Junction installs some 70 sculptures for display each May.

Statewide, outstanding art institutions include the Aspen Art Museum, the Colorado Springs Fine Arts Museum, the Denver Art Museum, Fort Collins' Lincoln Center Art Museum, Grand Junction's Western Colorado Center for the Arts, and Pueblo's Sangre de Cristo Arts Center. The Denver Art Museum has a fine Native American collection, while the Colorado Springs Fine Arts Museum specializes in Hispanic folk art.

Standouts among performing arts venues include Denver's Center for the Performing Arts, home to the Colorado Symphony Orchestra, Opera Colorado, the Colorado Ballet and a variety of theaters. The Central City Opera House, a granite gem constructed in 1878, has been restored for summer opera, as has the Wheeler Opera House in Aspen. The Aspen Music Festival was the first, and remains the foremost, of a growing number of music festivals in mountain towns including Boulder, Breckenridge, Beaver Creek, Steamboat Springs, Telluride, Winter Park and Vail. Jazz, bluegrass and dance festivals are also popular.

To learn more: The Colorado Council on the Arts sponsors Art in Public Places (303-894-2618), community programs (303-894-2670), arts organization programs (303-894-2673), individual artist programs (303-894-2619) and the Artists in Residence program (303-894-2670).

Arvada
Town founders Benjamin Franklin and Mary Wadsworth named this Jefferson County town after her brother-in-

law Hiram Arvada Haskin. For decades a farm hamlet of several hundred, it became the county's fastest-growing town after World War II.

With a population of more than 102,000, this Denver suburb is now Colorado's seventh largest city. The large, modern, multipurpose Arvada Center for the Arts and Humanities, the active Arvada Historical Society, the Arvada Pride Flour Museum and a rejuvenated downtown make this one of Denver's most distinctive, progressive suburbs.

Asian Americans

Ancient peoples crossed the prehistoric Bering Land Bridge from Asia to North America (present-day Alaska) between 40,000 and 15,000 years ago and evolved into the Indian and Eskimo groups of America today.

Chinese. The Chinese were the first Asians to come to the United States in historic times, arriving with 19th-century mining rushes and railroad construction crews. Although well-behaved and hard-working, the Chinese were often treated poorly. Central City blamed its 1874 fire on a Chinese laundry and ran all of the Chinese out of town. In Denver, Colorado's only major race riot occurred Oct. 31, 1880. Non-Asians who resented the skilled, cheap Chinese labor grew into a mob that ransacked and burned Denver's "Hop Alley." Ironically, Chinese who often ran laundries and did housekeeping or gardening were stereotyped as "dirty." Anti-Chinese sentiment in Colorado, as well as national discrimination in immigration laws, kept the Chinese population from growing in Colorado until the 1980s.

Japanese. Fewer than 100 Japanese came to Colorado before 1900, when they were recruited by labor broker Harry Hokasano to work in the sugar beet industry of the South Platte and Arkansas River valleys. By 1910 there were 2,300 Japanese men, women and children working in Colorado. Families saved money to buy their own farms or businesses. During World War II, a total of 7,657 Japanese Americans from California, Oregon and Washington were held at the Amache relocation camp (see entry). After the war, some of the Amache internees stayed in Colorado. Many headed for Denver, where a tiny Japanese settlement emerged on Larimer Street around the Tri-State Buddhist Church. That church remains the religious focus of a commercial and cultural center built in the 1980s as the modern block known as Sakura Square. Although Japanese Americans make up less than 1 percent of the Colorado population, Japan itself became a major trading partner with Colorado and in 1999 opened a consulate in Denver.

Cambodians, Hmong, Laotians and Vietnamese. Since the 1970s, a new wave of immigration from Southeast Asia has brought Cambodians, Hmong, Laotians and Vietnamese, as well as Chinese and Koreans, to Colorado. "Little Saigon" sprang up along Federal Boulevard in Southwest Denver and "Little Korea" along East Colfax Avenue in Aurora.

Aspen is a center for snow sports and skiing competitions. From Ski the Rockies; *photo by Marc Muench.*

aspen because the leaves flutter in the slightest breeze. Aspen grow into large thickets created by suckering roots and only rarely propagate from their seeds.

As a pioneering species, aspen are usually the first tree to reappear after evergreen forests are downed by fire or humans. They thrive anywhere between 8,000 and 10,000 feet, and as the only deciduous upland tree, nurse the evergreens that will replace them. Although aspen can grow as tall as 90 feet, they are usually much shorter. Their soft, fast-burning wood is undesirable as building material or fuel, but makes them favorite scratching posts of bears and a favorite food and construction material of beavers.

Aspen, Colorado

Silver seekers founded the Pitkin County seat after they struck pay dirt in the valley of the Roaring Fork of the Colorado River. Aspen's population peaked in 1893 at around 12,000, when it rivaled Leadville as Colorado's premier silver city. The silver crash of 1893 began a decline, with the town reaching a population low of 705 in 1930.

Since the 1950s, development of skiing, the Aspen Institute for the Humanities, the Aspen Music Festival and restoration of the town's 19th-century buildings has sparked Aspen's renaissance as Colorado's most fashionable resort. Some 6,000 locals play host to hordes of tourists during the ski and summer seasons.

Aspen Trees

The western trembling aspen (*Populus tremuloides*) is easily identified by its smooth white trunk and light-green, heart-shaped leaves, which turn bright yellow or orange in September. They are called trembling, or quaking,

---

Dr. Colorado's List of Aspen Gold for Leaf Peepers

Here are 10 top places to watch aspen turn from pale green to brilliant gold and sometimes orange. Traditionally the last week in September is the best time for leaf peeping.

- Guanella Pass between Georgetown and Grant
- Boreas Pass between Breckenridge and Como
- Tennessee Pass between Leadville and Vail
- Imogene Pass between Ouray and Telluride
- McClure Pass between Redstone and Paonia
- Cache la Poudre Canyon west of Fort Collins
- Independence Pass between Aspen and Twin Lakes
- State Hwy. 67 between Divide and Cripple Creek
- Cucharas Pass between Trinidad and Walsenburg
- Lizard Head Pass between Dolores and Telluride

Aspen trees. Photo by Susan Dupere.

Authors (SEE ALSO BOOKSTORES)

Of some 300 published Colorado-based novelists, Clive Cussler is probably the best known and most popular, with best-sellers such as *Raise the Titanic*. Among others who have attracted national attention are William E. Barrett, Rex Burns, Marian Castle, Margaret Coel, Sandra Dallas, Diane Mott Davidson, Warwick Downing, John Dunning, Joanne Greenberg, Kent Haruf, Manuel Ramos, Belle Turnbull, Frank Waters and Stephen White. Mary Coyle Chase, author of the Pulitzer Prize-winning play *Harvey*, was a Denverite.

A number of prominent novelists have set some of their fiction in Colorado, including Hal Borland, Willa Cather, Mary Hallock Foote, Hamlin Garland, Zane Grey, Louis Lamour and Wallace Stegner. James A. Michener's novel *Centennial* is the all-time best-selling introduction to the state.

Colorado produced the premier poet of the Rocky Mountain region, Thomas Hornsby Ferril (see entry), whose verse often focuses on mountains and the erosiveness of geological and historical time. Among nonfiction writers, David Lavender and Marshall Sprague excelled at popularizing Colorado history, while the most prolific and reliable academic historians writing on Colorado have included LeRoy R. Hafen and Duane A. Smith.

Avalanches Colorado

perennially leads the nation in avalanche deaths, averaging six fatalities a year. Backcountry skiers, snowboarders and snowmobilers are often victims of "white death." The worst avalanches have been in the San Juan Mountains of southwestern Colorado, particularly along U.S. Hwy. 550 where named avalanche routes such as the East Riverside Slide, the Oh Boy and the Riley Boy regularly block the road, and have killed snowplow operators trying to reopen it.

Avalanches have destroyed whole towns. On March 10, 1884, an avalanche killed 13 people and wiped out the town of Woodstock in Gunnison County. An avalanche killed 12 people at the Shenandoah Mine in San Juan County on March 24, 1906. The Silver Plume Cemetery in Clear Creek County has an 18-foot-high monument to 10 miners killed in a February 1899 snow slide.

Herman Goetinger, a boarding house cook outside Telluride in the winter of 1902, was filling a dishpan with snow for drinking water when a slide carried him off. Rescuers found him 1,200 feet down a gulch, sitting in the dishpan, wide-eyed but unhurt.

Colorado's 1998–1999 avalanche fatalities occurred on the west side of the Eisenhower– Johnson Tunnel, at Aspen Highlands Ski Area, on Grand Mesa, on Cumberland Pass and at Ophir.

The state's identified heavy avalanche zones are the towns of Aspen, Crested

Butte, Frisco, Marble, Ophir and Rico, the Camp Bird Mine and Red Mountain Pass near Ouray, Independence Pass, Mount Zion in Lake County, Twin Lakes,

Hoping to capture more tourists, Fraser, Colo., finally took down its old sign, "Ice Box of the Nation."

the Vail area, and in Hinsdale County at Rose's Cabin, Henson Creek and Sherman.

An average of more than 2,000 avalanches are reported annually in Colorado. The Colorado Department of Transportation purposely triggers avalanches as a safety measure. The state originally used howitzers to set off the slides, then developed a compressed air gun and helicopter-dropped explosives.

To learn more: Colorado Avalanche Information and Forecast Center; (303) 499-9650; www.caic/state.co.us.

Aviation and Aerospace (SEE ALSO AIRPORTS; DENVER INTERNATIONAL AIRPORT) U.S. air-mail contracts first made flying profitable in Colorado and led to the establishment in 1926 of the state's first postal route, from Denver to Pueblo's Heinshon Field. In 1927, Colorado Springs welcomed its first air-mail service to Nichols Field. Aviationists in Pueblo launched an annual air show in the 1940s and opened the B-24 Museum in 1986.

Aerospace and aeronautics firms have become important in the Boulder-Denver-Colorado Springs region. The first major firm, the Alexander Aircraft Co., made Eaglerock airplanes. Started in

Englewood in 1925, the firm later moved to Colorado Springs.

Lockheed Martin, an aerospace giant based in Bethesda, Md., opened a Denver office in 1959. The company built a $27 million plant near Littleton and became one of Colorado's largest employers, making rockets, missiles and satellites. Reorganized as Lockheed Martin Astronautics, the firm continues to garner huge defense and NASA contracts.

Ball Aerospace, Jeppesen-Sanderson Instruments/Maps and Hughes Aviation are among other Colorado aviation and aeronautical firms.

To learn more
Fred E. Weisbrod/B-24 International Museum, Pueblo Municipal Airport, 31001 Magnuson Ave., Pueblo 81001. Open Mon.–Fri. 10 A.M.–4 P.M., Sat. 1–4 P.M.; free admission. (719) 948-9219.

Peterson Air and Space Museum, Peterson Air Force, 150 E. Ent Ave., Colorado Springs 80914. Tues.–Sat. 8:30 A.M.–4:30 P.M.; free admission. (719) 556-4916.

Wings over Rockies Air and Space Museum, 7711 E. Academy Parkway, Denver 80220. Mon.–Sat. 10 A.M.–4 P.M., Sun. 1–4 P.M.; $2–$4. (303) 360-5360.

Banks Reborn No matter how shaky Colorado's mining, farming and ranching towns might become, sturdy masonry banks lent an air of stability and permanence. Posing as stately, neoclassical temples, these banks allowed dusty little tumbleweed towns to bask in the reflected glory that was Greece and the grandeur that was Rome.

No more. In the 1960s, Colorado changed its laws to allow branch banking and ultimately out-of-state ownership. Subsequently most hometown banks were gobbled up. All too often, the Main Street bank landmarks were abandoned for generic modern office boxes and automatic teller machines. The old classical banks are mostly gone.

In order to survive, the grand old Greek Temple banks—the banks that looked like banks—have turned themselves into hotels and saloons, into visitor centers and casinos.

The old First National Bank of Denver, at 17th and Stout, underwent a $16 million face-lift in 1995. The lobby is now a drive-in auto garage and the 13 upper stories have been converted to 250 luxury hotel rooms.

In Delta, the old First National Bank on Main Street with its three-story corner tower survived as the Last Chance Saloon. In recent years Deltans have restored it as the Visitors Center and Chamber of Commerce. Across Main Street, the former Colorado Bank and Trust Co. (1914), in similar stony Neoclassical garb, is now the elegant Delta City Hall.

In Elbert County, the Kiowa Town Hall likewise occupies the Kiowa State Bank (1907), at 228 Comanche St. This structure of concrete, chicken wire, plaster and stucco is a Lilliputian Greek temple with square columns imitating the Ionic order.

The First National Bank of Fort Collins (1897) retains its red sandstone facade with an arched doorway topped by a stone lion. Part of the bank houses The Town Pump, Fort Collins' oldest operating saloon. The old bank lobby is now Beau Jo's Pizza.

Fort Collins' old Commercial Bank and Trust is a miniature Neoclassical gem recycled as a restaurant, retaining its Ionic pilasters, oak wainscoting, fireplace and walk-in vault. The Poudre Valley Bank has been gorgeously reincarnated as a boutique in Old Town Fort Collins.

In Central City, the 1874 First National Bank at Main and Eureka streets became a casino. In Cripple Creek, the Nolon Block (1896) at 301 E. Bennett Ave. was the site of popular watering holes and gambling halls. After Johnny Nolon left for the goldfields of Nevada in 1904, David Moffat converted the joint into the Cripple Creek

This building in Cripple Creek first served as a gambling hall, then later housed a bank, and now is back in use for gambling. Photo by Tom Noel.

State Bank. The place returned in 1991 to its original uses. Turning banks into casinos seems appropriate in a state where banks were often gambling on gold and silver, on molybdenum and oil, on water and wheat, just as recklessly as their customers.

Bears

There has not been a documented sighting of grizzly bears in Colorado since 1979. That year a female grizzly attacked a guide, Ed Wiseman, near Platoro Reservoir in the remote northeastern edge of the San Juan Mountains. Although severely injured, Wiseman managed to kill the grizzly with a hand-held arrow. Grizzlies, one of the fiercest of mammals, earned the Latin name *Ursus horribilis.*

Black bears (*Ursus americanus*) inhabit brushy and forested areas of Colorado. They weigh as much as 450 pounds but average around 220. Black bears can be light brown or even blond, but are usually dark brown or black in Colorado. These shy creatures avoid humans but can be dangerous if surprised or cornered.

Bear diets vary with the seasons— emerging grasses in the spring, berries and acorns in the summer and fall, and human food and garbage anytime they can find it. Bears suffer and often die of starvation during Colorado droughts when they cannot find the vegetable matter that is the mainstay of their diet. Pregnant females going into hibernation may lack the body fat to nourish their young. Bears also feed on insects, carrion and small mammals, such as rodents, rabbits and young deer and elk, all of whose populations are also diminished by drought.

Black bears hibernate during the high-country Colorado winters for as long as 200 days without eating, drinking, defecating or urinating. During hibernation, females give birth to two or three cubs in January or February in the den. Although sleek and fat

Black bear. From *The Great Rocky Mountain Nature Factbook;* illustration by Marjorie C. Leggitt.

when they begin hibernation, bears emerge thin and voracious in the spring.

Signs of bear activity include large piles of scat, rotten logs ripped open and scooped out in search of insects and larvae, and broken, bent, or stripped branches of fruiting bushes or trees. During the mating season, males mark their territory by clawing aspen trees.

Colorado black bears live roughly eight to ten years in the wild. Because they are shy and solitary, these bears are extremely hard to count. Wildlife officials guesstimate there are between 8,000 and 12,000 in Colorado. In 1992, Coloradans voted to outlaw spring bear hunting and the use of bait and dogs for autumnal hunting.

The Colorado Division of Fish and Wildlife kills about 70 bears a year after they become accustomed to foraging around human habitations, which are increasingly moving into bear country. After two violations, a bear is shot. During Colorado drought years, such as 2000, bears unable to find food in the wild greatly increase their search for human food, resulting in a record number of bear executions.

Beer and Brewpubs

Colorado claims to brew more beer per capita than any other state and to have the world's largest brewpub (Wynkoop Brewing Co. in Denver). Anheuser Busch opened its giant brewery near Fort Collins in the 1980s. Anheuser Busch offers free tours and free samples in the beer garden and Clydesdale stables of their plant on I-25 just north of Fort Collins. Coors Brewery has also offered free tours and tastings since it opened in 1873 in downtown Golden (see entry for Adolph Coors). Coors, the third-largest U.S. sudsmaker, says its Golden plant is the world's largest single brewery. Concentrate brewed there is shipped to the other Coors Brewery, in Virginia.

Prohibition, which lasted from 1916 to 1933 in Colorado, wiped out most of some 200 old-time breweries. Four survived until the 1950s: Walter's in Pueblo, Schneider's in Trinidad, Tivoli in Denver and Coors in Golden. By 1970, only Coors remained. After brewpubs began springing up in the 1990s, towns once again began gaining their own breweries. Since Wynkoop Brewing Co. opened in 1989 as the state's first brewpub, more than 100 others have opened across the state. Microbreweries (where beer is made but not sold for consumption on premises) also provide Coloradans with a variety of ales, lagers, porters and stouts.

The following list of breweries and associated brewpubs attempts to be comprehensive, but the brewing and restaurant business is very fluid so operations can quickly come, go, or change operations.

Arvada
The Cheshire Cat, 7803 Ralston Road; (303) 431-9000.

Boulder
Avery Brewing Co., 5763 Arapahoe Ave.; (303) 440-4324.

BJ's Pizza, Grill and Brewery, 1125 Pearl St.; (303) 402-9294.

Mountain Sun Pub and Brewery, 1535 Pearl St.; (303) 546-0886.

Redfish New Orleans Brewhouse, 2027 13th St.; (303) 440-5858.

Rockies Brewing Co., 2880 Wilderness Place; (303) 444-8118.

Twisted Pine Brewing Co., 3280 Valmont Road; (303) 786-9270.

Walnut Brewery/Rock Bottom Brewery, 1123 Walnut St.; (303) 447-1345.

Breckenridge
Breckenridge Brewery and Pub, 600 S. Main St.; (970) 453-1550.

Colorado Springs
Back Alley Brewing Co., 3200 North Stone Ave.; (719) 520-1980.

Blicks Brewing Co., 625 Paonia St.; (719) 596-3192.

Bristol Brewing Co., 1647 South Tejon; (719) 535-2824.

Cheyenne Mountain Brewing Co., 3025-3029 Delta Drive; (719) 390-9100.

Il Vicino Wood Oven Pizza and Brewery, 11 South Tejon St.; (719) 475-9224.

Palmer Lake Brewing Co., 25 West Cimarron; (719) 475-8880.

Phantom Canyon Brewing Co., 2 East Pikes Peak; (719) 635-2800.

Sharkey's Brew Pub, 3231 Chelton Circle; (719) 623-2337.

Thunder Ridge Brewing Co., 20 N. Tejon St.; (719) 475-2739.

Cortez
Main Street Brewing Co., 21 E. Main St.; (970) 564-9112.

Crested Butte
The Crested Butte Brewery and Pub, P.O. Box 1089; (970) 349-5026.

Denver
Breckenridge BBQ and Brewery, 471 Kalamath St.; (303) 623-2739.

Breckenridge Brewery and Pub, 2220 Blake St.; (303) 295-2739.

Champion Brewing Co., 1442 Larimer Square; (303) 534-5444.

The Denver Chop House and Brewery, 1735 19th St.; (303) 296-0800.

Great Divide Brewing Co., 2201 Arapahoe St.; (303) 296-9460.

High Point Brewing Co., 4910 Fox St.; (303) 297-8568.

Lonetree Brewing Co., 375 E. 55th Ave.; (303) 297-3832.

Rock Bottom Brewery, 1001 16th St.; (303) 534-7616.

Sandlot Brewing Co., 2145 Blake St. in Coors Field; (303) 298-1587.

Wynkoop Brewing Co., 1634 18th St.; (303) 297-2700.

Dillon

Dillon Dam Brewery, P.O. Box 4845; (970) 262-7777.

Durango

Carver Brewing Co., 1022 Main Ave.; (970) 259-2545.

Ska Brewing Co., 545 Turner Drive; (970) 247-5792.

Steamworks Brewing Co., 801 E. Second Ave.; (970) 259-9200.

Englewood

Walnut Brewery/Rock Bottom Brewery, 9627 County Line Road; (303) 792-9090.

Estes Park

Estes Park Brewery, 470 Prospect Drive; (970) 586-5421.

Fort Collins

Big Horn Brewing Co., 1427 W. Elizabeth St.; (970) 221-5954.

Bohemian Breweries Inc., 236 Linden St.; (970) 482-3037.

Coopersmith's Pub and Brewing, 5 Old Town Square; (970) 498-0483.

H.C. Berger Brewing Co., 1900 E. Lincoln Ave.; (970) 493-9044.

Linden's Brewing Co., 214 Linden St.; (970) 482-9291.

New Belgium Brewing Co., 500 Linden St.; (970) 221-0524.

Odell Brewing Co., 800 East Lincoln Ave.; (970) 498-9070.

Glenwood Springs

Glenwood Canyon Brewing Co., 402 Seventh St.; (970) 945-1276.

Greeley

The Smiling Moose Brewpub and Grill, 2501 11th Ave.; (970) 356-7010.

Union Colony Brewery, 1412 Eighth Ave.; (970) 356-4116.

Idaho Springs

Tommyknocker Brewery and Pub LLC., 1401 Miner St.; (303) 567-4419.

Littleton

Columbine Mill Brewery, 5798 S. Rapp St.; (303) 347-1488.

Longmont

Left Hand/Tabernash Brewing Co., 1265 Boston Ave.; (303) 772-0258.

Overland Stagestop Brewery, 526 Main St.; (303) 772-3734.

Pumphouse Brewery, 540 Main St.; (303) 702-0881.

Loveland

Namaqua Brewing Co., 437 Garfield Ave.; (970) 635-9288.

Pueblo

Irish Brewpub and Grille, 108 W. Third St.; (719) 542-9974.

Salida

Il Vicino Wood Oven Pizza and Brewery, 136 E. Second St.; (719) 539-5219.

Steamboat Springs

Steamboat Springs Brewery and Tavern, 434 Lincoln Ave.; (303) 879-2233.

Telluride

Baked and Brewed in Telluride, 127 S. Fir St.; (970) 728-4775.

San Juan Brewing Co., 300 S. Townsend St.; (970) 728-0100.

Westminister

CB Potts/Bighorn Brewing Co. of Colorado, 1257 W. 120th Ave.; (303) 451-5767.

To learn more: www.colorado beer.org.

Bent's Fort

Charles and William Bent, two St. Louis traders doing business on the Santa Fe Trail, built this trading post on the Arkansas River in southeastern Colorado. Measuring 142 by 122 feet, it was a prairie castle with adobe walls 2 feet thick and 15 feet high. Between 1834 and 1849, this was the regional trade center for French, Indian, Mexican and U.S. trappers and traders.

The army later used the fort, overgrazed its environs and chased away the Indians with whom the Bents traded. When the army refused to adequately compensate him or to buy the fort at his price, William Bent blew it up in 1849 in frustration. Bent's Old Fort became a model for later structures, ranging from forts St. Vrain and Vasquez on the South Platte River to The Fort, an adobe restaurant in Morrison.

To learn more: The National Park Service reconstructed Bent's Fort in 1976 as a living history museum. Bent's Old Fort National Historic Site along U.S. Hwy. 50

The reconstructed Bent's Fort in southeastern Colorado. Photo by Tom Noel.

between La Junta and Las Animas is open 8:30 A.M.–5:30 P.M. summer and 9:00 A.M.–4:00 P.M. winter. (719) 383-5010; www.nps.gov/beol.

Bighorn Mountain Sheep

Designated in 1961 as Colorado's state mammal, these acrobatic rock scramblers are also called mountain sheep, Rocky Mountain bighorn sheep or bighorns (*Ovis canadensis*).

The distinctive horns become massive and heavily ridged on males, sweeping sharply outward, backward and downward with tips curling back up to frame the face. The horns are not shed but continue to grow throughout the life of the animal. Females are about half the size of males and more slender, less hairy, with smaller, slightly curled horns.

The sheep vary in fur color from grayish white to brown with white rump patches. Partly to avoid humans, they generally gravitate to high mountains and steep canyons, although large herds graze along I-70 around Georgetown, on the Mount Evans Highway, and along State Hwy. 24 in the Big Thompson Canyon west of Loveland.

Scattered throughout the mountains and foothills of central Colorado, they feed on grasses and travel in herds noted for sociable rubbing, dusting and scratching. They spend their lives in one location, rarely migrating beyond 10 miles of their birthplace.

Bighorns live up to 17 years, although in the wild they rarely survive more than 10 to 12 years. Predators include coyotes, bobcats, mountain lions, eagles and humans. Hunters almost exterminated Colorado's bighorns, leading to a complete closure of hunting from 1887 to 1953. Hunting is now directed toward mature rams whose trophy horns are prized. Lungworm pneumonia is now the deadliest enemy of bighorns.

Rocky Mountain bighorn sheep. Tom Noel Collection.

Boettcher, Charles

Colorado's most successful and diversified industrialist came to the United States at the age of 17 in 1869. This German immigrant first made money selling hardware to miners. Avoiding dicey mining ventures, he focused on mining equipment, tools, household goods and merchandise of every kind. His slogan: "Hard Goods. Hardware. Hard Cash."

When the economy shifted from mining to agriculture, Boettcher and some

Charles Boettcher, 19th-century industrialist and philanthropist. Tom Noel Collection.

associates formed the Great Western Sugar Co., Colorado's most lucrative agricultural operation by the 1920s. To build sugar processing factories of high-grade cement, Boettcher formed another profitable enterprise, the Ideal Cement Co. Besides sugar and cement, Boettcher invested in everything from cattle ranching to life insurance, from the Brown Palace Hotel to the Denver Tramway Co.

Even after his death at age 96, he helped bankroll Colorado through the Boettcher Foundation. After making millions in Colorado, he insisted that the foundation fund only projects in the state. He is commemorated by Boettcher Halls at the Colorado History Museum, Denver Museum of Nature and Science and Denver Performing Arts Center, as well as the Boettcher Conservatory at the Denver Botanic Gardens.

Bookstores and Publishers (SEE ALSO AUTHORS)

During the 1858–59 gold rush, the wooden arrow sign at the confluence of Cherry Creek and the South Platte River supposedly read "To California." All those who could read, legend has it, pushed on to the Golden State.

The dearth of books and readers ended soon after Arthur E. Pierce set up a pine workbench under a cottonwood tree on 11th Street between Market and Larimer in old Auraria City. Pierce, Colorado's first book dealer, had ordered two cases of books, magazines and newspapers. Lacking the money to pay shipping charges for both, he took one and sold it in his open air shop, quickly raising enough to return to the stage office to pay for the second case.

"I soon sold the stock out to the mentally hungry pilgrims," Pierce recalled before his death in Denver 50 years later. Pierce told pioneer historian Alice Polk Hill,

"In providing the new town with reading matter, I had struck a pay streak."

During the cold, lonely winter of 1860, most gold seekers joined the "go-backs," abandoning Colorado as a humbug. To relieve the cabin fever of those sticking it out in Denver, Pierce opened the Denver and Auraria Library and Reading Room Association in February 1860. For a 50-cent membership, readers could borrow any book Pierce owned. Colorado's modern libraries trace their origins to Pierce's outdoor bookshop and library, which he finally moved into a log cabin.

Hundreds of book dealers have subsequently sought to find a "pay streak" and made book lovers feel at home in Colorado. Tattered Cover Books, with more than 200,000 titles in stock and two huge Denver stores, has been recognized by the *New York Times* as the finest general bookstore in the United States. Besides the ubiquitous chain bookstores, Colorado still boasts some 200 independent booksellers.

Approximately 60 Colorado antiquarian bookshops specialize in previously owned works. These dealers trace their origins to A. E. Pierce and also to a 1922 cross-country train trip of a young Jewish immigrant. Fred Rosenstock lost his spectacles on that trip to California and stopped in Denver to buy a new pair. He fell in love with the Mile High City and never left. His bookshop became nationally noted for Western Americana, Coloradiana and Western art. Linda Lebsack, who worked for Fred, took over after his death in 1986.

Alan Culpin's Abracadabra Bookshop, Dan Larsen's Colorado Pioneer Books, Polly Hines and Linda German's Mad Dog and Pilgrim, Bob Topp's Hermitage, all in Denver, as well as Chinook Books in Colorado Springs and the Southwest Trader in Durango are notable purveyors of out of-print treasures. One antiquarian dealer and author, John Dunning, wrote a best-selling murder mystery about the Colorado rare book market, *Booked to Die.*

Publishers have gravitated to Boulder, the home of the University of Colorado. The University Press of Colorado, which originated in 1915 as the University of Colorado Press, issues about 35 to 40 titles a year. Boulder's Johnson Publishing Co. has specialized in guidebooks, history, natural history and outdoor recreation since its establishment as a commercial printer in 1946. Pruett Publishing, founded in 1966 by Frederick Pruett, issues about a dozen titles annually, mostly on outdoor recreation and Colorado history.

> **The University of Denver started with a gift of land and $500 from Rufus "Potato" Clark, whose motto was, "Work the ground instead of your mouth."**

Denver has no large, nationally noted publishers. Golden, however, has been the home of Fulcrum Publishing since Robert C. Baron founded that press in 1984. Fulcrum publishes around 50 books a year, notably works on Colorado and the American West, biography, gardening, guidebooks, history, natural history and tomes for teachers and children. Of some 300 other Colorado book publishers, most are small outfits, often home businesses sporadically issuing a volume or so.

To learn more: Colorado Center for the Book, 2123 Downing St., Denver 80205; www.coloradobook.org.

Botanical Gardens

Colorado has four botanical gardens, plus many nature areas where plants are cultivated for the public to enjoy.

Denver Botanic Gardens. Sprouting from the well-fertilized soil of what was Denver's pioneer cemetery, the gardens founded in 1951 showcase more than 14,000 plant species on a 23-acre site with a large tropical plant conservatory. DBG also maintains a high-altitude site on Mount Evans (see entry) and the 700-acre Chatfield Arboretum at Chatfield Reservoir. DBG is at 1005 York St., Denver. Open daily 9 A.M.–8 P.M., Oct.–April 9 A.M.–5 P.M. (303) 331-4000; www.botanicgardens.org.

Western Colorado Botanical Gardens. Founded in 1997, the area has a 4,000-square-foot greenhouse with 600 varieties of tropical plants and many butterflies and a 12-acre outdoor garden along the Colorado River. 1803 S. Seventh St., Grand Junction. (970) 243-7337.

Betty Ford Alpine Gardens. Named for the former First Lady and opened in 1987, this is the highest public alpine garden in North America, with perennial, rock and meditation gardens. In the town of Vail. Open daily sunrise to sunset, free admission. (970) 476-8702.

Hudson Gardens. Colorado plants are showcased in 16 different gardens on a 30-acre site along the South Platte River at these gardens founded in 1993. 6115 S. Santa Fe Drive, Littleton. Open daily 10 A.M.–dusk; $3–$4. (303) 797-8505.

Boulder

Thomas Aikins and a party of gold seekers named the town they founded in 1858 for rocky Boulder Creek. The town grew slowly but steadily by balancing mining and agricultural interests and by donating land for the University of Colorado, founded in 1876. Boulder, at an elevation of 5,363 feet, also emerged as a summer resort and a health resort with its sanitaria and nearby Eldorado Mineral Springs.

Boulder has become Colorado's growth management model by limiting new housing permits and tightly controlling other development. Greenbelts insulate the city from the suburban sprawl of metro Denver. Boulder began acquiring the state's earliest mountain park system in 1898, and later augmented it with farm and ranch lands on the plains. The Flatirons, massive, uplifted stone slabs that have become Boulder's logo, are also preserved as a mountain park.

University of Colorado scientific research after World War II helped attract large plants for IBM, Ball Aerospace, Beechcraft, the National Bureau of Standards, the Rocky Flats Nuclear Weapons Plant and the National Center for Atmospheric Research. A giant Qwest Advanced Technologies Research Center

Boulder's Scott Carpenter Park honors the hometown boy who became an astronaut.
Photo by Tom Noel.

and other federal and private industries give the city a steady, prosperous job base. The post-World War II population of 12,000 increased to almost 95,000 by 2000, not including most of the 26,000 students at the University of Colorado.

Bridges

As a high, dry state without navigable waterways, Colorado has fewer and shorter bridges than most states. Foremost among them is the country's highest suspension bridge, standing 1,053 feet above the Royal Gorge of the Arkansas River. Constructed in 1929 by nearby Cañon City, the 1,220-foot-long Royal Gorge Bridge is the centerpiece of a 5,000-acre municipal park that includes an incline railway, an aerial tram and a diesel excursion train.

Among other notable Colorado spans is the Rainbow Arch Bridge over the South Platte River in Fort Morgan. This concrete, art deco beauty has been restored and reilluminated with replicas of its original street lamps. Manitou Springs boasts several rustic stone arch bridges complementing that resort town's picturesque foothills setting.

The Burro Canyon three-arch bridge near Madrid in Las Animas County is one of the best preserved and most picturesque of some 30 stone Colorado roadway bridges built by the Works Progress Administration during the 1930s. Of 7,228 bridges in Colorado, 62 have been declared eligible for the National Register of Historic Places because of their design, engineering or historical merits. Many bridges, especially wooden railway trestles, have been lost. Other railroad bridges have been recycled as pedestrian/bicycle path bridges.

To learn more: The State Historic Preservation Office sponsors the Adopt A Bridge program for saving endangered edifices; (303) 866-5786.

Brown, Aunt Clara

(SEE ALSO AFRICAN AMERICANS) "Aunt" Clara Brown, as she was affectionately called, was born to slave parents who were sold to separate owners when she was three. She went with her mother to Ambrose Smith, a farmer in Logan County, Kentucky. Smith, a devout Methodist, took Clara and her mother to his church services.

Clara was 18 and a tall, strong woman with warm brown eyes when the Smiths bought an 18-year-old slave carpenter, Richard. The two were encouraged to marry and produce children to work the Smiths' farm. Clara was separated from her husband and children when she was sold to George Brown. Following southern custom, she, like other mature female slaves, was called "Aunt" and given the last name of her new owner.

The Browns liked Clara's intelligence and spunk and helped her buy her freedom. She moved to St. Louis, where Missouri law protected free blacks, and later went with the Browns when they emigrated to Kansas. There she joined a wagon train headed to Colorado, earning her way by cooking. She arrived in Denver in June 1859.

Former slave Clara Brown became an inspiration to early residents of Colorado. Colorado Historical Society.

Denver's first black woman opened a laundry shop, worked hard, and scraped together $5,000 to go back to Kentucky to look for her husband and children. She returned to Colorado with one daughter and other relatives and friends newly freed from bondage. Aunt Clara moved to then-booming Central City and resumed her laundering work, toiling long hours and denying herself any luxuries. With the money she saved she helped fund construction of St. James Methodist Church, which thrives to this day.

She died in her sleep in 1885. At Denver's Riverside Cemetery, Colorado Gov. James B. Grant, Denver Mayor John L. Routt and other dignitaries praised Aunt Clara as "the kind old friend whose heart always responded to the cry of distress, and who, rising from the humble position of slave to the angelic type of noble woman, won our sympathy and commanded our respect."

Brown, Margaret "Unsinkable Molly"

Born in Hannibal, Mo., in 1867, Molly started out as Maggie, in a shack on the Mississippi River bottoms. At age 13 this Irish lass went to work in a cigar factory. At 19 she ran away to the silver city of Leadville, Colo. In the two-mile-high Magic City, the red-haired, blue-eyed, buxom young woman found work sewing drapes.

She also found a wealthy, handsome husband, Leadville mine manager James Joseph Brown. After the silver crash of 1893, Brown's resourceful mining of gold in the Little Jonny Mine enriched the couple. Like the Boettchers, the Tabors and many other mining millionaires, the Browns moved from Leadville to Denver's swanky Capitol Hill neighborhood. She joined other society ladies in fund raising for St. Joseph's Hospital and Immaculate Conception

Cathedral, where pew number 6 was reserved for the Brown family.

Molly's legendary assault on Denver society was foiled, in part, by the fact that her roots were all too evident as she shared her home with her aging father, John Tobin,

an Irish-born day laborer, and her Irish-born mother, Johanna, who smoked her clay pipe on the front porch. After her husband twice tried to shoot her, Molly permanently separated from J.J. and began a life of travel that led to her 1912 heroics aboard the *Titanic*. When the ship sank after hitting an iceberg, Molly courageously calmed the panicking passengers of a lifeboat, persuading them to row to safety.

Molly undertook Denver's first well-known preservation project in 1927. When the cottage of poet-journalist Eugene Field faced demolition, Molly bought it and moved it in 1927 to Washington Park, where it still stands restored next to the Wynken, Blynken and Nod fountain inspired by Field's best known poem. Molly was also an early feminist, suffragist and philanthropist. She overcame her humble origins with lifelong learning, studying music, opera, French, German, Italian, Spanish and literature to make herself a polished lady.

After Molly died in New York City in 1932, her house was converted to a home for wayward girls, then became a boarding house for single men. In 1969 developers planned to raze Molly's house for a modern office building. Historic Denver Inc. was established in 1970 to save and restore the house, which has become Denver's most popular house tour.

To learn more: Molly Brown House Museum, 1346 Pennsylvania St., Denver. Open Tues.– Sat. 10:30 A.M.–3:30 P.M., Sun. noon–3:30 P.M.; $1.50–$5.00. (303) 832-4092; www.mollybrown.org.

Buffalo

The buffalo or, more properly, the American bison (*Bison bison*) is the largest Colorado mammal. They were once common throughout Colorado before being hunted nearly to extinction in the late 1800s. During the 1900s, buffalo were reintroduced to Colorado and have made a huge comeback on ranches and game preserves.

Bulls stand as high as 6 feet and weigh 2,000 pounds or more, although cows rarely weigh over 1,200 pounds. Fur on the huge, bearded head and front quarters is black to brown and long, dense, and woolly, contrasting with the lighter, shorter, smoother coat on the much smaller hindquarters. The shoulders rise into a large humpback, and the small ropelike tail ends in a tufted tip. Both sexes have a pair of smooth, permanent short horns that curve upward and forward.

Buffalo travel in large herds in search of grass and water. They are good swimmers and may be seen frolicking about in water on warm summer days. To escape insect pests and relieve skin irritations, bison roll in dirt or sand, creating bare buffalo wallows. Bison wallowing and dusting helped spread seeds of grasses and other plants, producing favorable habitats for prairie dogs, ferrets, burrowing owls, rattlesnakes and other Colorado creatures.

Bison breed in mid to late summer, when the bulls become noisy and aggressive, roaring and pawing the earth with their front feet and butting heads. The calves are born the next spring. They live to an average age of about 30 years, with some animals surviving into their 40s. Wolves and human beings are their main enemies in Colorado, along with disease and intestinal parasites.

Native Americans relied on bison for food, shelter, blankets and clothing. The Indians found a use for every part of the buffalo, using the brains to tan the hides, the dung as fuel, the tail as a brush. As Francis Parkman noted in *The Oregon Trail*, "The buffalo supplies them [Indians] with the necessaries of life [including] strings for their bows, glue, thread, cordage, trail ropes for their horses, saddles, vessels to hold water, boats to cross streams and the means of purchasing all they want from traders."

Buffalo once occupied most of North America, but reached their maximum numbers on the Great Plains. After white hunters began pursuing them, vast herds once numbering more than 30 million animals were decimated.

Colorado ranchers have found that bison survive much better in the wild than cattle. They use their large, bearded heads to sweep snow away from the dried grass below. They do their own calving and can survive Colorado blizzards that devastate cattle herds. Buffalo typically head into a storm—unlike cattle, which let prairie

American bison, or buffalo. Lithograph by George Catlin; University of Colorado.

blizzards drive them into fences and natural barriers where they suffocate beneath snowdrifts.

The bison's deep footprints capture seeds and the water that lets them grow, with bison waste providing moisture and fertilizer to get plants started. Buffalo move around and do not overgraze an area or befoul waterholes as do domestic cattle. Buffalo meat, which is lower in calories, cholesterol and fat than beef, chicken or pork, is gaining in popularity.

The Colorado Department of Wildlife classifies bison as a big game mammal and sells a very limited number of permits every year for hunting in a few designated government preserves.

To learn more: The 20th-century comeback of the buffalo includes protected Colorado herds like those at Genesee Mountain Park bordering I-70, 20 miles west of Denver; at Daniels Park in Douglas County; in Colorado National Monument; and at Zapata Ranch next to Great Sand Dunes National Park. (303) 697-4545.

Burros
This small member of the horse family is also known as an ass, donkey or jackass and, in Colorado, as the Rocky Mountain canary because of its noisy braying. Burros have a large head, long ears and small hooves. The dun-colored creature has a black stripe down its back and an erect mane of short, stiff hairs. Averaging about 4½ feet in height, they are hardy and surefooted pack animals.

Domesticated by the ancient Mesopotamians and Egyptians, ridden by Mary while she was with child and by her son Jesus when he rode into Jerusalem on Palm Sunday, burros have long been a favorite beast of burden. Burros thrive in desert and mountain conditions where they feed on almost anything they can sink their teeth into. In Colorado mining towns, they did much of the work both above and below ground.

How to Choose a Burro

George Cowell, an old-timer in the mining town of Gold Hill, recalled: "People would put their egg shells and coffee grounds and potato peelings out in the street. About 6 o'clock at night the burros would come down out of the timber and eat up all this garbage, even the paper off the cans. Then they'd go down to the saloon and drink from the watering trough. If you wanted a burro you never bought one. You picked one out and put your brand on him." ✻

A male is called a jack or jackass; a female is a jenny. Their proverbial stupidity, obstinacy and patience have endeared them to Coloradans. A burro named Prunes is enshrined in Fairplay as "A burro, 1867–1930, who worked All Mines in this District." Fairplay and Leadville stage annual "get your ass over the pass" burro races.

Colorado burro tales center on prospectors and their trusty burros and on burro pack trains loaded with mine machinery, household furniture, boxes of food and kegs of alcohol. Burros, routinely burdened with twice their own weight in freight, took siestas whenever they could, giving rise to their name, which means "get up" in Spanish.

Business
(SEE ALSO ECONOMY; EMPLOYMENT) The top ten Colorado companies in total revenues are all, except for the Adolph Coors brewing company, relative newcomers that in many cases have acquired or replaced older Colorado firms. In 2000, for instance, the old Bell company U.S. West became part of Qwest, a new telecommunications company founded by Denver billionaire Philip Anschutz. Only three of the firms were on Colorado's 1990 top-ten list. The boom, bust and

consolidation tradition that began with mining continues to characterize Colorado business.

1. Qwest Communications, Denver. Founded in 1994 by Philip Anschutz, this company's vast fiber optics network offers Internet communications and long distance phone service. After acquiring U.S. West in 2000, Qwest became the giant of Rocky Mountain communications. 1999 revenue: $17 billion.

2. Ball Corp., Broomfield. The Ball Brothers fruit jar company founded in 1880 has become the world's second-largest maker of aluminum cans and a big aerospace firm. 1999 revenue: $3.5 billion.

3. Xcel, Minneapolis. This regional gas and electric utility originated in 1869 as the Denver Gas and Electric Co. and later became the Public Service Co. of Colorado. During the 1990s it was acquired by New Century Energies of Texas. In 2000, New Century merged with Northern States Power Co. of Minneapolis to form Xcel, the most recent parent company of Public Service. 1999 revenue: $3.3 billion.

4. Liberty Media Group, Englewood. A telecommunications firm founded in 1995 by cable TV mogul John Malone; merged with AT&T. 1999 revenue: $3.3 billion.

5. Transmontaigne Inc., Denver. An oil and natural gas pipeline company founded in 1996 by Denver native Cortlandt S. Dietler. 1999 revenue: $3 billion.

6. MediaOne Group, Englewood. This cable television company, founded in 1995 and with more than 5 million customers, merged with AT&T and TCI. 1999 revenue: $2.5 billion.

7. Storage Technology Corp., Louisville. Founded in 1969, this is one of Colorado's oldest and most resilient high-tech companies, specializing in computer storage. 1999 revenue: $2.3 billion.

8. Johns Manville Corp., Denver. Founded in New York in 1858, this construction materials giant moved to Colorado in 1971 and, after surviving the asbestos debacle, is riding the current construction industry boom. 1999 revenue: $2.2 billion.

9. Adolph Coors Co., Golden. Now headed by Adolph's great-grandson Peter, the family brewery founded in 1873 has become the nation's third-largest suds-maker. 1999 revenue: $2 billion.

10. Newmont Mining Co., Denver. Newmont became America's largest gold mining company following its merger in 1999 with Cyprus Minerals. 1999 revenue: $1.4 billion.

Looking Back

July 14, 1874

Pi-ah and his Utes conducted the last scalp dance in Denver. A thousand whites gathered at Sloan's Lake to watch some 200 Utes dance around three bloody Cheyenne scalps dangling from poles. "Lots of ladies, prominent in church and society circles," reported the *Rocky Mountain News* on July 15, 1874, were "straining for a sight of the reeking scalps which they scanned as eagerly as if they had been new bonnets."

Byers, William Newton (SEE ALSO NEWSPAPERS)

Byers, founder of Colorado's first newspaper, was born in Ohio in 1831. He worked as a land surveyor in Iowa, Oregon, Washington and Nebraska before moving to Denver. He hauled a printing press with him from Omaha and issued the initial issue of the *Rocky Mountain News* on April 23, 1859.

Ever since then, the *News* has been a major voice for Colorado. Byers used his boosterish newspaper to champion railroad construction, mining, agriculture, statehood and tourism. Active on many fronts, Byers accompanied the first recorded party to climb Longs Peak, introduced grapes and other crops to Colorado, promoted Hot Sulphur Springs as a resort and helped found the Colorado Historical Society. He died in Denver in 1903.

The Byers–Evans House Museum, Byers School and Byers Place, all in Denver, as well as Byers Peak, the town of Byers and a stained glass window in the state Capitol, commemorate a man who not only recorded but also made much Colorado history.

Calendar of Events

Many Colorado communities established festivals in the 19th century. A few of these events, often harvest festivals, have survived. Since the 1976 U.S. bicentennial and Colorado statehood centennial, Coloradans have created many more fairs and festivals. Tiny Telluride, for instance, has launched enough festivals to make itself the festival capital with galas nearly every weekend between Memorial Day and Labor Day devoted to such things as bluegrass, film, futurology, hang gliding, ideas, jazz, mushrooms, and wine—and one No-festival Festival weekend when townsfolk can relax.

Many other towns have created festivals in recent decades to attract tourists and give locals a chance to celebrate unique community assets. Colorado is also alive with annual ski races, ethnic celebrations, parades, rodeos and other doings.

Camp Hale *(See also Skiing and Snowboarding)* In the Pando Valley near Leadville, the U.S. Army opened this

(Continued on page 45)

Denver's National Western Stockshow attracts top rodeo performers. Photo by Martin Weiker.

Calendar of Annual Events 2002

JANUARY

Aspen
Wintersköl: *Second weekend in January. This "toast to winter" emphasizes family fun and winter sports. Four ski areas and downtown Aspen host a parade, ski splash, fair, fireworks and a canine fashion show. (970) 925-1940.*

Breckenridge
International Snow Sculpture Championships: *Third week in January. Teams from around the world create enormous, exquisitely detailed sculptures from 20-ton blocks of packed snow. (970) 453-6018.*

Ullr Fest: *Fourth week in January. This weeklong carnival honors the Norse god of snow with a wacky snow Olympics, skating, parade and freestyle events. (970) 453-6018.*

Denver
National Western Stock Show: *Two weeks in mid-January. Since 1906, Denver's largest and longest festival includes rodeos, livestock shows and auctions, parades, children's events and hundreds of exhibits. (303) 297-1166.*

Greeley
Colorado Farm Show: *Last weekend in January. The second-largest agriculture-related exhibition in Colorado (after Denver's National Western Stock Show), with exhibitors and patrons from many states and Canadian provinces. (970) 356-9426.*

Steamboat Springs
Cowboy Ski Race: *Third week in January. This zany end to Denver's National Western Stock Show has cowboys racing on skis towed by horses.*

Winter Park
Winter Park Snowboard Series: *January–April. Eight event dates feature snowboard cross, slopestyle, half-pipe and dual-mogul events. Riders compete for series points and prizes. (888) 760-7529; www.ridewinterpark.com.*

FEBRUARY

Frisco
Frisco Gold Rush: *Second week in February, since 1971. The Frisco Nordic Center hosts 5-, 10- and 15-kilometer Nordic races, as well as snowshoe races. (800) 424-1554.*

Loveland
Sweetheart City Festival: *Feb. 14. St. Valentine's Day is a gala with special mailings of cards from the Sweetheart City.*

Winter Park
Wells Fargo Bank Cup at Winter Park: *Second weekend in February, since 1976. This invitation race for disabled skiers benefits the National Sports Center for the Disabled. Parties, silent auctions, and pro-am ski races. (888) 760-7529; www.skiwinterpark.com.*

MARCH

Denver
Rocky Mountain Book Festival: *First weekend in March, since 1993. The Colorado Center for the Book hosts this literary extravaganza that draws 10,000 biblioholics to the Denver Merchandise Mart with talks from nationally noted and local authors, storytellers, performers, book arts craftspeople, skits, impersonations and children's activities. (303) 839-8320; www.coloradobook.org.*

St. Patrick's Day Parade: *Saturday closest to March 17, since 1961. Denver's largest parade attracts thousands of participants and as many as 300,000 spectators along the downtown route. Thousands of horses, marching bands, floats and numerous ethnic groups participate. (303) 789-3333.*

Denver March Pow Wow: *Third weekend in March, since 1974. One of the nation's largest Native American gatherings features more than 700 dancers, a drumming contest, Native American food, storytelling and arts and crafts such as traditional buckskins, buffalo robes, turquoise jewelry, Navajo blankets and Pueblo pottery. (303) 455-4575.*

More Calendar of Annual Events

Springfield

Spring Equinox Festival: *Third weekend in March. Includes tours of Picture Canyon, with its ancient rock art, and the Farm, Ranch, Home and Garden Show. (719) 523-4061.*

APRIL

Morrison

Easter Sunrise Service: *In Red Rocks Amphitheater.*

Winter Park

Spring Splash: *Last week in April. This annual closing-day tradition for the ski season includes a zany ski race, colorful costumes and a finish line in the middle of an icy pond. (888) 760-7529; www.skiwinterpark.com.*

MAY

Cañon City

Fremont County Days: *Third weekend in May. A spring fling at the Royal Gorge Suspension Bridge and Park, complete with bed races. (719) 275-7507.*

Cripple Creek

Hot Time in the Gold Camp: *Last weekend in May. Old-time fire company races, chili blaze-off, live entertainment. (877) 858-4653.*

Denver

Cinco de Mayo Parade and Festival: *First weekend in May. Parade, exhibits and Mexican food in Civic Center to celebrate Mexican independence. Strolling mariachi bands, dancers and several stages of traditional and contemporary entertainment help make this the state's largest Latino event. (303) 534-8342.*

Durango

Iron Horse Bicycle Classic: *Last weekend in May. Colorado's oldest continuous cycling event features a road race and tour along the Durango & Silverton Narrow Gauge Railroad, mountain bike races and kids' races. (970) 259-4621.*

Greeley

Cinco de Mayo/Semana Latina: *First week in May. Dancing, music, art and Mexican food for all ages and ethnic backgrounds. (970) 350-9451.*

Telluride

Mountain Film Festival: *Last weekend in May. Brings together legendary mountaineers with filmmakers and photographers and an eclectic blend of film screenings, speakers, exhibits, slide presentations and seminars. (888) 783-0263.*

Vail

Whitewater Festival: *Memorial Day weekend. The Vail Valley's annual kickoff to summer offers whitewater rafting and kayaking races and public parties in Vail and Dowd Junction.*

JUNE

Aspen

Aspen Summer Music Festival: *June–August, since 1949. Although the music tent is often sold out, you can listen for free on the lawn outside to world-renowned classical musicians. (970) 425-3254.*

Boulder

Colorado Shakespeare Festival: *June–August, since 1960. Hosted by the University of Colorado in the outdoor Mary Rippon Theater. (303) 492-0544.*

Colorado Music Festival: *June–August. In historic Chautauqua Auditorium, world-class musicians perform classical music. (303) 449-1397.*

Carbondale

Mountain Festival: *Last weekend in June, since 1971. A 16-stage pop music festival with art booths and international foods. (970) 963-1680.*

More Calendar of Annual Events

Central City
Madame Lou Bunch Day: *Third Saturday in June, since 1974. Honors a celebrated madam. Males push scantily clad women in a bed race through town. Evening dance and costume contests. (303) 582-5251.*

Crested Butte
Fat Tire Bike Week: *Third week in June. America's mountain bike capital hosts the country's original mountain bike festival with bicycle rodeos, clinics, trail tours and races up Mount Crested Butte. (970) 349-6817.*

Cripple Creek
Donkey Derby Days: *Fourth weekend in June, since 1931. The golden city of Cripple Creek offers donkey races, gold panning and a pack burro race. (877) 858-4653.*

Denver
Capitol Hill People's Fair: *First weekend in June, since 1972. This hippie street festival has evolved into one of Colorado's biggest and most eccentric urban celebrations. Capitol Hill United Neighborhoods sponsors this extravaganza in Civic Center Park. Six stages with continuous entertainments, arts and crafts booths, food, drink and bizarre goods and services are highlighted in more than 500 exhibit booths. (303) 830-1651.*

Cherry Blossom Festival: *Last weekend in June, since 1973. Traditional Japanese food, dance, martial arts, flower show and music, in Sakura Square. (303) 295-0305.*

Glenwood Springs
Strawberry Days: *Third weekend in June, since 1898. Glenwood Springs celebrated its spring harvest with berries, food, and arts and crafts. (970) 945-6589.*

Greeley
Greeley Independence Stampede: *Last week in June and first weekend in July. Features music, rodeos, cowboys and cattle. (800) 982-2855.*

Heeney
Tick Festival: *Second weekend in June, since 1981. Looking for something that no one else celebrated, the tiny mountain town of Heeney came up with an annual tribute to the blood-sucking bug.*

Ignacio
Ute Indian Bear Dance: *Every June for centuries, the Utes have gathered for this ritual honoring their sacred mammal. The Ute Mountain Ute and Southern Ute Reservations host these dances. (303) 565-3751.*

Larkspur
Renaissance Festival: *Eight weekends in June and July, since the 1970s. This celebration of medieval days, ranging from jousting to eating large chucks of meat with your hands, has become one of Colorado's most popular festivals. The re-created 16th-century marketplace includes several hundred artisans and stunts by the Society for Medieval Anachronisms. (303) 688-6010; www.coloradorenaissance.com.*

Salida
Art Walk: *Third weekend in June, since 1990. Historic downtown Salida bristles with artists showing off their work. (877) 772-5432; www.salidaartwalk.org.*

Snowmass
Snowmass Balloon Festival: *Late June, since 1975. Billed as the world's largest high-altitude hot-air balloon race, with more than 50 balloonists; also champagne brunch and classical music. (800) 598-2003.*

Trinidad
Santa Fe Trail Festival: *Mid-June. A gala with dancing, living history, food, artists and craftspeople, on Main Street. (719) 846-9285.*

JULY

Central City
Central City Opera: *Early July through mid-August, since 1932. Now has three operas (in English) per season, with matinees and evening performances. (800) 851-8175.*

More Calendar of Annual Events

Colorado Springs
Pikes Peak Hill Climb: *July 4, since 1916. The first Hill Climb automobile race was held the year Spencer Penrose completed construction of this challenging road snaking up the 14,110-foot peak. (719) 685-4400.*

Denver
Cherry Creek Arts Festival: *July Fourth weekend. The festival has become the state's largest art show in terms of sales and attendance. Denver's Cherry Creek North neighborhood hosts some 250,000 art fanciers and 200 artists picked by a jury. (303) 555-2787.*

Four Mile Historic Park Traditional Fourth of July Festival: *July 4. Stagecoach rides, rifle and cannon fire from an encampment of the 1860s'-style Colorado Volunteers, recitation of the Declaration of Independence, numerous re-enactors, terrific food and a carnival atmosphere make Four Mile House, Denver's oldest structure, the place to be. (303) 399-1859.*

Fairplay
Burro Days Race: *Last weekend in July. Runners try to coax burros 31 miles up 13,188-foot Mosquito Pass; also llama races and a mountain man rendezvous. (719) 836-4279.*

Golden
Buffalo Bill Days: *Last weekend in July. A celebration of the man buried just west of town atop Lookout Mountain, with a parade, games, history exhibits and a duck race. (303) 278-7789.*

Gunnison
Cattleman's Days: *Last weekend in July, since 1900. Gunnison celebrates with a rodeo, carnival, parade and horse races. (800) 323-2453.*

Monte Vista
Ski-Hi Stampede Rodeo: *In July, since the 1920s. (800) 562-7085.*

Montrose
Lighter Than Air Balloon Affair: *July 4. This hot-air balloon gala displays a graceful, colorful flotilla. (800) 873-0244.*

Paonia
Cherry Days: *July 4. Features a cherry pancake breakfast and parade in Town Park. (970) 527-3886.*

Steamboat Springs
July 4th Week: *Since 1903. Cowboy roundup offers a flapjack feed, parade and fireworks. (970) 879-0880.*

Victor
Gold Rush Days: *Third weekend in July. Features hard-rock mining contests such as two-person mucking, jackleg drilling, hand steeling and a gold rush car race. (719) 689-3211.*

AUGUST

Buena Vista
Contin-Tail Rock and Gem Show/Gold Rush Days: *Second week in August. A free gem, rock and jewelry show featuring 100 vendors, western singers and dancers, burro races, bed races, gold panning, gunfights and pancake breakfast. (719) 395-6612.*

Colorado Springs
Pikes Peak or Bust Rodeo: *First week in August, since 1936. Rodeo competition, street breakfast and the city's largest downtown parade. (800) 888-4748.*

Denver
Rocky Mountain Book Festival: *First weekend in August, since 1985. Over 100 antiquarian book dealers from across America exhibit rare and unusual literary treasures in Denver's Merchandise Mart. (303) 561-0035.*

Grand Lake
Lipton Cup Yacht Regatta: *Second week in August, since 1905. The Grand Lake Yacht Club hosts one of the world's highest regattas, at 8,369 feet above sea level. (970) 627-3402.*

More Calendar of Annual Events

Highlands Ranch
Colorado Scottish Festival: Second weekend in August, since 1963. The St. Andrew Society sponsors the festival of kilts, bagpipes, highland dancing, and Scottish athletic competitions, food and drink. (303) 238-6524.

Leadville
Boom Days: August. Burro races and rock drilling contests. (719) 486-2997; www.leadville.com/boomdays.

Littleton
Western Welcome Week: Second week in August. Celebrates Littleton's well-preserved Main Street, arts, and Littleton History Museum. (303) 794-4870.

Louisville
La Festa: Second Sunday in August, since 1988. Celebrates the Italian heritage shared by many Louisvillians. (303) 666-6565.

Loveland
Sculpture in the Parks Festival: Second weekend in August, since 1983. This has grown into one of America's largest sculpture shows. (800) 551-1752.

Olathe
Sweet Corn Festival: In early August. This small town offers crafts, games, concerts, fireworks and all of Colorado's sweetest corn you can eat free. (970) 323-6006.

Palisade
Peach Festival: August, since about 1900. Includes a peach-recipe cookoff, parade, craft fair and town-grouch contest. (970) 464-7458.

Pueblo
Colorado State Fair: August–September, since 1872. The biggest fair has grown into a 17-day extravaganza with nationally known music stars, stock showings, rodeos, rides and games. (719) 561-8484.

Rocky Ford
Melon Days: In mid-August, since 1877. This is an orgy of feasting on free honeydew melons and watermelons. (719) 254-7723.

Silverton
Great Western Rocky Mountain Brass Band Festival & Hardrockers Holidays: Every August, since 1950. Features music by brass bands from all over the world, and a miner's carnival with rock drilling contests. (800) 752-4494.

SEPTEMBER

Delta
Council Tree Pow Wow & Cultural Festival: Last weekend in September. Named for the Ute Council cottonwood tree, where peace treaties were negotiated, this American Indian event offers dancing, singing, jewelry, fry bread and an art show. (800) 874-1741.

Denver
Festival of Mountain and Plain: A Taste of Colorado: Labor Day Weekend. Denver's Festival of Mountain and Plain, celebrated between 1895 and 1911, was revived in the 1980s as a "Taste of Colorado," offering samples from hundreds of restaurants. Attracts some 400,000 to Civic Center Park. (303) 892-7004.

Durango
Cowboy Days: Last weekend in September. Musicians, storytellers and cowboy poets. (800) 525-8855.

Estes Park
Longs Peak Scottish/Irish Highland Festival: First weekend following Labor Day, since 1976. Ethnic entertainers, bagpipes, food from the United Kingdom, caber tossing, and tartans and kilts galore. (800) 443-7837.

Greeley
Potato Day Harvest Festival: Second Saturday in September, since the 1890s. A parade, largest-potato contest and other spudfun. (970) 350-9220.

Ignacio
Iron Horse Motorcycle Rally: Every Labor Day since 1992. Ignacio resident and

More Calendar of Annual Events

Northern Cheyenne Chief Ben Nighthorse Campbell, a U.S. Senator, champions this rally of bikers, which draws some 30,000 participants.

Leadville
St. Patrick's Day Practice Parade: *Saturday closest to Sept. 17. Because March is snowy and cold in two-mile-high Leadville, townsfolk celebrate St. Patrick's Day on the warmer, sunnier Saturday closest to Sept. 17 with a parade, corn beef and cabbage, music and green beer. (719) 486-3900.*

Longmont
Pumpkin Pie Days: *September, since 1899. Harvest festival features "pie in the sky" floats, postcards, poetry, political addresses and samples served "by the prettiest girls in Longmont, which means the prettiest girls in Colorado." (303) 776-6050.*

Palisade
Colorado Mountain Winefest: *Second weekend in September. A sampling of locally grown wines at Colorado's premier wine event. (800) 704-3667.*

Pueblo
Chile and Frijoles Festival: *Fourth weekend in September. This harvest celebration honors the hottest local crops. (800) 233-3446.*

Saguache
Handmade Tour: *Second weekend in September, since 1994. Artists display and sell handmade arts and crafts. Live music, food, beer garden and fresh produce in Otto Mears Park on U.S. Hwy. 287. (719) 655-2805.*

Telluride
Telluride Film Festival: *First week in September, since 1974. World-renowned festival celebrates the art of film with premieres, tributes, restored old films, shorts, foreign films and seminars with film stars and critics. (888) 783-0263.*

OCTOBER

Denver
Great American Beer Festival: *First week in October. Hundreds of brewers and brewpubs exhibit and taste malt beverages and award medals to most meritorious.*

Lafayette
Oatmeal Festival: *October, since 1996. This city's ode to wholesome living includes an oatmeal breakfast and lunch, a 5-kilometer walk and run, and samples of myriad oatmeal products, from oatmeal pancakes to musical instruments made from oatmeal tubes.*

NOVEMBER

Cripple Creek
Gold Camp Christmas: *Nov. 21–Dec. 31. Mining headframes are lighted and bonfires ignited for caroling and reenactments of "Ghosts of Christmas Past." (877) 858-4653.*

Pueblo
Christmas at Rosemont: *November and December. Historic 37-room Victorian Rosemont Mansion is decorated for the holiday season and tours. (719) 545-5290.*

Woodland Park
Mountain Holiday Festival Arts & Crafts Fair: *Third weekend in November, since 1954. Artists and craftspeople demonstrate and sell handmade works at the Ute Pass Cultural Center. (719) 687-9885.*

DECEMBER

Burlington
Old Town Country Christmas Jubilee: *First Sunday in December. An afternoon of bells ringing, a choir of women singing, and kids performing in Old Town's historic buildings.*

Denver
Parade of Lights: *First week in December, since 1978. Tremendous floats, marching bands and giant balloons highlight this Christmas-time parade that brings people downtown for a light show, including the lavish lighting of the City and County Building with 40,000 floodlights, as well as "Wild Lights" at the Denver Zoo and "Blossoms of Light" at the Denver Botanic Gardens. (303) 534-6161.*

(Continued from page 38)

camp in 1942 to train the ski troops of the Tenth Mountain Division. A few hundred experienced skiers, including both Ivy League skiers and coaches and Colorado mountaineers, trained thousands of volunteers. These ski troops helped liberate northern Italy and the Alps from the Germans in 1944 and 1945.

Camp Hale was closed and dismantled after World War II, although commemorative markers and a National Register site remain today on U.S. Hwy. 24 seven miles north of Tennessee Pass. One of Camp Hale's ski training hills has evolved into the Ski Cooper winter sports area. Many veterans of Camp Hale returned to Colorado to establish or work in ski areas after the war. During the 1990s, Tenth Mountain Division veterans helped construct a hut-to-hut cross-county skiing/hiking route (970-925-5775; www.huts.org).

Cats
Domestic cats, unlike dogs, were reluctant to leave the genteel, regular refinements of the East. Western frontier towns infested with rodents, however, were desperate, offering as much as $25 for felines. Rev. Jacob Adriance, a pioneer Methodist minister, reported that Denver's first cat, Tabby, arrived in 1860. The bidding war started at $10.

Three species of wild cats also reside in Colorado:

Mountain lions *(Felix concolor)*. These are the largest of the state's cats, measuring from 5 to 9 feet from whisker tip to tail tip. Also known as cougars, painters, panthers and pumas, these felines are brownish to reddish brown with paler undersides. They occupy western and central Colorado, commonly in rough, broken foothills, canyon lands and montane forests. Their favorite prey is deer, but they will settle for domestic livestock, foxes, porcupines, raccoons, beavers and other rodents as well

Mountain lion. From *The Great Rocky Mountain Nature Factbook*; illustration by Marjorie C. Leggitt.

as birds and fish. These cats range 20 to 30 miles in a day.

Humans are the chief cause of mountain lion mortality, although starvation is also a factor, especially for older cats with worn or broken teeth. From 1929 to 1965, mountain lions were listed as predators in Colorado and a bounty was paid for their hides. They are now hunted, with a controlled Colorado harvest of about 200 animals annually. Mountain lions rarely attack humans. They killed an Idaho Springs jogger in 1991 and a boy in Rocky Mountain National Park in 1998. As suburbs and developments sprawl into mountain lion habitats, conflicts with humans intensify.

Lynx *(Lynx lynx)*. Rarest and most solitary of Colorado cats, the lynx spends its life in a small ecological band around 9,000 feet, just above bobcat range. With tufted ears pointed like radar, it patrols a 50-square-mile range, searching for snowshoe hares. The lynx, a bobtailed animal, measures about 3 feet long and weighs 20 to 30 pounds. Its long legs and large feet serve as snowshoes. Its long, fine fur is gray to reddish brown, often tinged with black, with paler undersides and a black tail tip.

Lynx were thought to be extinct in Colorado in 1999, when the Colorado Division of Wildlife introduced 41 animals

45

from Canada and Alaska to the San Juan Mountains. Of these, six died of starvation, three were shot, two were hit by motor vehicles, one was killed by a predator and five died from unknown causes. Another 33 radio-collared lynx were released in 2000. In the March 2000 mating season, Division of Wildlife officials jubilantly reported that two pair of lynx were keeping company.

Cemetery near Crested Butte. Photo by Susan Dupere.

Bobcats *(Lynx rufus).* About twice the size of a domestic cat, the bobcat has a bobbed tail, long legs and grayish to reddish fur with dark stripes and spots. Bobcats prowl rocky, broken terrain in the foothills and canyon lands, piñon-juniper woodlands and montane forests. They have also been seen in river and creek bottoms on the eastern plains. They relish rabbits, but will eat deer, mice, chipmunks, squirrels, prairie dogs, porcupines, birds, amphibians, crayfish and young domestic sheep, goats, poultry and household pets. Bobcats are generally solitary except during mating season. Human hunters, starvation, mountain lions and coyotes are the leading causes of death.

Caves
Colorado has 265 known caves. Prehistoric Coloradans lived in these caves, the state's oldest residences, and left pictographs and petroglyphs like those in Sweetwater Indian Cave in Garfield County.

Groaning Cave in the White River National Forest near Dotsero is Colorado's largest known cave—almost 10 miles long. The Cave of the Winds in Manitou Springs and the Fairy Caverns in Glenwood Springs are commercially operated and open to the public. The Caverna del Oro near Westcliffe is the best known of many caves to contain legendary—and very elusive—lost treasure.

To learn more: The Colorado Grotto of the National Speleological Society, 680 Emerson St., Denver 80218.

Cemeteries
These are good places to study not only the people of the past and their monuments, but also nature. Denver's Fairmount Cemetery, for instance, is also the state's biggest arboretum and an urban preserve for birds, foxes, rabbits and other wildlife. Architecturally distinctive mausoleums and artistic tombstones commemorate the lives of prominent and ordinary folk. Paupers, on the other hand, are buried in unmarked rows in low-lying cemetery nooks and crannies. Many cemeteries include ethnic burial sections, mirroring the enclaves of their communities.

Most burial grounds are small family sites in rural areas. While ghost towns may have overgrown and disheveled boneyards, larger cities and towns have generally well-kept, landscaped burial grounds. Visitors can inspect a full spectrum of funeral markers, including stone lambs for children, broken tree stumps for Woodmen of the World members and communal markers for victims of mine disasters. Larger cemeteries often have guidebooks or maps for tombstone tourists. Cemeteries traditionally are free and open dawn to dusk.

Chambers of Commerce (SEE ALSO TOURISM)

Because of the importance of business and tourism to almost every community, even small towns often have a chamber of commerce eager to provide information on local conditions and attractions. Information on Colorado chambers of commerce is available at (800) 265-6723 or www.state.co.us/business_dir/chambers.html.

Charities

Philanthropy had a slow start in Colorado, a state founded by gold rushers who came to "get and git out." Most planned to take whatever wealth they could find back to their former homes. Native Americans generously welcomed palefaced pilgrims. Little Raven, Niwot and Friday, three Southern Arapaho chiefs, greeted white newcomers in English. They followed the tradition, common among many tribes, of honoring an individual for how much he gave away rather than for how much he hoarded.

While Colorado men seemed preoccupied with ripping riches from the earth and selling off parcels of Colorado as the promised land, some pioneer women grew concerned about the less fortunate. One of them, Elizabeth Byers, wife of the founder of the *Rocky Mountain News*, set up Colorado's first charity, the Ladies' Union Aid Society. The ladies made underwear, nightshirts and bandages for Civil War soldiers. After the war, they continued to aid the poor, tend the sick and bury the dead. In 1876, the Society built Denver's Old Ladies Home, which still serves its original mission of housing, feeding and amusing indigent widows and elderly ladies.

Tuberculosis victims flocked to Colorado for the curative high, dry, sunny air. Some arrived with few resources and found that their highly contagious, deadly disease made them outcasts. Locals criticized these "lungers" and the "one-lunged army" and threatened to put bells on them to warn healthy citizens. The plight of these ostracized people touched Frances Wisebart Jacobs (see entry), Colorado's "mother of charities." She spearheaded establishment of a free dispensary and of what has become National Jewish Hospital, still a leader in treating respiratory disorders.

By the 1880s, more than a dozen charities were active in Colorado. To

Father Woody

When the Christmas blizzard of 1982 was followed by months of bitter cold, Rev. Charles B. "Woody" Woodrich of Holy Ghost Catholic Church in downtown Denver let the homeless sleep in the pews of his luxurious onyx and gold sanctuary. He burned incense to hide the odor and ignored parishioners who complained that the homeless fouled the church. Father Woody became legendary for giving 20-dollar bills to panhandlers who asked for spare change. ✷

coordinate them, Rev. Myron Reed, a leading Congregational minister, and Frances Jacobs established an interfaith umbrella group to consolidate fund raising and dispensation. They enlisted Dean Martyn Hart of St. John's Episcopal Church, Father William J. O'Ryan of St. Leo's Catholic Church and Rabbi William S. Friedman of Temple Emanuel. This ecumenical team organized the Charity Organization Society, now the United Way.

Charity is now also dispensed by more than 200 philanthropic foundations and some 10,000 nonprofit groups in Colorado. Foundations are a product of federal tax law as well as *noblesse oblige.* Establishment of a federal income tax in 1913 and of a federal inheritance tax in 1916 sparked the first flurry of foundations.

During the 1930s, President Franklin D. Roosevelt's heavy New Deal inheritance taxes led to a proliferation of tax-exempt charities. Mining tycoon Albert E. Humphreys set up the first Colorado philanthropic foundation, the Humphreys Foundation in 1922, followed by Irish milling millionaire John K. Mullen's Mullen Foundation in 1924, the Denver Foundation in 1925, the Colorado Springs Community Trust Fund in 1928, the Boettcher Foundation and El Pomar Foundation in 1937 and the Coulter Foundation in 1938.

In Colorado, 15 foundations dominate the dollar amounts given each year for Colorado causes: El Pomar, The Colorado Trust, Rose Community, Boettcher, Gates, Coors, Johnson, Denver, Daniels, Bonfils-Stanton, Buell, Monfort, Hunter, Taylor and Schlessman. Each makes annual grants of more than $1 million.

Church groups, such as Catholic Charities and Lutheran Family Services, also contribute substantially to improving the condition of Colorado's needy and underserved, including a growing homeless population and refugees from around the world.

Chase, Mary McDonough Coyle

(*SEE ALSO* AUTHORS) The author of the Pulitzer Prize-winning play *Harvey,* one of Broadway's most popular and longest running hits, wrote more than a dozen other comedies. She satirized contemporary American life, earning praise from Dorothy Parker as "the greatest unacclaimed wit in America."

Mary Coyle, born in Denver in 1907, learned storytelling from her Irish-born family. Their tales of banshees, leprechauns and pookas would later appear in her stories and plays. She attended Denver schools, graduating from West High in 1922 at the age of 15. She attended the University of Denver and the University of Colorado before joining the *Rocky Mountain News.* An attractive, raven-haired woman who dressed stylishly, she wrote a newspaper column, "Society Notes."

In 1931, she left the newspaper to write plays, while also working as a freelance writer of articles, short stories

Denverite Mary Coyle Chase won the Pulitzer Prize in 1945 for her play Harvey. *Denver Public Library, Western History Department.*

and children's books. Hoping to bring laughter to wartime America, Chase wrote a comedy about a 6-foot-tall imaginary white rabbit. *Harvey* opened on Broadway in 1944 and ran for 1,775 performances, also becoming a Universal-International Pictures movie starring Jimmy Stewart in 1950.

Chase died in Denver in 1981. Her childhood home, a small one-story cottage at 532 W. Fourth Ave., has been designated a landmark by the City of Denver.

Cheeseburger

Hamburgers garnished with cheese were invented by Denver's Louis E. Ballast at his Humpty Dumpty Drive In. Ballast sent in his patent application Jan. 1, 1932, after supposedly making the historic discovery by accident when cheddar cheese spilled onto his hamburger grill. The Humpty Dumpty at the corner of Speer and Federal boulevards in North Denver later burned down, but the cheeseburger lives on worldwide.

Cities and Towns

(*SEE ALSO* COUNTIES; GHOST TOWNS; PLACE NAMES) Colorado's first sizable towns may have been the pueblos and cliff dwellings that prehistoric Indians built in southwestern Colorado and abandoned around A.D. 1300. Cliff Palace, the largest known settlement, had a population estimated at 500.

Colorado's oldest continuously occupied town, San Luis, was established by Spanish-speaking settlers from New Mexico in 1851. With the gold rush, Denver, Boulder and many other towns were founded in 1858. Perhaps half the cities in Colorado began as real estate subsidiaries of railroads, which hoped to support railroad construction by town development and real estate sales. The Denver & Rio Grande Railroad helped

found Colorado Springs, Alamosa, Durango and many other towns along its tracks. When the railroads pulled up tracks, and mines, farms and ranches failed, over half the post office towns in Colorado became ghosts.

Largest Cities	Elev. (ft.)	Population
1. Denver (1858)	5,280	554,636
2. Colorado Springs (1870)	6,012	360,890
3. Aurora (1891)	5,342	276,393
4. Lakewood (1892)	5,440	144,126
5. Fort Collins (1873)	4,984	118,652
6. Centennial (2001)	5,382	103,014
7. Arvada (1871)	5,337	102,153
8. Pueblo (1859)	4,695	102,121
9. Westminster (1911)	5,280	100,940
10. Boulder (1858)	5,363	94,673
11. Thornton (1953)	5,268	82,384
12. Greeley (1870)	4,663	76,930
13. Longmont (1872)	4,979	71,093
14. Highlands Ranch (1976)	5,461	70,931
15. Loveland (1877)	4,982	50,608
16. Grand Junction (1881)	4,586	41,986
17. Littleton (1861)	5,362	40,340
18. Broomfield (1884)	5,420	38,272
19. Wheat Ridge (1913)	5,445	32,913
20. Englewood (1903)	5,306	31,727
21. Northglenn (1959)	5,460	31,575
22. Parker (1877)	5,870	23,558
23. Lafayette (1889)	5,237	23,197
24. Commerce City (1952)	5,150	20,991
25. Brighton (1871)	4,982	20,905
26. Castle Rock (1871)	6,202	20,224
27. Louisville (1878)	5,350	18,937
28. Golden (1859)	5,675	17,159
29. Cañon City (1859)	5,343	15,431
30. Durango (1880)	6,512	13,922
31. Montrose (1882)	5,794	12,344

Source: 2000 U.S. Census

The state's ten largest cities housed about two-fifths of Colorado's 4.3 million residents in 2000. Sprawling cities such as Arvada, Aurora, Colorado Springs, Fort Collins, Lakewood and Pueblo have annexed dozens of smaller surrounding towns. Six once-tiny suburbs of Denver (Aurora, Arvada, Lakewood, Littleton,

Thornton and Westminster) are now thriving cities themselves. (See the separate entries in this book for Arvada; Aspen; Boulder; Denver; Durango; Grand Junction; Leadville; Loveland; Pueblo; Trinidad.)

Colorado's most populous cities lie in the state's more temperate lower elevations. Although high-country towns such as Aspen, Leadville, Central City and Cripple Creek were once in the top five for population, the long, hard winters at such elevations as well as the collapse of the mining industry led to their decline. The list on page 49 includes each city's date of founding in parentheses.

Climate (SEE ALSO SNOW; WIND)

Colorado weather varies wildly depending on elevation, season and time of day. The state's high altitude makes for thin, dry air conducive to intense solar radiation and rapid evening cooling that generally leads to a daily temperature fluctuation of at least 25 degrees Fahrenheit. The sudden arrival of a Canadian cold front can drop temperatures within a few hours by 40 degrees. Chill factors from high winds can make actual temperatures sink far below thermometer readings. On the other hand, Chinook (an Indian word for "snow eater") winds may elevate the temperature 40 degrees.

Elevation greatly influences moisture as well as temperature. For every 1,000 feet gained, temperatures drop about 3 degrees Fahrenheit, and the annual precipitation rate rises about 3 inches. The mean annual temperature difference between the summit of Pikes Peak and the lower Arkansas Valley towns 100 miles away is 35 degrees—the difference between Florida and Iceland. Yet on winter days, when Canadian cold fronts bring subzero temperatures and blizzards to the plains, the foothills and mountain valleys can be balmy since upslope weather rarely penetrates beyond the foothills.

Elevation also affects humans: babies born in Colorado weigh about half a pound less than those born at sea level. People with acute heart or lung problems are advised to avoid Colorado's high country with its shortage of oxygen.

Colorado has three seasons: winter, summer and fall. Spring is lost amid late winter snows that melt suddenly on hot summer-like days. Dry, sunny, mild weather often lingers into November, although Halloween snowstorms are one of Mother Nature's favorite tricks for trick-or-treaters. Colorado's long, pleasant autumn is decorated with golden aspen, cottonwood and willow, as well as red scrub oak. Even in the mountain towns, snow usually does not become a winter-long blanket until December. Atop the western plateaus and on the eastern plains, snow rarely covers the ground for more than a week at a time.

Colorado's yearly average temperature is 44 degrees Fahrenheit, but the records show an all-time high of 118 at Bennett, near Denver, and an all-time low of 61 below zero at Maybell, in Moffat County. Drastic temperature changes have brought snow and killing frosts to Denver as late as Memorial Day and as early as Labor Day. Summer highs over 90 are common along the Front Range; Denver sweltered through a record-breaking 61 days of 90 degrees or more in 2000. Hundred-degree days have been recorded at all the eastern plains weather stations.

In a Flash

Flash floods can punish those who complain about Colorado's dryness. As much as a third of the annual rainfall for Colorado locales may fall in a single storm dumping 3 to 6 inches of rain in just a few hours. Flash flooding is the number one weather hazard in Colorado between July and September. ✳

Colorado Temperatures and Precipitation

Highest Temperatures, Degrees F

Data through 1999	Yrs*	Jan	Feb	Mar	Apr	May	Jun	Jul	Aug	Sep	Oct	Nov	Dec	Ann*
Alamosa	54	62	66	73	80	85	95	96	90	87	81	71	61	96
Colorado Springs	51	73	76	81	87	93	100	100	99	94	86	78	77	100
Denver	61	73	76	84	90	96	104	104	101	97	89	79	75	104
Grand Junction	53	60	68	81	89	95	105	105	103	100	88	75	64	105
Pueblo	58	81	81	86	93	99	108	106	104	101	94	84	82	108

Lowest Temperatures, Degrees F

Data through 1999	Yrs*	Jan	Feb	Mar	Apr	May	Jun	Jul	Aug	Sep	Oct	Nov	Dec	Ann*
Alamosa	54	−50	−35	−20	−6	11	24	30	29	15	−10	−30	−42	−50
Colorado Springs	51	−26	−27	−11	−3	21	32	42	39	22	5	−8	−24	−27
Denver	61	−25	−30	−11	−2	22	30	43	41	17	3	−8	−25	−30
Grand Junction	53	−23	−18	5	11	26	34	44	43	29	18	−2	−17	−23
Pueblo	58	−29	−31	−20	2	25	36	44	40	21	4	−17	−25	−31

Normal Daily Maximum Temperatures, Degrees F

1961–1990	Yrs*	Jan	Feb	Mar	Apr	May	Jun	Jul	Aug	Sep	Oct	Nov	Dec	Ann*
Alamosa	30	33	40	49	59	68	78	82	79	73	62	47	35	59
Colorado Springs	30	41	45	50	60	69	79	84	81	74	64	51	42	62
Denver	30	43	47	52	62	71	81	88	86	77	66	52	44	64
Grand Junction	30	36	45	56	66	76	88	94	90	81	68	51	39	66
Pueblo	30	45	51	57	68	76	88	93	90	81	70	57	47	69

Normal Daily Minimum Temperature, Degrees F

1961–1990	Yrs*	Jan	Feb	Mar	Apr	May	Jun	Jul	Aug	Sep	Oct	Nov	Dec	Ann*
Alamosa	30	−4	5	16	24	33	41	48	45	37	25	12	−1	23
Colorado Springs	30	16	19	25	33	42	51	57	55	47	36	25	17	35
Denver	30	16	20	26	34	44	52	59	57	48	36	25	17	36
Grand Junction	30	14	24	31	38	48	57	64	62	53	42	29	19	40
Pueblo	30	14	20	26	36	46	54	61	59	50	37	24	16	36

Normal Monthly Precipitation (inches)

1961–1990	Yrs*	Jan	Feb	Mar	Apr	May	Jun	Jul	Aug	Sep	Oct	Nov	Dec	Ann*
Alamosa	30	0.3	0.3	0.4	0.6	0.6	0.7	1.2	1.1	0.9	0.7	0.4	0.4	7.6
Colorado Springs	30	0.3	0.4	0.9	1.3	2.2	2.2	2.9	3.0	1.3	0.8	0.5	0.5	16.3
Denver	30	0.5	0.6	1.3	1.7	2.4	1.8	1.9	1.5	1.2	1.0	0.9	0.6	15.4
Grand Junction	30	0.6	0.5	0.9	0.8	0.9	0.5	0.6	0.8	0.8	1.0	0.7	0.6	8.7
Pueblo	30	0.3	0.3	0.8	0.9	1.2	1.2	2.1	2.0	0.9	0.6	0.4	0.4	11.1

Snowfall: Average Total in Inches (including ice pellets and sleet)

Data through 2000	Yrs*	Jan	Feb	Mar	Apr	May	Jun	Jul	Aug	Sep	Oct	Nov	Dec	Ann*
Alamosa	51	4.4	4.0	5.9	4.5	1.6	0.0	0.0	0.0	0.2	3.3	4.3	5.5	33.1
Colorado Springs	50	5.0	5.1	9.3	6.6	1.4	0.0	0.0	0.0	1.0	3.5	5.5	5.3	42.5
Denver	61	8.1	7.5	12.5	8.9	1.6	0.0	0.0	0.0	1.6	3.7	9.1	7.3	60.3
Grand Junction	52	6.9	4.0	3.7	1.1	0.1	0.0	0.0	0.0	0.1	0.5	2.7	5.1	23.8
Pueblo	56	5.7	4.3	7.0	4.1	0.6	0.0	0.0	0.0	0.6	1.4	4.7	5.3	33.3

*Yrs: Number of years from which statistics have been calculated

*Ann: Annual extreme or average

Source: www.ncdc.noaa.gov/ol/climate/online/ccd

Bitter cold grips every part of the state for at least a few days every year, killing off many insect pests. Mountain-valley towns often have the dubious distinction of being the coldest communities in the contiguous 48 states.

Winds, sometimes dangerously high, characterize the entire state but especially the Front Range foothills. Denver's average wind speed, 9 miles per hour, can be a blessing when it blows away air pollution.

Throughout much of Colorado, winter days may be surprisingly warm, permitting outdoor activities in January. Summer nights are generally cool because the dry, thin atmosphere rapidly loses heat after sunset. Once a leading state for tuberculosis victims chasing the "climate cure," Colorado now has smog along the Front Range that may chase away people wanting to breathe easier. Overall, Colorado's cool, sunny climate generally delights residents and visitors. Unexpected changes in the climate are common, however, so it is advisable to dress in layers.

Coal (SEE ALSO MINING) This fossil fuel is created from decomposing vegetable and animal matter. Its discovery is a reminder of an ancient past when now-extinct creatures roamed a swampy, lushly vegetated Colorado. Approximately 88 percent of Colorado's coal is bituminous, 10 percent sub-bituminous and only 2 percent anthracite. Gold seekers first found coal along Clear Creek, near Golden, in 1859, and prospectors have frequently stumbled across it since then. One indication of the mineral's abundance is the 45 different Colorado streams named Coal Creek.

Coal has been found both in the mountains and on the prairies, where black prairie dog mounds have been a clue. Between the 1870s and the 1930s, coal mining centered on the northern fields around Boulder and the southern fields around Trinidad. Today those fields are largely played out; production has shifted to huge open-pit mines in northwestern Colorado and the upper Gunnison River valley. Of more than 50 coal-mining towns, the handful that have survived have done so by switching to other pursuits. These include Crested Butte, Erie, Lafayette, Louisville, Redstone and Walsenburg.

Railroad builders looked for coal to fuel steam locomotives, launching an intensive search for deposits. By carrying and burning coal, trains helped transform Colorado production from 13,500 tons in 1870 to 1,229,593 tons in 1883. Coal mining also provided coke for smelters and steel mills. Besides fueling trains and factories, coal heated most Colorado homes and businesses. Acrid coal smoke, coal ash, clinkers and the constant need for more coal were part of nearly everyone's life until the introduction in 1928 of cheaper, cleaner, more-efficient natural-gas heating. Natural gas and electricity have since replaced coal for heating and cooking in most homes.

Coal mining revived during World War II, but slumped during the 1950s and 1960s. The industry was bolstered by the energy crisis of the early 1970s, which increased the demand for coal to fuel power plants. In 1999, Colorado miners produced 30 million tons of coal, an all-time high. Twelve mines, including three northwestern Colorado giants—Foidel Creek, West Elk and ColoWyo—provide coal primarily for power plants, which provide 82 percent of Colorado's electric power. Colorado ranks 12th nationally in coal production.

Cody, William Frederick "Buffalo Bill"

William Cody was born in Iowa in 1846. His career began when he ran away from home at age 13 to join the Colorado gold rush. A year later he became a Pony Express rider who boasted that he covered 322 miles in 21 hours and 40 minutes using 21 horses. In the book *Life & Adventures of Buffalo Bill,* (1917), Cody claims railroad construction crews nicknamed him after he fed them by killing, according to his own count, 4,280 buffalo.

For helping to defeat the Cheyenne at Summit Springs in eastern Colorado in 1869, Cody received the Congressional Medal of Honor. He slew Yellow Hair, a Cheyenne leader, in 1876 and boasted: "Jerking his war-bonnet off, I scientifically scalped him in about five seconds.... As the soldiers came up, I swung the Indian chieftain's top-knot and bonnet in the air, and shouted 'The first scalp for Custer!'"

After gaining national attention, Cody became the hero of more than 500 dime novels and Broadway plays, where he sometimes played himself. In 1883, he organized Buffalo Bill's Wild West Show, which toured the United States and Europe for three decades. Audiences flocked to see cowboys, Indians, reenactments of Indian battles and stagecoach robberies, trick shooting, rope work and fancy horseback riding.

During his final years, Cody's show became the possession of Fred Bonfils and

"Buffalo Bill" Cody went from Pony Express rider to showman. Buffalo Bill Memorial Museum, Lookout Mountain.

Harry Tammen of the *Denver Post*, who foreclosed on the bankrupt, aging showman. Tammen kept Cody the star, although the creaky, bewigged hero had to be lifted onto his horse. He died in his

> In 1976 the Colorado Historical Society officially ended the long controversy over whether the people who live in Colorado are Coloradans or Coloradoans. They're Coloradans. The *Fort Collins Coloradoan* disagrees.

sister's house at 2932 Lafayette St. in Denver. Some 25,000 people viewed his body as it lay in state inside the gold-domed Colorado state Capitol. Another 25,000 joined the funeral procession June 3, 1917, to the top of Lookout Mountain in Golden, where a graveside museum commemorates his life.

To learn more: Buffalo Bill Museum and Grave, 987½ Lookout Mountain Road, Golden 80401; (303) 526-0747.

Colorado Historical Society (SEE ALSO HISTORICAL

PRESERVATION) Since 1879, the historical society has been collecting, preserving and interpreting artifacts. In Denver, its Colorado History Museum and headquarters contains exhibits on the state's varied peoples, occupations, modes of transportation and buildings.

The society's library includes the most complete collection of Colorado newspapers and 600,000 photos, as well as books, pamphlets and manuscript collections. Its Denver headquarters also houses the State Historic Preservation Office, with extensive materials on thousands of National and State Register historical and archaeological sites.

The society maintains regional museums at Fort Garland, Leadville, Montrose, Platteville, Pueblo and Trinidad, as well as the Byers–Evans House in Denver. It also owns and operates the Georgetown Loop Railroad and Lebanon Mine as well as Pikes Stockade, some 20 miles south of Alamosa. The Society has installed and maintains more than 500 historical markers around the state.

To learn more: Colorado History Museum, 1300 Broadway, Denver 80203. Open Mon.–Sat. 10:00 A.M.– 4:30 P.M., Sun. noon–4:30 P.M.; $1.50–$3.00. (303) 866-3682; www.coloradohistory.org.

Colorado Railroad Museum (SEE ALSO RAILROADS)

Puffs of white incense regularly rise skyward out of Clear Creek Valley when the Iron Horse cult congregates to honor the mighty steam locomotive at its greatest Rocky Mountain shrine, the Colorado Railroad Museum. The CRM, since 1958, has been preserving and publicizing Colorado's rail history by the trainload. The museum in Golden is owned and operated by a nonprofit corporation, the Colorado Railroad Historical Foundation. CRM volunteers lay track, restore grungy old rolling stock and keep the museum open.

Just east of the Coors Brewery, the railroad museum lives in a replica of an 1880s' depot at the foot of North Table Mountain. The museum shop has the largest collection of rail antiques, publications and gifts in the Rocky Mountains, not to mention posters,

calendars, timetables, lanterns, postcards, belt buckles, badges and patches.

Downstairs, the museum houses exhibits, dioramas, an HO model railroad and a research library. Outside is the largest collection of narrow and standard gauge stock in the Rockies: 56 locomotives, cabooses, cars and passenger coaches. These antiques are exercised regularly on a half-mile of track rimming the 12-acre site, including a steam-fired Santa Claus excursion for youngsters.

To learn more: Colorado Railroad Museum, 17155 W. 44th Ave., Golden 80402. Open every day except Thanksgiving and Christmas, 9 A.M.–5 P.M. $3 adult, $1.50 under 16, or $6.50 per family. (800) 365-6263; www.crrm.org.

Colorado Springs

The El Paso County seat was founded in 1871 by William Jackson Palmer, president of the Denver & Rio Grande Railroad. Palmer planted his model town at the eastern base of Pikes Peak around the junction of Monument and Fountain creeks and named it for nearby Manitou Springs.

Palmer purchased the 10,000-acre townsite for $10,000 and built a spacious residential city of broad, tree-lined streets. Smoke, sweat and noise would be banished to Denver, Colorado's rail and smelter hub, and to Pueblo, the steel city. Initially, Colorado Springs attracted English settlers and wealthy tuberculosis patients.

Palmer provided land for Colorado College, the Colorado School for the Deaf and Blind, and an extensive system of parks, which has come to include the Garden of the Gods (see entry) with its spectacular red stone formations. Colorado Springs grew slowly until the Cripple Creek gold rush of the 1890s and early 1900s caused it to boom. Since World War II, military installations (the Air Force Academy, Ent Air Force Base, Fort Carson, the North American Air Defense Command and Peterson Air Force Base) and high-tech industries have transformed Colorado Springs into the second-largest city in Colorado. The city's population climbed nearly 31 percent during the 1990s to 360,890 in 2000.

Other attractions include the Broadmoor Hotel, Colorado College, Colorado Springs Fine Arts Museum, the Colorado Springs Museum, the Fountain Valley School, the ProRodeo Hall of Fame and Museum, the University of Colorado's Colorado Springs campus, the Western Museum of Mining and Industry and the World Figure Skating Museum and Hall of Fame.

To learn more: Colorado Springs Convention and Visitors Bureau; (800) 368-4748; www.coloradosprings-travel.com.

Colorado Tick Fever

Avoid Colorado tick fever by wearing long pants, boots and long-sleeve shirts in wooded or grassy areas and by wearing tick repellent. If potentially exposed to these tiny blood-sucking insects, inspect the scalp, groin, armpits, behind the knees, around the waistband and other potentially moist, sheltered body parts. Most tick bites are not infectious, but an average of 50 to 60 Colorado tick fever cases are reported each year.

Although Colorado tick fever has never been fatal, it is hard to cure. The symptoms are flu-like: chills, fever, aches, headache and fatigue will appear for three or four days, disappear, and then reappear for several more days. Once the disease is gone, patients cannot be reinfected.

Two other tick-transmitted diseases are more serious. They are Rocky Mountain spotted fever (see entry) and Lyme disease. Cases of Lyme disease, a neurological disease spread by ticks, were first diagnosed in the northeastern U.S. and are rare in Colorado.

Columbine Plant

Edwin James, botanist and physician of the 1820 Long Expedition to eastern Colorado, discovered near Palmer Lake what he called *Aquilegia* (Latin for "eagle") *coerulea* ("blue"). Five distinctive knobbed spurs and showy white and blue blossoms make the columbine easy to recognize. A member of the buttercup family, its flowers are 1 to 3 inches in diameter and bloom between May and August.

On Arbor Day in 1891, schoolchildren chose the columbine as the Colorado state flower by a landslide 15,000 votes. The

Columbine. Photo by Gail Brooks.

closest competitors included goldenrod, mariposa lily, wild rose and yucca. Once much more common, the columbine has suffered from sheep grazing in high mountain meadows and wildflower plucking excursions. To curb the latter, the 1924 Columbine Law made it illegal to pick from public property more than 25 buds or blossoms in one day or to uproot the plants.

In its native environment from 6,000 to 12,000 feet elevation, the blue columbine is as blue as the Colorado sky. In other states and at lower elevations, it fades into paler colors. Columbines inspired Arthur J. Flynn to write the state song, "Out Where the Columbines Grow," in 1915.

At Columbine High School in suburban Jefferson County, the 1999 killings of one teacher and 12 students by two students, who then killed themselves, gave a tragic new connotation to the columbine, widely worn afterward as a symbol of grief and concern.

Congressional Delegation (SEE ALSO ELECTED OFFICIALS; GOVERNORS; LEGISLATURE)

As early as 1858, Coloradans elected and sent back to Congress a representative of what was then called the Pikes Peak Region to lobby for territorial status. After Colorado Territory was created in 1861, a representative was elected for each session of Congress.

With statehood in 1876, Colorado received two Senate seats and a single U.S. representative. Not until 1890 did the population increase warrant a second congressional district. In 1902, Colorado received a third congressional seat, with the fourth seat in 1913, the fifth in 1972 and the sixth in 1982. The fast-growing state gained a seventh congressional district after the 2000 census.

Colorado Congressional Districts

MOFFAT

ROUTT

JACKSON

LARIMER

Fort Collins

WELD

LOGAN

SEDGWICK

PHILLIPS

RIO BLANCO

GRAND

BOULDER

Boulder

GILPIN

BROOM-FIELD

1

MORGAN

ADAMS

DENVER

WASHINGTON

YUMA

GARFIELD

3

EAGLE

SUMMIT

2

ARAPAHOE

PITKIN

CLEAR CREEK

JEFFERSON

DENVER

DOUGLAS

6

ELBERT

KIT CARSON

4

Grand Junction

LAKE

MESA

DELTA

GUNNISON

PARK

CHAFFEE

5

TELLER

EL PASO

Colorado Springs

LINCOLN

CHEYENNE

FREMONT

MONTROSE

OURAY

SAN MIGUEL

HINSDALE

SAGUACHE

CUSTER

Pueblo

PUEBLO

CROWLEY

KIOWA

Las Animas

PROWERS

DOLORES

SAN JUAN

MINERAL

RIO GRANDE

ALAMOSA

HUERFANO

OTERO

BENT

MONTEZUMA

LA PLATA

ARCHULETA

CONEJOS

COSTILLA

LAS ANIMAS

BACA

— COUNTY LINE
— DISTRICT BOUNDARY

U.S. Senators

Ben Nighthorse Campbell was first elected in 1992 to the Senate as a Democrat; he was reelected in 1998 as a Republican. Earlier he served three terms in the U.S. House of Representatives as a Democrat and was a member of the Colorado Legislature. Campbell, a rancher and jewelry maker from Ignacio, is the only Native American in Congress and the first to ever serve in the Senate. He is a member of the Council of Chiefs of the Northern Cheyenne tribe. Office: 6950 E. Belleview Ave., Suite 200, Englewood 80111; (303) 843-4100; www.senate.gov.

Wayne Allard, a Republican, was elected to the Senate in 1996 after three terms in the

House of Representatives. Allard is a veterinarian from Loveland who served earlier in the Colorado Legislature. Office: 734 E. Caley Ave., Suite 215, Englewood 80111; (303) 220-7414; www.senate.gov.

U.S. Representatives

District 1 (Denver):
Diana DeGette (D)
This district has traditionally voted Democratic, although Republican James McKevitt captured the office from 1971 to 1973, when he was replaced by Colorado's first congresswoman, Patricia Schroeder. During her 1973–1996 tenure in the House, she was hailed as one of the most powerful women in Washington and promoted as a

presidential candidate. DeGette has represented the Denver area since 1997. An attorney, she previously served in the Colorado legislature. Office: 1400 Glenarm Place, Suite 202, Denver 80202; (303) 844-4988; www.house.gov/degette.

District 2 (Boulder, Gilpin and parts of Jefferson County): **Mark Udall (D)**
Voters have twice elected Udall, a former Boulder city councilman and former director of Colorado Outward Bound, who replaced fellow Democrat David Skaggs in 1998. Udall is the son of former U.S. representative and presidential aspirant Morris K. Udall. Office: 1333 W. 120th Ave., Suite 210, Westminster 80234; (303) 457-4500; www.house.gov/markudall.

District 3 (Western Slope and San Luis Valley): **Scott McInnis (R)**
McInnis, a former Glenwood Springs police officer and lawyer, has represented District 3 since 1988. He served in the Colorado House of Representatives, where he was Republican majority leader. Office: Hotel Colorado, 526 Pine St., Suite 100, Glenwood Springs 81601; (970) 945-6511; www.house.gov/mcinnis.

District 4 (Larimer and Weld counties, Fort Collins, eastern Colorado): **Bob Schaffer (R)**
The district has been Republican controlled since its creation in 1982. Schaffer has represented the district since 1996. Schaffer ran without a Democratic opponent in 2000 and said he would retire in 2002, voluntarily observing a three-term limit. He previously served in the Colorado Senate. Office: 315 W. Oak St., Suite 307, Fort Collins 80521; (970) 493-9132; www.house.gov/schaffer.

District 5 (Colorado Springs, and El Paso, Elbert, Douglas, Chaffee and Lake counties): **Joel Hefley (R)**
A two-to-one Republican registration kept Democrats from nominating a candidate in 1996 and 2000. Hefley has won easily since 1987. He previously served in the Colorado Senate and House. Office: 104 S. Cascade Ave., Suite 105, Colorado Springs 80903; (719) 520-0055; www.house.gov/hefley.

District 6 (eastern, southern and western suburbs of Denver in Adams, Arapahoe and Jefferson counties): **Tom Tancredo (R)**
Tancredo, of Littleton, has represented this heavily Republican district since 1996. A veteran of the Colorado House, he also served as regional director for the U.S. Department of Education and director of the Independence Institute in Golden. Office: 5601 S. Broadway, Suite 370, Littleton 80121; www.house.gov/tancredo.

Continental Divide

Colorado straddles the Continental Divide at its highest point. This divide separates waters flowing eastward via the Arkansas, Platte and Rio Grande Rivers into the Atlantic Ocean and those flowing westward via the Colorado River into the Pacific Ocean. This backbone of North America separates Colorado's Eastern Slope from the Western Slope.

Coors, Adolph (*See also* BEER AND BREWPUBS; BUSINESS) Adolph Kohrs was born in Germany in 1847. Orphaned at 15, he became an apprentice brewer. He came to the United States as a stowaway and changed his name to Coors.

Adolph Coors' brewery in Golden, Colorado, about 1879. From 1880 edition *History of Boulder and Clear Creek Valleys, Colorado.* Tom Noel Collection

The young man reached Denver in 1872 and went to work making bottles, but remained more interested in what might fill them. In 1873 he opened a brewery in Golden with partner Jacob Schueler, whom he bought out in 1878. Coors made the brewery a success, but, troubled by Prohibition and health problems, he committed suicide in a Virginia hotel in 1929. His son, Adolph Coors Jr., grandson William K. Coors and great-grandson Peter Coors subsequently directed the brewery, which became Colorado's largest by 1940.

The use of tight quality control, refrigerated cars, cork tops and pop-top aluminum cans helped Coors become the industry leader in the Rockies. The Golden plant claims to be the world's largest single brewery operation. During the 1980s and 1990s, Coors expanded to national marketing and became the country's third-largest beer maker.

To learn more: The Coors brewery at 13th and Ford Street in Golden is open Mon.–Sat. for free tours, 10 A.M.–4 P.M. (303) 277-2337.

Counties (SEE ALSO CITIES AND TOWNS)

When Colorado became a state in 1876, it consisted of 17 counties: Arapahoe, Boulder, Clear Creek, Conejos, Costilla, Douglas, El Paso, Fremont, Gilpin, Huerfano, Jefferson, Lake, Larimer, Park, Pueblo, Summit and Weld.

Rapid growth soon led to creation of the mining counties of Custer, Gunnison, Ouray, and Routt in 1877. Lucrative silver strikes around Leadville led to subdivision of the original Lake County as Chaffee (1879) and Pitkin (1881). The removal of

Looking Back

1894

The Army Signal Corps built a balloon station at Fort Logan in southwest Denver that housed the nation's entire air force: a single tethered hydrogen-filled balloon.

Ute Indians to reservations in 1881 opened up northwestern Colorado, leading to the 1883 formation of Delta, Eagle, Garfield, Mesa and Montrose counties. The San Juan mining boom continued, resulting in the new counties of Dolores (1881), San Miguel (1883), Archuleta (1885) and Montezuma (1889).

Large counties, occupied primarily by ranchers and farmers, prevailed on the eastern plains. Stock growers generally opposed the formation of new counties, reckoning that the convenience of a closer courthouse was not worth the cost of building and staffing it. Furthermore, many rural folk reasoned that creation of a new county government only attracted politicians, lawyers, bureaucrats and other undesirables.

Railroads steaming westward into Colorado during the 1880s promoted heavier settlement of the plains by farmers who would become customers both as passengers and as shippers of crops and livestock. The Atchison, Topeka, and Santa Fe Railroad built through the Arkansas Valley, leading to the creation of Baca, Otero and Prowers counties in 1889. The Union Pacific built along the South Platte River through northeastern Colorado, sparking formation of Logan, Morgan, Phillips, Sedgwick, Washington and Yuma counties in the late 1880s. The Burlington and other roads laid tracks through the central eastern plains, encouraging the establishment of Cheyenne, Kiowa, Kit Carson and Lincoln counties in 1889.

A silver strike at Creede gave life to Mineral County (1893), and the last and greatest gold rush, at Cripple Creek, led to the creation in 1899 of Teller County. When

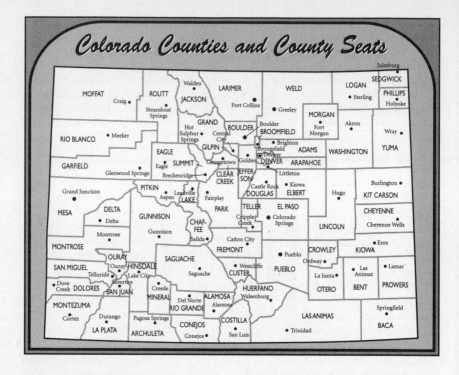

Colorado Counties and County Seats

the Denver & Salt Lake "Moffat" Railroad reached northwestern Colorado in 1911, a county was named in honor of rail tycoon David Moffat. Development of lumbering, mining and ranching led to the formation of Jackson County from Larimer County in 1909.

Passage of a state home-rule amendment permitted the City and County of Denver to be carved from Arapahoe County in 1902. Further dismemberment of once-vast Arapahoe County created Adams County (1902). Crowley (1911) and Alamosa (1913) counties originated as, and remain, agricultural areas. As of 1913, Colorado had 63 counties, a configuration that persisted until voters approved establishment of a new county for Broomfield in 2001 after that city had sprawled into four counties—Adams, Boulder, Jefferson and Weld—leading to a jurisdictional morass. El Paso County, with fast-growing Colorado Springs as its hub, is projected to be the largest county in population by 2020.

All counties are governed by three- or five-member boards of county commissioners, elected to four-year terms, except for the City and County of Denver, which is governed by a mayor and a city council.

Largest Counties by Population

County	2000	2020 (est.)
1. Denver	554,636	655,744
2. Jefferson	527,056	617,760
3. El Paso	516,929	703,381
4. Arapahoe	487,967	587,430
5. Adams	363,857	586,801
6. Boulder	291,288	394,344
7. Larimer	251,494	355,353
8. Weld	180,936	344,774
9. Douglas	175,766	361,813
10. Pueblo	141,472	184,851

Smallest Counties by Population

County	2000	2020 (est.)
1. San Juan	558	826
2. Hinsdale	790	1,179
3. Mineral	831	1,090
4. Jackson	1,577	2,451
5. Kiowa	1,622	1,937
6. Dolores	1,844	2,539
7. Cheyenne	2,231	2,564
8. Sedgwick	2,747	3,160
9. Costilla	3,663	4,316
10. Ouray	3,742	6,074

Largest Counties by Area (acres)

1. Las Animas	3,070,720
2. Moffat	3,047,040
3. Weld	2,581,120
4. Mesa	2,133,760
5. Rio Blanco	2,088,960
6. Gunnison	2,075,520
7. Saguache	2,013,440
8. Garfield	1,920,000
9. Larimer	1,689,600
10. Grand	1,196,160

Coyotes

Coyotes *(Canis latrans)* are becoming increasingly common in Colorado, even in settled areas. Their growing numbers, which threaten pet dogs and cats as well as sheep and mule deer, led the Colorado Division of Wildlife to champion aerial hunting of coyotes in 2001, despite widespread protest.

These slender mammals have sharp pointed ears and a black-tipped, bushy tail that hangs low. The fur is generally brownish to tannish intermixed with black. The face, ears, forelegs and undersides are tan to pink. Shy and secretive, coyotes are active mostly at night. They will eat almost anything they can catch, from rabbits to berries to carrion, from domestic sheep and domestic pets to fish and bugs. Coyotes bark, whimper, yip, howl and, especially at dusk or dawn, sing hauntingly mournful songs.

This singing may be part of an extended courtship of two to three months before actual mating. Coyotes generally mate for life. A few have mated with domestic dogs, making positive identification of some specimens almost impossible. Litters average five to six pups. Natal dens are generally dug into shrubby thickets, downed timber, steep banks or rocky areas. Their Colorado life expectancy in the wild can be 13 to 15 years, but is generally much shorter. Human predators eliminate from 38 to 90 percent of studied Colorado coyote populations.

Colorado (and many other states) defines coyotes as predators because of the damage they do to livestock, especially sheep. Although trapped, hounded, gassed, dynamited, drowned, poisoned and shot on general principle, coyotes have survived, even thrived. There are now more coyotes in more Colorado locales than ever before. Cagey, capable, resourceful and independent, these creatures have become accustomed to humans and may be found practically anywhere.

Coyotes haunt western literature, notably Hope Ryden's book *God's Dog*, J. Frank Dobie's *The Voice of the Coyote* and Mark Twain's *Roughing It*. Twain, echoing the contempt of many westerners, described the coyote as "a long, slim, sick and sorry looking skeleton, with a gray wolf-skin stretched over it, a tolerably bushy tail that forever sags down with a despairing expression of forsakedness and misery, a furtive and evil eye, and a long, sharp face, with slightly lifted lip and exposed teeth. The coyote is a living, breathing allegory of Want. He is always hungry. He is always poor, out of luck and friendless."

Crime

Colorado Territory originated hundreds of miles from any court or jail and became a haven for desperadoes. Early Coloradans formed miners' and peoples' courts to bring law and order to the territory. These informal courts often used vigilante action to quickly—if sometimes erratically—punish criminals.

Colorado has seen its share of celebrated criminal cases. The 1996 murder of 6-year-old Jon Benet Ramsey remains unsolved. Revered schoolteacher Emily Griffith (see entry) was killed in her Boulder County mountain cabin in 1947 and the perpetrator still remains a mystery. After Alfred Packer denied eating his five companions on an 1873 prospecting trip into the San Juan Mountains, the judge supposedly said, "Packer, you son of a bitch, there were only seven Democrats in Hinsdale County, and you ate five of 'em. I sentence you to hang until you are dead, dead, dead." Packer steadily maintained his innocence in this most bizarre of all Colorado crimes. He got a new trial on a technicality and eventually served only five years in the Colorado State Penitentiary, released on parole after being a model prisoner. Another Colorado celebrity criminal was the "king of western con men," Jefferson Randolph "Soapy" Smith (see entry).

Colorado enforces the death penalty with a gas chamber at the state penitentiary in Cañon City, where the Women's Territorial Prison is now a museum. Cañon City and nearby Florence now host America's largest federal prison complex, which has housed such notorious inmates as Timothy McVeigh and Terry Nichols (the Oklahoma City bombers), Ted Kaczynski (the Unabomber) and former Panamanian President Manuel Noriega. Crime in Colorado, as in the rest of the nation, has been declining on a per capita level for the past decade, with credit given to tighter gun controls, better law enforcement and widespread economic prosperity.

Murder Victims (1999)

Gender	Percentage
Male	71
Female	29

Race	Percentage
White	76
Black	19
Asian	4
Indian	1

Age	Number
Under 1	5
1–10	11
11–17	20
18–20	18
21–29	50
30–39	31
40–49	31
50–59	13
60–69	4
70 and over	4

Murder Perpetrators (1999)

Gender	Percentage
Male	71
Female	12
Unknown	17

Race	Percentage
White	61
Black	17
Asian	3
Indian	1
Unknown	18

Age	Number
Unknown	41
1–10	0
11–17	22
18–20	34
21–29	50
30–39	28
40–49	14
50–59	7
60–69	0

Homicides

Year	1990	1991	1992	1993	1994	1995	1996	1997	1998	1999
Number of Murders	138	197	213	194	189	205	176	176	178	187

Robbery

Year	1990	1991	1992	1993	1994	1995	1996	1997	1998	1999
Number of Robberies	2,982	3,630	4,131	4,040	3,404	3,551	6,253	3,403	3,187	3,034

Robbery. The Colorado Bureau of Investigation defines a robbery as taking or attempting to take anything of value under a confrontational circumstance from another person by force or threat of force or violence and/or by putting the victim in fear of immediate harm.

1882

Butch Cassidy held up his first bank, the San Miguel Valley Bank in Telluride.

Burglary. In 1998, Colorado law enforcement agencies reported 30,248 burglaries. Since 1986, this crime has decreased from the 58,441 burglaries reported in that year. Burglary is the most common type of major crime in Colorado, making up 59.2 percent of the major offenses reported.

Method of Threat (1999)

	Percentage
Firearm	37.4
Knife	8.7
Other weapon	13.9
Strong-arm tactics	40.0

Type of Burglary (1998)

	Percentage
Forced entry	53.6
Non-forced entry	34.9
Attempted burglary	8.1
No description available	3.4

Rape. The following figures may not be indicative of the actual number of forcible rapes committed, as victims may not report an assault.

Forcible Rape

Year	1985	1991	1998
Number of Rapes	1,317	1,589	1,818

Motor Vehicle Theft. Motor vehicle theft accounts for over 30 percent of the major crimes committed in Colorado.

Sex Offender Registration. There is no statewide sex offender registry, but residents may check their community registry by contacting local law enforcement.

To learn more: Colorado Bureau of Investigation; www.cdpsweb.state.co.us.

Motor Vehicle Theft

Year	1990	1991	1993	1994	1995	1996	1997	1998	1999
Number of Thefts	14,093	14,337	15,559	12,565	14,401	14,723	16,314	15,687	14,633

Day, David Frakes

With ferocious wit, this pioneer journalist sassed Colorado's tycoons and honored its working class.

Day, born in 1847 in Ohio, enlisted at age 15 in the Union Army, earning a Congressional Medal of Honor for his bravery at Vicksburg. After the war, Day settled in the southwestern Colorado mining town of Ouray. There he named his weekly newspaper the *Solid Muldoon* for a hoax of the time, a 7½-foot-tall "petrified" man "discovered" in 1877 near Pueblo and exhibited to the gullible public as the missing link between *Homo sapiens* and hairier, more distant ancestors.

Day termed his newspaper "A Dead Sure Thing. Democratic in Politics. Neutral in Religious and Domestic Affairs only." When politicians arrived from Denver to give speeches, the portly Day took delight in sprawling over front-row seats to take a nap. When questioned, he shot back: "I can lie down here, as long as you can lie up there."

In 1892, Day moved to Durango to edit the *Durango Democrat*, one of the few papers in the state to defend striking miners. Day criticized the Denver & Rio Grande Railroad, which had an economic stranglehold on many Colorado towns. In 1907, he complained that the D&RG's Durango Depot (now elegantly restored for the Durango & Silverton narrow-gauge excursion trains) was so dilapidated that it rivaled the nearby Mesa Verde ruins. One of Colorado's most admired, despised and quoted inkslingers died in Durango in 1914 and was buried in Denver's Riverside Cemetery.

Denver (SEE ALSO CITIES AND TOWNS) Colorado's capital city was founded

Nov. 22, 1858, after the William Green Russell party found gold in Cherry Creek and the South Platte River. Town founders named the baby town for James W. Denver, governor of Kansas Territory, of which eastern Colorado was then a part.

Denver's aggressive leadership, headed by William N. Byers (see entry) of the *Rocky*

> Cats were critical to Colorado development. They controlled rodents, kept humans warm and comfortable on cold nights and even helped sniff out gold veins. As Mark Twain noted, "If a man could be crossed with the cat, it would improve man, but it would deteriorate the cat."

Mountain News and Territorial Governor John Evans (see entry), dispossessed the native Arapaho and Cheyenne, then built a network of railroads that made Denver the regional banking, minting, supply and processing center. Between 1870, when the first railroads arrived, and 1890, Denver grew from 4,759 residents to 106,713, becoming the most populous city in the West after San Francisco.

The depression of 1893 and repeal of the Sherman Silver Purchase Act ended Denver's first boom with the collapse of mining and smelting. Civic leaders promoted economic diversity—the growing of wheat and sugar beets, manufacturing, tourism and service industries. The Denver Livestock Exchange and National Western Stock Show confirmed the city's role as the cow town of the Rockies. Denver began growing again

Denver sits at an elevation of 5,280 feet at the eastern base of the Rockies. Photo by Michael Gamer.

after 1900 as stockyards, brickyards, canneries, flour mills, and manufacture of leather and rubber goods nourished the city.

Regional or national headquarters of many oil and gas firms fueled much of Denver's post-World War II growth, including an eruption of 40- and 50-story highrises downtown. Denver's dependence on nonrenewable natural resources returned to haunt the city during the 1980s oil bust. When the price of crude oil nose-dived from $39 to $9 a barrel in 1982, Denver lost population and experienced the nation's highest office vacancy rate.

Flush times returned during the 1990s, aided by newcomers from California, Texas and other states. Downtown Denver enjoyed an urban renaissance thanks to successful historic districts such as LoDo (Lower Downtown), which attracted loft dwellers, art galleries, brewpubs, night clubs and Coors Field, home of the Colorado Rockies National League baseball club. On the fringe of the city, residential subdivisions and shopping malls proliferated.

Denver's economic base has come to include tourism, electronics, computers and the largest U.S. telecommunications industry. Federal jobs are a mainstay as Denver boasts more federal employees than any city besides Washington, D.C.

Sited at 5,280 feet on high plains at the eastern base of the Rocky Mountains, Denver has a sunny, cool, dry climate averaging 14 inches of precipitation and 300 days of sunshine a year. Warm chinook winds erase some of winter's chill. The usually benign climate and nearby Rocky Mountain playground have made tourism one of the Mile High City's economic anchors.

Visually, Denver is notable for its predominance of single-family brick housing. Good brick clay underlies much of the area, while local lumber is soft and scarce. Even in the poorest residential neighborhoods, single-family detached housing prevails, reflecting the western interest in elbow room. The city's location on a spacious, relatively flat plains allows sprawling growth unimpeded by any large body of water or geographic obstacle.

Notable institutions include the Denver Museum of Nature and Science, Denver

Public Library, Colorado History Museum, Denver Art Museum and Denver Center for the Performing Arts, as well as the U.S. Mint and major league baseball (Colorado Rockies), basketball (Denver Nuggets), football (Denver Broncos), hockey (Colorado Avalanche) and soccer (Colorado Rapids).

As one of the most isolated major cities in the United States, Denver has been obsessed with transportation systems. Fear of being bypassed began early when railroads and, later, airlines originally avoided Denver because of the 14,000-foot-high Rocky Mountain barrier just west of town. To secure Denver's role as the Rocky Mountain transportation hub, the city in 1995 opened its $5 billion Denver International Airport (see entry).

In 2000, the six-county metro area reached a population of 2.4 million, three-fourths of whom live in the suburban counties—Adams, Arapahoe, Boulder, Douglas and Jefferson. Of the core city population, 52.1 percent was white, 28.8 percent Hispanic, 11.1 percent African American, 2.9 percent Asian, 1.3 percent Native American and 3.8 percent multiracial.

The Rocky Mountain metropolis boomed during the 1990s as its eastern suburb of Aurora became Colorado's third-largest city and the western suburb of Lakewood became the fourth-largest. Even the core City and County of Denver showed a 16 percent growth in the 1990s, climbing to a 2000 population of 554,636. Thanks to vibrant core business and residential areas, as well as the 1990s opening of Coors Baseball Field, Elitch Gardens Amusement Park, Ocean Journey Aquarium, the Pepsi Center, many new core city housing projects, and prosperous suburbs, the Mile High City is booming at the dawn of the 21st century.

To learn more: Denver Metro Convention and Visitors Bureau, 1555

California St., Denver 80210; (800) 462-5280; www.denver.org; www.denvergov.org/aboutdenver.

Denver International Airport

In 1995, Denver opened the first major new state-of-the art U.S. airport since Dallas–Fort Worth in 1973. Located 23 miles northeast of downtown Denver, the $5 billion municipal airport contains five 12,000-foot runways and three concourses on a 53-square-mile site, America's largest.

Denver architects C. W. Fentress, J. H. Bradburn and Associates designed the distinctive Teflon-coated fiberglass roof of Jeppesen Terminal to reflect both the snowcapped Rockies and the Indian tipis that once occupied the site. Nautical illusions are also fostered by the billowing white textile roof and the crow's nests of its masts. The energy-saving translucent roof admits diffused daylight and solar warmth. The novel automated baggage handling system, after some initial problems and delays, generally has baggage waiting on time at the carousels for disembarking passengers.

By 2001, DIA had become the sixth-busiest airport in the United States (behind Atlanta, Chicago, Los Angeles, Dallas–Fort

Denver International Airport's tent-like terminal was inspired by Indian tipis and by the nearby mountains. Fentress, Bradburn and Associates.

Worth and San Francisco) and the 10th busiest in the world, with 38 million passengers. United Airlines is the major carrier with about two-thirds of the passengers. Frontier Airlines, Denver's only surviving hometown carrier, is the second-largest DIA user. Other scheduled commercial carriers are AirBC, Air Canada, Air Wisconsin, America West, American, American Trans Air, Big Sky, British Airways, Continental, Delta, Frontier, Great Lakes, Korean, Lufthansa, Mesa, Mexicana, Miami, Midwest Express, Northwest, TWA, US Airways and Vanguard Airways. Direct flights connect Denver with Canada, Mexico, Germany and Great Britain.

Fast Facts about Denver International

- This 53-square-mile airport is twice the size of Manhattan.
- DIA's 327-foot-high control tower is the tallest in North America.
- The five runways, taxiways and aprons consist of 2.5 million cubic yards of concrete.

- The Jeppesen Terminal is named for Elrey B. Jeppesen, a Denverite who began flying in 1930. Concerned about air crashes and lost pilots, Jeppesen began making notebook maps. In 1934, he started to share copies of his aviation maps, which soon became—and remain—the best air navigational maps and charts available worldwide.
- Jeppesen Terminal's roof rises 126 feet from the floor to its highest point. It is supported by 34 masts and 10 miles of steel cable.

Denver Museum of Nature and Science

(SEE ALSO MUSEUMS) This largest and most popular museum in the Rocky Mountain region is best known for its many life-size dioramas of wildlife and of Native Americans. The museum also plays a major role in research and, since 1915, has published scholarly reports. In 1927, a museum crew excavated, identified and reported the discovery of Folsom Era projectile points, proving that human beings had been in North America since 11,000 B.C., much longer than previously thought.

The museum's geology department has one of America's finest collections and exhibits of rocks and minerals, including fabulous specimens of gold and silver. The paleontology department showcases skeletons of Tyrannosaurus rex, stegosaurus and other prehistoric monsters. The museum harbors a permanent collection of almost 500,000 specimens and artifacts, a library and archives, and a 500-seat restaurant.

Known as the Denver Museum of Natural History from 1948 to 2000, it opened in 1900 with 3,300 bird and mammal specimens of pioneer Colorado naturalist Edwin Carter as the Colorado Museum of Natural History. The first building of the current complex opened in 1903, with sizable additions in 1908 (Central Wing), 1918 (Standley Memorial Wing), 1928 (William H. James Memorial Wing), 1940 (Phipps Auditorium), 1955 (Gates Planetarium), 1968 (Boettcher Memorial Wings), 1982 (45-foot-high IMAX theater screen), and several more recent additions. The Denver Art Museum and Denver Botanic Gardens, once part of this science museum, have evolved into separate institutions.

To learn more: The Denver Museum of Nature and Science is on the east side of Denver's City Park, at Colorado and Montview boulevards. Open seven days a week, 9 A.M.–5 P.M.; $4–$6. (303) 322-7009; www.dmnh.org.

Dinosaurs
Colorado is a paleontological paradise and the first western state to yield dinosaur bones for museums, including the Smithsonian Institution, Yale's Peabody Museum and the Denver Museum of Nature and Science. Dinosaur tracks and bones found throughout Colorado help explain not only dinosaurs but also the Jurassic (135–200 million years ago) and Cretaceous (65–135 million years ago) periods. A then-swampy, lushly vegetated Colorado included the Western Interior Seaway. Dinosaurs thrived, leaving evidence in sediments of the fossil-bearing Morrison formation.

One of the world's largest single dinosaur trackways lies in the Picketwire Canyonlands along the Purgatoire River in southeastern Colorado. These tracks are believed to be that of an apatosaurus mother and her youngsters being chased by an allosaurus.

Would-be paleontologists can experience a real dinosaur dig at Rabbit Valley, near Grand Junction. Participants work beside professionals unearthing

paleo-treasures. The Garden Park Dinosaur Quarry, discovered in 1877, 10 miles north of Cañon City, yielded a partial diplodocus and a complete stegosaurus now at the Denver Museum of Nature and Science. An ultrasaurus and supersaurus were discovered near Fruita at Dry Mesa Quarry, as were as the birdlike dinosaurs *Ornitholestes* and *Coelurus*.

The state dinosaur, the stegosaurus, or "plated lizard," roamed Colorado during the Jurassic period, but died out before the disappearance of all dinosaurs about 65 million years ago. The stegosaurus ranged in height from 8 to 25 feet, with a double row of plates along the spine and spikes on the tail. These plates may have been protective armor or for heat regulation, either absorbing or dissipating heat.

Stegosaurus bones have been excavated in Dinosaur National Monument in the northwestern part of the state and Dry Mesa Quarry near Fruita. The Denver Museum of Nature and Science is home to Spike, a 140-million-year-old stegosaurus skeleton from the Garden Park Quarry.

To learn more
Dinosaur National Monument, 4545 U.S. Hwy. 40, Dinosaur 81610. A huge glassed-in museum includes a working excavation of dinosaur bones. (970) 374-3000.

Dinosaur Depot Museum, 330 Royal Gorge Blvd., Cañon City 81212. Open daily 9 A.M.–5 P.M. (Wed.–Sun. in winter); $1–$5. (719) 296-7150.

Dinosaur Ridge Visitor Center, 16831 W. Alameda Parkway, Morrison

80465. A two-mile interpretive trail explains tracks, fossil bones and geology, including exposed Iguanodontid tracks and dinosaur bones at Morrison where the bones of stegosaurus, diplodocus, apatosaurus and other giant lizards were first discovered in 1877. Free admission. (303) 697-3466.

Dinosaur Valley Museum, 362 Main St., Grand Junction 81502. Exhibits include robotic dinosaurs and a paleontology laboratory. Open daily 9 A.M.–4 P.M. (Tues.–Sat. 10 A.M.–4 P.M. in winter); $2–$4. (970) 243-3466; www.mwc.mus.co.us.

Dude Ranches Colorado

ranchers have hosted paying guests since the gold rush days, when many pilgrims knocked on ranch house doors, seeking food and shelter. Ranchers initially put up such visitors for free but as their numbers grew, began charging. Sundowning, the pioneer practice of looking for the nearest ranch as evening approached, has evolved into dude ranching. Many Colorado dude ranches are for adults only and most are pricey but with autumn discounts.

To learn more: Colorado Dude and Guest Ranch Association, P.O. Box 2120, Granby 80446; (970) 887-3128; www.colorado-ranch.com.

Dr. Colorado's List of Rip-snortin' Dude Ranches

C Lazy U Ranch. This is the only U.S. dude ranch to regularly receive the Mobil Five Star and AAA Five Diamond Ratings. P.O. Box 379, Granby 80446; (970) 887-3344.

Drowsy Water Ranch. A traditional 600-acre ranch that offers guests the usual horsey stuff and also hayrides, sing-alongs and square dancing. P.O. Box 147A, Granby 89446; (800) 845-2292.

Focus Ranch. This 6,000-acre ranch near the Wyoming border is open year-round despite the 7,000-foot elevation and welcomes dudes who can work daily with wranglers tending cattle. Slater 81653; (970) 583-2410.

Historic Pines Ranch. Englishman Reginald Cusack opened this guest ranch in 1893. Handsomely sited at the base of the Sangre de Cristo Mountains, this family-style resort provides horseback riding, fishing and square dancing, with wintertime cross-country skiing, sleigh rides and indoor pool and whirlpool bath. Pines Road, P.O. Box 131, Westcliffe 81525; (800) 446-9462.

Lake Mancos Ranch. A casual ranch owned by the same family since the 1950s. 42686 County Road N, Mancos 81328; (800) 325-9462.

Latigo Ranch. Sited at 9,000 feet, this ranch offers more than 200 miles of mountain trails and whitewater rafting. Box 237, Kremmling 80459; (800) 227-9655.

Rawah Ranch. This ranch straddling the Colorado–Wyoming line has been family owned since 1950. The fishing, scenery and terrain illustrate the Ute word rawah (meaning wilderness or abundance). 11147 N. County Road 103, Jeln, WY 82063; (800) 820-3152.

Skyline Guest Ranch. This 160-acre ranch is nestled in a mountain meadow at 9,600 feet, beneath 14,000-foot mountains. The Farny family also keeps it open as a cross-country ski resort in winter. Eight miles south of Telluride off Colorado 145, Telluride 81435; (970) 728-3757.

Stapp Mountain Lakes Guest Ranch. In 1986, after a century of dude ranching, this 320-acre spread became the Truth Consciousness

Ashram. It is the first of several ranches to offer spiritual as well as physical exercise. In Ward; (303) 459-0469.

Wilderness Trails Ranch. Next to the remote Weminuche Wilderness Area, the ranch offers superb horses for galloping through some of the most rugged mountain terrain in southwest Colorado. 23486 County Road 501, Bayfield 80122; (800) 527-2624.

Durango

The La Plata County seat was founded in 1880 as a Denver & Rio Grande Railroad hub for southwestern Colorado. William J. Palmer and other railroad town promoters named Durango after the city in Mexico that they hoped the railroad would someday reach.

In the Colorado town, the railroad controlled the land, a smelter site and nearby coalfields. Durango was platted with two parks, a county courthouse site, church sites and the fashionable Third Avenue Parkway residential district. By 1890, horse-drawn trolleys clanged up and down Main Avenue. The "sagebrush metropolis," cheered the *Durango Record*'s feisty editor, Caroline Romney, "is really attaining metropolitan proportions."

Coal-rich Durango boomed as a rail and smelter hub, with the San Juan Smelter processing silver and gold ores and later uranium. After the smelter closed in 1963, Durango concentrated on tourism. Fort Lewis College, established in 1933, is the town's single largest employer, followed by the Durango & Silverton Narrow Gauge Railroad. The railroad draws 220,000 passengers a year, helping to keep Main Avenue the town's activity center.

Eagles

These large, predatory members of the hawk family have wingspans up to 7½ feet. They are solitary birds who tend to mate for life. The nest, or aerie, of twigs and sticks is built high in a tree or on a cliff and used year after year to hatch two to three eggs each spring.

Rufus Sage, the explorer, mountain man and trader, provided the first report on Colorado eagles. On North St. Vrain Creek in the winter of 1843, he found the bodies of 36 golden and bald eagles, which Indians had killed for their feathers. Since then ranchers have slaughtered thousands of eagles, which feed on young livestock. The population has also been severely reduced by pesticides and by the extermination of many prairie dogs, a staple food for eagles.

The American bald eagle (*Haliaeetus leucocephalus*), with its prominent white head on a uniformly dark brown body, has been the U.S. national emblem since 1782, when an estimated 75,000 existed in the United States. By 1967, when there were only 418 nesting pairs left, the national bird was placed on the endangered species list.

The bald eagles' decline was attributed primarily to DDT, a pesticide that washed off crops and fields and into water. Eagles ate DDT-contaminated fish and it made their eggshells so thin that they would break before the young could hatch. By 2000, the species had recovered to about 5,000 nesting pairs, including hundreds in Colorado. Bald eagles are often found near water as they feed on fish, notably at Barr Lake State Park near Denver and along the Colorado River.

Whereas bald eagles are nearly always found near water, the golden eagle (*Aquila chrysaetos*) may be found even in the driest parts of Colorado. Golden eagles are noted for majestic, flat-winged gliding and soaring with only occasional wingbeats. This uniformly dark brown bird has a wash of gold on the hind neck, a white wing flash and a white tail with a dark terminal band. It is the largest Colorado bird. Golden eagles are spotted statewide but particularly in northwestern and northeastern Colorado. They occupy cliffs and canyons near open grasslands, shrublands and pine forests, feeding on prairie dogs, jackrabbits, small mammals, snakes and birds.

Economy (SEE ALSO

AGRICULTURE; BUSINESS; EMPLOYMENT; ENERGY; EXPORTS AND IMPORTS) Born in a gold rush, Colorado has long attracted get-rich-quick individuals pursuing wealth. Coloradans strove to make fortunes in gold and silver, coal and oil, railroads and real estate. Most recently telecommunications and other high-tech industries have created new billionaires.

The median household income of Coloradans in 1999 was $47,987, sixth-highest in the United States. Per capita income was $22,821. Colorado had the 10th-lowest poverty rate, according to the U.S. Census Bureau, with 8.7 percent of the population living below the poverty level.

Pitkin County, with the glitzy resort of Aspen as its centerpiece, is the state's wealthiest county. Several other resort villages, along with Cherry Hills Village, a Denver suburb in Arapahoe County, rank among the wealthiest U.S. communities. Even Denver's former skid row has been transformed since 1990 into Lower Downtown (LoDo), a rich community of loft dwellers.

Of the wealthiest counties, four (Pitkin, Eagle, Summit and Routt) house Colorado's major mountain ski and summer resorts.

The remaining six wealthiest counties are in the Denver metro area and reflect its prosperity. The poorest counties are located in primarily agricultural areas, either on the eastern plains or in the southeastern and central portions of the state.

Colorado Counties with highest per capita income (1997)

1.	Pitkin	$49,266
2.	Douglas	34,264
3.	Arapahoe	34,233
4.	Denver	33,727
5.	Eagle	31,890
6.	Boulder	31,393
7.	Summit	30,894
8.	Jefferson	29,497
9.	Routt	28,361
10.	Clear Creek	26,508

Colorado Counties with lowest per capita income (1997)

1.	Saguache	$12,561
2.	Crowley	13,362
3.	Conejos	13,585
4.	Archuleta	15,510
5.	Fremont	15,526
6.	Costilla	15,660
7.	Las Animas	16,233
8.	Huerfano	16,674
9.	Lincoln	16,798
10.	Bent	16,990

Colorado is developing a more diverse economy with the rise of service-sector companies. The state's traditional dependence on a handful of key industries such as energy, aerospace, mining, agriculture and government has decreased in recent years. High technology research has been a growing sector in the state economy. Never a prominent manufacturing center, Colorado has maintained its status as the primary distribution center for the Rocky Mountain West.

The economy's diversification is reflected in the percentage of residents working in various nonfarm categories: services (30.5), trade (23.8), government (15.4), manufacturing (9.3), construction (7.6), transportation (6.4), finance (6.4) and mining (0.6). Agriculture, once Colorado's number one employer, is now roughly fourth; the exact number of employees is unknown because of unreported use of undocumented workers and family members.

To learn more: Colorado Department of Local Affairs; www.dola.state.co.us

Education *(SEE ALSO GRIFFITH, EMILY; UNIVERSITIES AND COLLEGES)*

Colorado's first school opened in a Denver log cabin, where the Auraria Higher Education Center now stands. Owen J. Goldrick (1833–1882) from County Sligo, Ireland, a teacher and newspaper reporter, arrived in Denver supposedly in a double-ox cart wearing a Prince Albert coat, striped trousers, white gloves and silk stovepipe hat. Goldrick rented a log cabin and on Oct. 3, 1859, opened Colorado's first school, with 13 students, including Hispanics and Native Americans, whom he collected in his wagon. Grateful Denverites elected him their first superintendent of schools in 1862.

While Denver boasted the first school, the town of Boulder built the first schoolhouse. Abner Roe Brown, a Yankee schoolteacher, recalled later that "as I passed through the little nest of some 20 log cabins in Boulder, Colorado, on June 1, 1860, [I wondered at] the number of school age children playing in the streets." Brown, a carpenter as well as a teacher, helped build a frame schoolhouse with a shingle roof. Townsfolk donated glass from their picture frames for the windows.

To reward Brown, Boulder mothers held a "Gold Dust Dance," charging 25 cents per person. They raised $42 to pay Brown, bought him a proper teacher's suit and persuaded him to forsake gold prospecting to teach in what was named Pioneer School. To the dismay of young students hoping to avoid homework, their parents even took turns housing schoolmaster Brown.

The Sisters of Loretto opened the first Colorado private school, Denver's St. Mary's Academy, in 1864, and it operates yet today. Catholic nuns also opened schools in many other communities, including St. Scholastica's (1890) in Cañon City, which closed in 2001.

Golden opened a tent school in 1860 and Pueblo a frame schoolhouse in 1872. Schoolhouses were often the first attempt at community cooperation. Their construction required collective effort, public expenditure and a consensus on the geographical boundaries of a school district. The first Colorado Territorial Legislature in 1861 pushed public education by providing for both district and county school taxes. Denver organized the first tax-supported school district in 1862, followed by Pueblo in 1866.

After statehood in 1876, Colorado created the office of State Superintendent of Public Instruction and saw to it that each county also had a superintendent. These officials were charged with enforcing a compulsory school attendance law for children aged 6 to 18. The attendance law was widely disregarded, as many children worked on farms and ranches, or in businesses, factories and mines until the 1911 Child Labor Law ordered children out of the workforce and into schools.

By 1900, nearly every Colorado community had a school—often a primitive one- or two-room schoolhouse with limited equipment. Boulder established the territory's first high school in 1872, followed

by Denver in 1874. During the 1900s, educational reformers worked to consolidate schools in order to provide better instruction and facilities, including libraries, playgrounds and expanded curriculums. During the governorship of Stephen L.R. McNichols (1957–1963), many schools were consolidated, often into city or countywide districts.

Colorado handled school financing from the beginning through property taxes raised either by the school district or the local government. Some $40 million a year in additional income currently comes from the state's 4 million acres of school lands, which are leased for mining, grazing, farming and other uses to generate income for education.

Denver Public Schools were the state's academic pacesetter until mandatory busing began in 1968. Although controversial, busing improved education for poor and minority children and exposed all children to more diverse populations. This mandatory busing ended in the 1990s.

Gov. Bill Owens pushed through a controversial state law in 2000 requiring that all schools be graded, based on student performance on standardized tests. Schools that consistently do poorly could be closed or turned into charter schools. The bill passed despite objections that economically poorer school districts would be discriminated against.

The first schoolhouse constructed in Colorado: Boulder, 1860. From 1880 edition *History of Boulder and Clear Creek Valleys, Colorado.* Tom Noel Collection.

Elected Officials (SEE

ALSO CONGRESSIONAL DELEGATION; GOVERNORS; LEGISLATURE) Colorado's executive branch is headed by five elected officials who serve four-year terms. Since the 1990s, when Roy Romer was the last governor to serve three terms, all five of these offices have been limited to two terms. Both the governor and the legislature are housed in the state Capitol (see entry).

Governor: Bill Owens, the first Republican to be elected governor in 28 years, became Colorado's 40th chief executive in 1999. He had previously directed an oil and gas trade association and served in the state House and Senate and as state treasurer.

The gubernatorial term was expanded from two to four years in 1964 and terms were limited in 1990 to eight years. As the chief executive officer, the governor prepares the state budget and appoints directors of the state administrative departments: Agriculture, Corrections, Education, Health Care Policy and Financing, Higher Education, Human Services, Labor and Employment, Law, Local Affairs, Military

Governor Bill Owens of Colorado.
Office of the Governor.

A Voice for Reform

Colorado's most controversial governor, Davis H. Waite, served one tempestuous term, 1892–1894. Waite, a former schoolteacher and editor of the Aspen Times, was a populist who strove to reform banks, mines, railroads and the corrupt city government of Denver.

An old man with a long beard and a loud voice, he promised to clean up Colorado even if "blood should flow to our horses' bridles." His attempt to oust crooked Denver officials almost did cause bloodshed. Among many proposed reforms, he achieved a few, most notably helping Colorado women get the vote in 1893. ⚜

Affairs, Natural Resources, Personnel, Planning and Budgeting, Public Health and Environment, Public Safety, Regulatory Agencies, Revenue and Transportation.

Office of the Governor. State Capitol Building, Room 136, 200 E. Colfax Ave., Denver 80203; (303) 866-2471. The governor's mansion at 400 E. Eighth Ave. is open for free tours on Tuesday afternoons; (303) 866-3682.

Lieutenant Governor: Joe Rogers, the highest-ranking African American official in Colorado, was the youngest lieutenant governor in the country when elected at age 34 in 1999. He is also the only African American lieutenant governor in the nation.

The lieutenant governor is first in line to succeed the governor if the governor dies, retires, is impeached or resigns. Whenever the governor is absent from the state, the lieutenant governor serves in his stead. The lieutenant governor supervises the State Commission on Indian Affairs. In 1999 some Colorado legislators tried to abolish the office of lieutenant governor as unnecessary and wasteful of tax dollars. Although the measure failed, the legislature did change the office from an elected position to one appointed by the governor beginning in 2002.

Office of the Lieutenant Governor: State Capitol Building, Room 130, 200 E. Colfax Ave., Denver 80203; (303) 866-2087.

Secretary of State: Donetta Davidson served as Bent County Clerk and Arapahoe County Clerk before being appointed secretary of state in 1999 by the governor upon the death of her predecessor, Vicky Buckley.

The secretary of state administers and enforces the Colorado Corporations Code, Colorado Elections Code, Voter Registration Law, Campaign Reform Act, Sunshine Law, Uniform Commercial Code, bingo and raffles laws, and laws relating to private detectives, dance schools, and fireworks manufacturers and wholesalers. The secretary's duties are divided between the Commercial Recordings Division and the Elections Division.

Office of the Secretary of State: Denver Post Building, 1560 Broadway, Suite 200, Denver 80202; (303) 894-2200; www.sos.state.co.us.

State Treasurer: Mike Coffman, a former U.S. Marine, founded the Colorado Property Management Group, then became a Colorado representative and a senator before being elected state treasurer in 1998.

The state treasurer manages the money of the state, receiving revenues, paying expenses and investing the surplus. During the 1990s, when Colorado had a surplus, the state treasurer also mailed refunds to taxpayers.

Office of the State Treasurer: State Capitol, Room 140, 200 E. Colfax Ave., Denver 80203; (303) 866-2441.

Attorney General: Ken Salazar, a fifth-generation Coloradan, has been a farmer, businessman, natural resources lawyer and director of the Colorado Department of Natural Resources.

The attorney general manages the Colorado Department of Law and more than 30 lawyers, investigators and administrative staff. He also chairs the Peace Officer Standards and Training Board, which certifies Colorado's 11,000 law enforcement officers.

Office of the Attorney General: 1525 Sherman St., Denver 80202; (303) 866-4500.

Elk

American elk *(Cervus elaphus)* were once common in Colorado, even on the plains. During the 1800s, however, they were hunted nearly to extinction, reaching an estimated low of around 1,000 in the early 1900s. With numerous reintroductions and protection during the past century, elk have made an enormous comeback to perhaps 250,000 in Colorado today. Elk have become so numerous as to be pests

Elk in Rocky Mountain National Park. Photo by Lenny Brooks.

in some places, consuming hay meant for domestic livestock, fouling golf courses and munching on the landscaping of mountain homes.

Among these large, deer-like mammals, males may weigh 800 pounds or more while females are smaller. The light tan fur is long and coarse with a longer, darker mane and a light-colored rump, which inspired the Algonquin and Shawnee Indian name for the animal: *wapiti* ("white rump").

The tail is short and inconspicuous with the same light fur as the rump. Males carry a multibranched rack of antlers that led Europeans to call elk the American stag. Older bulls may have up to six or seven tines (branches) on the two main beams (horns). Their legs are long and their ears large and conspicuous.

Elk favor semi-open forests, parks, meadows and tundra. They travel in large herds in search of grasses and shrubs. In winter, heavy snowfall drives them to lower valleys and parks in search of edible plants.

During the fall mating season, bulls emit a musical call or "bugle" to attract females, which they shield from other males with much noise, display and occasional fighting, using their antlers as weapons. The Colorado mating (rut) peaks in the last week of September and first week of October, when many people flock to areas such as Rocky Mountain National Park to listen to the bugling and watch the competition between bulls. The calves are born in the spring, usually one per female with occasional twins.

Elk die, according to one Colorado study, from starvation of calves (17 percent), hunting (13 percent) and predation, primarily by bears and coyotes feasting on calves. Elk can live as long as 20 years, but less than 25 percent survive in the wild beyond age 5. Chronic wasting disease has become a major threat in recent years. Elk are now found in all counties of central and western Colorado at elevations above 6,000 feet. An experimental herd has also been introduced to Baca County on the prairie, a habitat where elk once were common.

Employment (SEE ALSO BUSINESS; ECONOMY)

Colorado's unemployment rate declined from 4.9 percent in 1990 to 3.1 percent in 2000, second-lowest rate in the United States.

Top Colorado Employers (1999)

Firm	Type of Business	Employees
1. Qwest (including U.S. West)	Telecommunications	15,501
2. MediaOne Group	Cable television	15,196
3. Ball Corp.	Aluminum cans, aerospace	12,500
4. Columbia	Health care, hospitals	10,059
5. Johns Manville	Construction materials	9,740
6. Centura Health	Health care, hospitals	9,000
7. King Soopers	Grocery stores	8,960
8. Storage Technology	Computer services	8,700
9. United Airlines	Airline	7,700
10. Lockheed Martin	Aerospace	7,382
11. Lucent Technologies	Telecommunications	6,000
12. Xcel	Gas and electric utility	6,000
13. Adolph Coors Co.	Beer	5,800
14. Safeway	Grocery stores	5,000

Source: Denver Metro Chamber of Commerce

Nonfarm Colorado Employment (1999)

Sector of Economy	No. of Workers	Percentage*
Services	673,600	30.5
Trade (retail and wholesale)	523,400	23.8
Government	338,800	15.4
Manufacturing	203,800	9.3
Construction	166,500	7.6
Transportation	141,500	6.4
Finance	140,500	6.4
Mining	12,900	0.6
Total	2,201,000	100.00

*Approximate, due to rounding
Source: Denver Metro Chamber of Commerce

Colorado ranked second among the states in 2000 in its percentage growth in the number of employed workers and total payroll, according to the U.S Census Bureau. Yet the average 1999 Colorado salary was $30,604, virtually the same as the national average of $30,609. Colorado employers have traditionally paid less because workers will sacrifice income to live in Colorado. Acute labor shortages are attracting many foreign workers, legal and illegal, to Colorado.

To learn more

Denver Metro Chamber of Commerce; www.denvernet.org.

U.S. Department of Labor, Bureau of Labor Statistics; http://stats.bls.gov/datahome.htm.

Endangered Places

(*SEE ALSO* HISTORICAL PRESERVATION; NATIONAL REGISTER OF HISTORIC PLACES)
Since 1997, Colorado Preservation Inc. has compiled an annual list of endangered places. Vandalism, neglect, natural weathering and encroaching development threaten these architectural, archaeological, cultural and historical treasures. The nine sites named for 2001 are:

Camp Amache, at Granada, Prowers County. Colorado's only World War II Japanese relocation camp is a neglected 300-acre site, haunted by foundations and a cemetery.

Shield Rock art site, near Rangely, Rio Blanco County. The pictographs and petroglyphs carved here by Native Americans date to around A.D. 1200. They have been shot at, chiseled and tagged with graffiti.

Durango Power House, in Durango, La Plata County. This 1893 plant, which still has its original boiler and generator, faces demolition despite a proposal to recycle it as a children's museum.

Snowstorm Gold Dredge, near Fairplay, Park County. The last dredge left in Colorado weighs 48.3 tons and is 50 feet wide by 86 feet long. Owners want to move it and mine the site for sand and gravel. The Park City Historical Society wants to move this gold boat to its Fairplay Museum, which would cost about $225,000.

Lime Kilns, in Thomasville, near Basalt, Pitkin County. Built in the 1880s by the Calcium Limestone Co. to process lime for gold and silver smelting, these kilns and some of the frame conveyor structures linger in a neglected condition.

Inter-Laken Resort, near Twin Lakes, Lake County. This 1879 lakefront resort, including a hotel, cabin and outhouses, was once restored by the U.S. Forest Service but now needs more attention on its isolated and weather-threatened original site.

Stranges Grocery Store, in Grand Junction, Mesa County. This rusticated sandstone store has survived—barely—since 1909.

Studzinski and Holden Blocks, in Pueblo, Pueblo County. These 1880s' commercial buildings face demolition for a parking lot needed by the adjacent Sangre de Cristo Arts Center.

San Rafael Presbyterian Church, in Mogote, Conejos County. Abandoned in 1965, this small adobe church faces demolition by neglect.

Of previously endangered sites identified by Colorado Preservation, (the Christian Science Church and much of the Colorado Fuel & Iron Company plant are now gone), here is the list of these sites:

- Alta Lakes, San Miguel County
- Black Hawk
- Central City
- Christian Science Church, Victor (demolished 2001)
- Colorado Fuel & Iron Company plant, Pueblo (partly demolished)
- Cripple Creek
- Currigan Exhibition Hall, Denver
- Dearfield
- Evans School, Denver
- Gold Hill
- Greeley downtown
- Hispanic cultural landscape, Purgatoire River Valley
- Leadville mining district
- Lewis Mill, Telluride
- Preston Farm, Fort Collins
- Red Mountain mining district, Ouray to Silverton
- Rock Creek Stage Stop, Routt County
- Trinidad downtown and the Toltec Hotel

The National Trust for Historic Preservation also listed two Colorado sites as threatened:

Mesa Verde National Park, threatened by inadequate funding and preservation efforts.

Black Hawk/Central City National Historic District, former mining towns threatened by the gaming industry construction boom.

To learn more

Colorado Preservation Inc., 910 16th St., Denver 80202; (303) 893-4260.

National Trust for Historic Preservation, 910 16th St., Denver 80202; (303) 623-1504.

Endangered Species

The U.S. Fish and Wildlife Service lists threatened and endangered species under the 1966 Endangered Species Act as expanded in 1973. Colorado became one of the first states to match federal funds to help protect these species, and the Colorado Division of Wildlife, like the United States agency, lists state as well as federal endangered and threatened species. In addition, Colorado in 1977 adopted a state income tax checkoff allowing taxpayers to contribute a tax deductible portion of their tax refunds to protect wildlife.

Colorado was the first state to appoint a biologist to research and manage raptors, including two formerly endangered species, the peregrine falcon and the bald eagle. Peregrine falcons have been introduced to many new environments, including downtown Denver skyscrapers, where they feed on pigeons.

White pelicans, reduced to only one Colorado nesting island in the 1960s, were classified as endangered. After conservation efforts, in 1985 these pelicans became the first Colorado species to be taken off the endangered list. Other threatened birds remain very rare; there are only 15 known survivors of the Mexican spotted owl in Colorado. Another threatened native is the state fish, the greenback cutthroat trout, which was nearly wiped out by rainbow trout and other introduced fish until a reintroduction program began in 1974.

Grizzly bears, listed as endangered in 1973, were thought to be extinct in Colorado until one was killed after mauling a sportsman in the San Juan Mountains in 1979. In 1998 the Preble's meadow jumping mouse was placed on the endangered list. Now found only in Colorado and Wyoming, this 3-inch-long brown rodent sports black markings and a 6-inch-long tail. It can jump as far as 3 feet. It occupies creekbeds and meadows along Colorado's Front Range, where new subdivisions and shopping malls are consuming its habitat.

Similar development is threatening the black-tailed prairie dog, which the National Wildlife Federation asked the U.S. Fish and Wildlife Service in 1999 to list as endangered in Colorado and nine other western states. Opposition from ranchers and farmers has kept the endangered designation from being granted.

Colorado Endangered Species
- Black-footed ferret
- Bonytail fish
- Boral toad
- Colorado pike minnow (formerly Colorado squawfish)
- Gray wolf
- Grizzly bear
- Lake chub
- Least tern
- Lynx
- Northern redbelly dace
- Plains sharp-tailed grouse
- Razorback sucker

- Rio Grande sucker
- River otter
- Southern redbelly dace
- Southwestern willow flycatcher
- Suckermouth minnow
- Swift fox
- Western boreal toad
- Whooping crane
- Wolverine

Colorado Threatened Species
- American peregrine falcon
- Arctic peregrine falcon
- Arkansas darter
- Bald eagle
- Brassy minnow
- Common shiner
- Greater prairie chicken
- Greater sandhill crane
- Greenback cutthroat trout
- Humpback chub
- Lesser prairie chicken
- Mexican spotted owl
- Piping plover
- Preble's meadow jumping mouse
- Western burrowing owl
- Wood frog

To learn more
Colorado Division of Wildlife; 6060 Broadway, Denver 80216; (303) 297-1192.

U.S. Fish & Wildlife Service; Denver Federal Center, Building 16, Denver 80225; (303) 236-7904.

Energy
Colorado ranks 28th among the 50 states in total energy consumption (Texas is the highest, Vermont the lowest). On a per capita basis, Colorado places 40th in energy usage, despite hot summers, cold winters and high per capita motor vehicle use. Colorado is a net energy exporter and delivers coal, petroleum, natural gas and electricity to other states.

Transportation consumes the largest amount of energy in Colorado, followed by industrial, residential and commercial uses. Of the four major energy sources, Colorado uses petroleum the most, then coal, natural gas and electricity. No nuclear power plants are operating or planned for Colorado after an experimental plant, the Fort St. Vrain High-Temperature Gas Reactor, was closed by the Public Service Co. of Colorado in the 1980s due to technical problems.

Xcel (formerly the Public Service Co.), the state's largest energy supplier, relies primarily on coal-fired electric plants. Transportation is dependent on petroleum products and heating relies heavily on natural gas. Colorado electricity is generated from coal, petroleum and natural gas.

Colorado obtains tiny portions of its electricity supply from in-state hydroelectric plants. Electricity users can have their own solar and wind systems feed into the power grid, and they can contract to buy wind-generated electricity from Xcel, which operates a wind farm north of Fort Collins. Both sunlight and wind are abundant energy sources in the state, and these projects are the first opportunity for residents to use renewable energy on a large-scale basis.

During the 1990s, New Century Energy of Texas acquired Public Service Co. of Colorado, ending home state control of Colorado's dominant utility. New Century subsequently merged with Northern States Power of Minnesota and changed its name to Xcel. In 2000, the utility contracted to build an $80 million, 83-megawatt power plant in Pueblo fired by used automobile tires. This plant is only the third power plant in the United States to recycle discarded tires into an energy source.

Looking Back

Dec. 25, 1858

The *New York Times* reported "Two Russell brothers and nine or ten others left Leavenworth, Kansas, about April 1, 1858 for Pike's Peak. They brought back specimens of surface gold, claiming they made $2 to $5 a day [and] found Cherry Creek the richest."

To learn more: Energy Information Administration; www.eia.doe.gov.

Evans, Anne

This social leader and civic benefactor was born in London in 1871 and educated at Miss Ferris' School in Paris, the Willard School in Berlin and the Art Students League in New York City. She moved to Denver in the early 1890s, joined the Denver Artists' Club in 1894, and served on the Denver Art Commission and the Denver Public Library Commission.

She never married, devoting herself to philanthropy and to her family. She was a vice-president and director of the Evans Investment Co., which handled funds in real estate, railroads, tramways and other assets. Although Evans never graduated from college, she earned honorary doctorates from the University of Denver and Colorado College.

The daughter of Territorial Governor John Evans (see entry), she helped make the Denver Art Museum one of the first to establish a Native American collection where Indian artifacts were treated not as curious relics of barbarians, but as art.

Evans cofounded the Central City Opera Association, for whom she recruited artist Allen True and architect Burnham Hoyt to help with restoration of the Opera House. She enlisted Robert Edmond Jones, the most famous stage designer in America, to come from New York City to enhance the Central City Opera.

A driving force in many civic organizations, she once said, "You have to get angry with people sometimes or they'll think they can run over you, especially if you're a woman." She died in Denver in 1941.

Evans, John
A Chicago developer and physician, Evans was appointed territorial governor of Colorado in 1862 by his friend President Abraham Lincoln.

Evans strove mightily to turn Denver, a dusty little town in the middle of nowhere, into the Queen City of the Mountains and Plains. He gave $100 to any congregation that would start a church in the godless town cursed by gunfire and drunken brawls. He founded the University of Denver, helped bring railroads to Colorado, and helped establish Denver's streetcar system.

Evans had been a respected Chicago doctor who cofounded Northwestern University in Evanston, Ill., a fashionable Chicago suburb he developed. Evans turned down the governorship of Washington Territory, wanting to serve in Colorado

John Evans, governor of the Territory of Colorado, 1862–1865. From 1902 edition of Representative Men of Colorado. Tom Noel Collection.

because it would be closer to his Chicago business interests. As territorial governor, Evans was responsible for Indian affairs and was dismissed after the Sand Creek Massacre (see entry) in 1864.

As a shrewd entrepreneur, Evans became involved in the development of the Denver Pacific, the Denver & New Orleans, and the Denver, South Park & Pacific railroads. Evans also founded the University of Denver as the Colorado Seminary in 1864 and was active in a wide variety of civic and commercial activities.

Colorado's most important state builder is commemorated by Mount Evans, which crowns the horizon west of Denver. Born in Ohio in 1814, Evans died in Denver in 1897.

Exports and Imports *(SEE ALSO ECONOMY)*

Although an inland state with no navigable rivers, Colorado has long aspired to do international business. Denver's Chamber of Commerce began lobbying the federal government in the 1880s for designation as an official port of entry, and in 1882 Washington built a U.S. Customs House in downtown Denver.

Foreign capital has played a major role since the pioneer days, when foreign, especially British, capitalists bankrolled many of the state's railroads, mines and ranches. Overseas interests continue to invest some $9 billion a year in Colorado while spending close to $6 billion a year on Colorado products. An English firm, Tomkins, PLC, bought one of Colorado's oldest and largest industrial firms, the Gates Rubber Co., in 1996, ending 85 years of family ownership. French, Canadian and German investors put up the money for downtown Denver's newest shopping mall, the Denver Pavilions, opened in 1999.

Colorado's economic boom in the 1990s inspired the Japanese to open a consulate in Denver in 1999, and the British and Peruvians did the same in 2000. They joined Canadian and Mexican consulates already handling a growing amount of international commerce. Increasingly, Colorado has become an exporter rather than an importer. While the state originally exported little but mineral wealth, by 1900 its largest exports were livestock, sugar (from sugar beets) and wheat. Since the 1970s, however, Colorado's booming telecommunications and high-tech industries have emerged as leading exporters.

Colorado's appetite for foreign business was enhanced by the global economic conference held in Denver in 1997, the Denver Summit of Eight. President Clinton praised "not only the breathtaking beauty of the Rockies, but the powerful optimism of a state proud of its past and focused on its future." International business has also been augmented by the huge Denver International Airport, opened in 1995.

In 2000, Colorado exported almost $6.6 billion in goods abroad, ranging from software to squashes. Almost 1,300 Colorado companies export goods abroad.

Colorado's Top Export Destinations (2000)

Canada	$ 1.1 billion
Japan	892 million
United Kingdom	481 million
Germany	445 million
France	417 million
South Korea	340 million
Netherlands	339 million
Singapore	318 million
Mexico	313 million
Hong Kong	233 million

Source: World Trade Center, Denver

Colorado's Top Exports (2000)

Integrated circuits	$989 million
Data processing machines	867 million
Office machine parts	569 million
Oscilloscopes/analyzers	448 million
Beef	286 million
Photo plates	236 million
Medical equipment	215 million
Telecom equipment	171 million
Electrical equipment	100 million
Aerospace equipment	88 million
Measuring instruments	84 million
Sound media	72 million

Source: World Trade Center, Denver

Samsonite Sells to the World

The Shwayder brothers, who were Polish Jews, founded Samsonite Luggage Company in Denver in 1910. The Denver company's ads featured all five chubby brothers standing on an indestructible suitcase made by Samsonite, which emerged as one of the nation's top luggage companies.

When sales dropped drastically in the 1980s and 1990s, Samsonite looked to Europe for a solution. Luc Van Nevel, a Belgian veteran of Samsonite's European operation, was brought to Denver to head the company in 1998. While the company's hard-sided luggage sales declined in the United States, they have increased in Europe.

European sales now account for more than 40 percent of Samsonite's revenues. French capitalists now own 30 percent of the company, which has manufacturing plants in Belgium, Canada, China, Hungary, India, Italy, Mexico, Slovakia and Spain. More than three-quarters of Samsonite's 7,300 employees are overseas. Internationalizing has enabled Samsonite to survive in a world economy while maintaining its headquarters in Denver. ✦

Ferril, Thomas Hornsby (*SEE ALSO* STATE CAPITOL)

The Rocky Mountains have inspired forests of bad poetry. As Oscar Wilde noted after a visit to Colorado, the Rockies seemed too high for poets to climb.

Thomas Hornsby Ferril also cringed at what he called the "God-finding" poetry and the "low grade mysticism" of most verse about the Rockies. The Denver poet wrestled for most of his life with the mountains. He knew them too well to be sentimental and sloppy. His work earned praise from Robert Frost, Carl Sandburg and others who crowned him "the poet laureate of the Rocky Mountains."

"Always Begin Where You Are," Ferril titled one poem, and Colorado usually was the setting for his poetry.

Ferril did not share the alienation, anger and negativism of many modern poets. His poetry was generally a positive analysis and celebration of grand themes in Rocky Mountain history and landscape.

Ferril wrote about out-of-the-way, offbeat Colorado places in poems such as "Magenta":

> Once, up in Gilpin County, Colorado,
> When a long blue afternoon was
> standing on end
> Like a tombstone sinking into the Rocky
> Mountains,
> I found myself in a town where no one
> was. . . .
> The town was high and lonely in the
> mountains;
> There was nothing to listen to but the
> wasting of
> The glaciers and a wind that had no
> trees. . . .

Ferril died in 1988 but his poetry lives on. His house at 2123 Downing St. in Denver is now the Colorado Center for the Book and also serves as a museum commemorating Colorado's premier poet.

Fish and Fishing

Colorado's 66,000 miles of streams and 550 lakes attract anglers, and a few hardy ice fishermen. Colorado designates its highest quality trout water as Gold Medal Water, where the giant trout await. The Division of Wildlife also maintains Wild Trout Water, which has only native populations. Colorado fishing licenses are required for fishing on public waters.

Anglers in Colorado catch bass, bluegill, carp, catfish, crappie (white and black), drum, kokanee, perch, pike, salmon, sauger, splake, sunfish, trout (brook, brown, golden, native cutthroat and rainbow), walleye and whitefish. Colorado squawfish, humpback chub and razorback sucker are endangered and, if caught, are to be thrown back immediately.

Fishing has long been a popular activity and growing numbers of anglers led to a diminishing supply of fish. Consequently, fish became the first managed wildlife resource. Efforts to keep waters fishy led to the earliest environmental efforts at conservation. Since the 1890s, federal and state fish and wildlife agencies have built fish hatcheries and stocked Colorado waters.

Colorado's Record Trout

Rainbow: 18 lbs.; 32 in.; South Platte River in Park County, 1972.

Brown: 30 lbs.; 36 in.; Roaring Judy Ponds in Gunnison County, 1988.

Cutthroat: 16 lbs.; 32 in.; Twin Lakes in Lake County, 1964.

Splake: 19 lbs.; 32 in.; Island Lake in Delta Co., 1976.

Golden: 3 lbs, 12 oz.; 22.5 in.; Kelly Lake in Jackson County, 1979. ✳

Colorado maintains 17 fish hatcheries and rearing units and the Federal Fish and Wildlife Service maintains several others, including the Leadville National Fish Hatchery. Built in 1890, the Leadville

Barney Ford, 19th-century businessman and African American leader. Colorado Historical Society.

station is the second oldest in the United States. The picturesque Queen Anne-style main building, now a National Register Landmark, is still used to raise eggs into fry, which then are reared in outside tanks. This facility and the other federal and state fish hatcheries welcome visitors.

To learn more: Colorado Division of Wildlife, 6060 Broadway, Denver 80216; (303) 291-7366; fishing reports (303) 291-7533; www.dnr.state.co.us.

Ford, Barney Lancelot (SEE ALSO AFRICAN

AMERICANS) Born in 1822 in South Carolina to a slave mother, Barney Ford had his father's blue eyes and light skin. While working on a Mississippi River steamboat, he escaped and made his way to Chicago, then headed to Colorado in 1860. After claim jumpers cheated him out of his gold claims in Mountain City and Breckenridge, he moved to Denver and opened his People's Restaurant and Barber Shop. Success there led to a career as a prosperous innkeeper in Denver, Breckenridge and Cheyenne, Wyoming.

Ford helped African Americans by establishing literacy classes and by opposing Colorado statehood until black suffrage was included. He served on the board of the Dime Savings Bank, became a member of the Colorado Association of Pioneers, and was listed in Denver's 1898 Social Register— the first Coloradan of color to be included. A credit report from R.G. Dun called Ford a "man of excellent character and standing, proverbial for his honesty and square dealing." Ford, who died in Denver in 1902, is commemorated by a stained glass window at the Colorado statehouse.

Ford, Justina (SEE ALSO

AFRICAN AMERICANS) Born in Illinois in 1871, the seventh and last child of a nurse, Justina Warren wanted to be a doctor from the beginning. "I wouldn't play with other children," she recalled, "unless we played hospital and I got to be the doctor."

Such determination helped her clear two major hurdles to a medical career: being a woman and being black. She graduated from Hering Medical College in Chicago and moved to Denver to practice in 1902. The Colorado Medical Society and local hospitals denied her privileges because of her color, so she set up a home practice and made house visits in central Denver where she lived. She specialized in gynecology, obstetrics and pediatrics.

She was married to Rev. John E. Ford, of Zion Baptist Church. During her 50-year practice in Denver, Dr. Ford delivered more than 7,000 babies. Many were newborns of color whose parents could not afford, or felt shy about using, white doctors. Not only blacks, but Hispanics, Asians and American Indians sought out Dr. Ford, who once said, "Whatever color they show up, that's the way I take 'em."

She accepted money only if the patients could afford to pay. When she doubted that the family could afford the fee they gave her, she used the money to buy things for the new baby.

After her death in 1952, the Ford home and Dr. Ford's office stood on Arapahoe Street until a demolition crew arrived in 1983. Fast work by Historic Denver Inc. and other parties saved the house and saw that it was moved to a new location.

To learn more: The Ford home has been restored as the Black American West Museum. 3901 California St.; (303) 292-2566.

Fourteen-thousand-foot Peaks (SEE ALSO

LONGS PEAK; MOUNT EVANS; MOUNT OF THE HOLY CROSS; PIKES PEAK) The "14ers," as Colorado's 54 peaks over 14,000 feet in elevation are called, are the highest points

A rambling fence and old buildings defy harsh elements before Colorado's highest mountain— Mount Elbert (14,433 feet). From The Rockies; photo by David Muench.

remaining from a plateau that once covered much of the state. Typically, they are stony bulwarks that have resisted erosion. Of the 14ers, only Grays and Torreys peaks are on the Continental Divide. The highest is 14,433-foot Mount Elbert; the lowest is Sunshine at 14,001.

Colorado's mountains have "grown" and "shrunk" over the years with measurement and remeasurement. Since 1950, Grizzly Peak and Stewart Peak have been demoted from 14er status. Mount Ellingwood, once considered a 14er, is now officially considered a part of Mount Blanca. Many mountains come close to 14,000 feet, and more than 600 Colorado peaks soar over 13,000 feet. To the chagrin of Coloradans, one peak in California is higher than Mount Elbert. That is 14,495-foot Mount Whitney, which lost its title as the nation's highest peak when Alaska, with 20,300-foot Mount McKinley, became the 49th state.

Native Americans probably climbed some of these peaks before Euro-Americans came to Colorado, but the first recorded ascent was by Dr. Edwin James, a member of the Long Expedition, who ascended Pikes Peak with some companions in 1820.

Among climbers, the 14ers are notorious for sudden changes of weather: glorious mornings can turn into afternoon electrical

Colorado's 14ers

Mt. Elbert	14,433	Mt. Sneffels	14,150
Mt. Massive	14,421	Mt. Democrat	14,148
Mt. Harvard	14,420	Capitol Peak	14,130
Blanca Peak	14,345	Pikes Peak	14,110
La Plata Peak	14,336	Snowmass Mountain	14,092
Uncompahgre Peak	14,309	Mt. Eolus	14,083
Crestone Peak	14,294	Windom Peak	14,082
Mt. Lincoln	14,286	Challenger Point	14,080
Grays Peak	14,270	Mt. Columbia	14,073
Mt. Antero	14,269	Culebra Peak	14,069
Torreys Peak	14,267	Missouri Mountain	14,067
Quandary Peak	14,265	Humboldt Peak	14,064
Castle Peak	14,265	Mt. Bierstadt	14,060
Mt. Evans	14,264	Sunlight Peak	14,059
Longs Peak	14,255	Handies Peak	14,048
Mt. Wilson	14,246	Mt. Lindsey	14,042
Mt. Shavano	14,229	Little Bear Peak	14,037
Mt. Princeton	14,197	Mt. Sherman	14,036
Mt. Belford	14,197	Redcloud Peak	14,034
Mt. Yale	14,196	Pyramid Peak	14,018
Crestone Needle	14,191	Wilson Peak	14,017
Mt. Bross	14,172	Wetterhom Peak	14,017
Kit Carson Peak	14,165	San Luis Peak	14,014
El Diente Peak	14,159	North Maroon Peak	14,014
Maroon Peak	14,156	Mt. of the Holy Cross	14,005
Tabeguache Peak	14,155	Huron Peak	14,005
Mt. Oxford	14,153	Sunshine Peak	14,001

storms with high winds, rain, sleet and snow.

Apprehensive sightseers wishing to conquer a 14er may enjoy scenic paved automobile roads open in summer to the top of Mount Evans and Pikes Peak.

To learn more: American Mountaineering Museum, 710 10th St., Golden 80401; (303) 384-0110; www.mountaincenter.org.

Franco Americans

French explorers, trappers, traders and missionaries were among the first Europeans to visit Colorado, leaving behind French place names such as the *Platte* (flat or shallow) and *Cache la Poudre* (gunpowder hiding place) rivers. Eastern Colorado north of the Arkansas River was part of French Louisiana before Napoleon sold it to the United States in 1803.

French mountain men familiar with Colorado's waterways and mountains guided Francis Parkman, Rufus Sage and other early visitors to Colorado. French, or French Canadians, were among the pioneers in many towns but often left, along with their Indian wives, as towns grew larger and less friendly to Indians, Frenchmen and their "half-breed" offspring. French-born residents made up the fifth most numerous group in Colorado until 1870, when they dwindled in relative numbers.

Among the French pioneers was a small, wiry French missionary, Joseph P. Machebeuf. Father Machebeuf came to Colorado in 1858 to say Mass at Our Lady of Guadalupe Church in Conejos, which today is Colorado's oldest church still in use. In 1860 he founded the first Catholic church in Denver and subsequently started parishes in many other communities. As the first pastor, and then the first bishop of Colorado, he started 102 churches, 9 schools, a college, an orphanage and 10 hospitals.

Other French notables include Joseph Bijeau, who guided Major Stephen Long through Colorado in 1820 and gave his name to Bijou Creek; mountain men and fort builders such as Antoine Roubidoux and Ceran St. Vrain; and Louis DuPuy, founder of Georgetown's legendary Hotel de Paris.

To learn more: Alliance Francaise, Denver; (303) 831-0304.

Front Range The Front

Range is the easternmost edge of the Colorado mountains, stretching roughly from Pikes Peak near Colorado Springs to Longs Peak near Denver and up to Rocky Mountain National Park near Fort Collins. More popularly, the term is used to describe the urbanized corridor at the eastern base of the mountains, from Colorado Springs to Fort Collins.

Fur Trade Many of the first

Euro-Americans to reach Colorado came in search of beaver pelts, which sold in the East and Europe for as much as $30. After beaver hats went out of style in the 1830s, the fur trade faded, although traffic in buffalo robes continued until bison, like the beaver, were almost extinct.

Loners like the mountain man James Purcell had poked into Colorado as early as 1805, but not until 1815 did Auguste P. Chouteau of St. Louis begin a large-scale, organized fur trade. Some 50 men came to trap and trade with the Native Americans,

holding trade fairs and rendezvous at various places, including Bear Creek in what is now southwest Denver and at the confluence of Fountain Creek and the Arkansas River at what in now the city of Pueblo.

Louis Vasquez, a trader from St. Louis, established a small, short-lived post in 1832 at the confluence of Vasquez Creek (now

> **Grand Lake, Colorado's largest natural lake, is surrounded by mountains that inspire tourists to ask about elevation. One lady viewing Grand Lake asked, "Which end is higher?"**

Clear Creek) and the South Platte where metropolitan Denver now stands. Five years later, Vasquez and Andrew Sublette erected a second, better-known Fort Vasquez a mile south of Platteville. This adobe fort has been reconstructed as a fur-trade museum by the Colorado Historical Society.

Other South Platte River fur trade posts were Fort Lupton, built in 1837 by Lancaster P. Lupton, and Fort St. Vrain, operated by Ceran St. Vrain between 1837 and 1846 as a branch of the Bent's Fort trading post. In western Colorado, Antoine Robidoux of the St. Louis fur-trade clan opened a log fort and trading post in the 1830s on the Uncompahgre River, near its confluence with the Gunnison. Known as Fort Roubidoux or Fort Uncompahgre, this outpost five miles southwest of modern-day Delta survived until 1846, when the Utes reduced it to ashes.

The mountain men generally got along well with the Native Americans, Hispanics and French, often intermarrying. Indeed, hard-working Indian women were indispensable to the fur trade. They processed the furs and negotiated acceptance of fur traders with their tribes. Most fur traders died young, but some survived to guide gold seekers and immigrants in Colorado and helped to establish many trails and towns. Kit Carson lived to age 59, James Beckwourth to 66, Jim Bridger to 71.

Gambling

In a state founded on a gamble on gold, Coloradans have long been risk takers. Native Americans fancied gambling, and archaeologists speculate that carved bones and stones found in ancient pit houses may have been used for gaming. Historic tribes also wagered on games such as Hand and Double Ball, as well as on horse races. The two tribes with Colorado reservations today, the Southern Utes and the Ute Mountain Utes, both opened casinos during the 1990s.

Gambling became a major amusement of miners who began arriving with the 1859 gold rush. Gambling saloons were ubiquitous, offering such card games as monte, rouge et noir, over and under 7, chuck-a-luck, poker and blackjack, as well as dice and roulette. Colorado Territory and most local governments outlawed gambling, but did not always enforce the laws. Indeed, many communities used fines on gambling as a source of income, simply conducting raids when the town treasury was low. Illegal gambling, of course, has always been a major, untaxed, uncalculated part of the underground economy.

Poker Alice, Edward Chase, Vaso Chucovitch, Doc Holiday, Bat Masterson, Soapy Smith and other noted gamblers operated in Colorado by bribing or eluding authorities. Gambling remained illegal in Colorado, although in 1982 a state lottery was established, with 50 percent of the revenues going for prizes and 40 percent for parks, recreation and open space programs.

In 1990 voters also approved limited legalized gambling in Black Hawk, Central City and Cripple Creek. Gambling is permitted seven days a week between 8 A.M. and 2 A.M. with maximum $5 bets. Revenues are taxed at up to 18 percent of the adjusted gross proceeds depending on the size of the business. Gaming tax income is awarded 50 percent to the Colorado general fund, 28 percent to the State Historical Fund for preservation projects, 10 percent to the three gaming communities and 12 percent to the involved counties, Gilpin and Teller.

In 2000, Black Hawk and Cripple Creek each had 19 casinos and Central City had 8. Almost 100 small operations have come and gone since 1991 as larger casinos have come to dominate the business. Black Hawk now generates more gaming revenue than Central City and Cripple Creek combined, although the latter were originally larger towns with more casinos. Black Hawk's advantage lay in larger casinos, such as the Isle of Capri with 1,100 slot machines.

With another $1 billion worth of new casinos projected in 2000, Black Hawk continues to outstrip Central City and Cripple Creek, collecting 70 percent of the gaming dollars. In 1999, Colorado's casinos posted adjusted gross revenues of $531 million, a 13 percent increase over the previous year.

Looking Back

1806

James Purcell, a mountain man from Kentucky, showed Zebulon Pike a bag of gold dust he had dug out of the South Platte River—a full half-century before the big Colorado gold rush.

Ever-increasing gaming revenues have pumped more than $80 million into preservation projects administered by the Colorado Historical Society. Ironically, the gaming construction boom has compromised the historical integrity of the three National Historic Landmark mining towns generating the funds. But despite some problems with gaming, Colorado state and local governments seem to have become addicted to casinos and lotto for revenues.

Garden of the Gods

This municipal park in Colorado Springs is far-famed for its spectacular upright stone slabs, pinnacles and mushroom rocks, which frame views of Pikes Peak to the west. These Paleozoic and Mesozoic sandstone formations are beach and shore deposits left by ancient inland seas. Solidified sandstone has been tilted upward by volcanic action and carved by subsequent erosion of softer rock beneath harder rock, creating features such as the famous balanced rock.

After white settlement began in nearby Colorado City in 1858, Melanchton S. Beach gazed over the red rock formations and told his companions Lewis Tappan and Rufus Cable, "This would be a capital place for a beer garden!"

"A beer garden, indeed!" Cable replied. "This is a place for the gods to assemble."

So the park came to be called the Garden of the Gods, although it first developed as a beer garden, dance hall and hodgepodge of commercial operations selling photos, rocks and trinkets.

Edwin L. "Fatty" Rice and his wife Phoebe opened Fatty's Place, a beer garden and curio shop specializing in gems and rocks. "Stop by and See the Fat Man," read the advertisements placed by the bushy-bearded, 300-pound proprietor.

In 1907, Fatty's widow sold the place to Colorado Springs town founder William J. Palmer, who worked with Charles Elliott

Perkins, president of the Chicago, Burlington and Quincy Railroad, to acquire the entire garden. Perkins' children donated it to the city in 1909 with the stipulation that it be used forever as a free public park. The original 700-acre gift has been expanded to 1,364 acres of park space that offers a variety of desert and foothills flora and fauna.

After acquiring the park, Colorado Springs did away with such commercial establishments as Billy Bryan's Dance Hall at the base of Gateway Rock. Billy had built a stairway to the top of the Gateway in 1887 and began promoting it as "the best sparking place in El Paso County." The city also discouraged Paul Goerke, who had set up a photography stand at Balanced Rock and Steamboat Rock, where he posed tourists on a burro for 25-cent photos. Another commercial establishment, the Garden of the Gods Trading Post founded in 1900, survives on the edge of the park, as does the Flying W Ranch with its dinner theater.

The Balanced Rock at Garden of the Gods park, Colorado Springs. Antique postcard, Tom Noel Collection.

In 1999, Colorado Springs demolished the old 1915 Pueblo Revival-style Hidden Inn, which was tucked between giant red sandstone formations. This quaint landmark, with its tea room and observation deck, had been upstaged by a new 10,000-square-foot visitor center, museum and restaurant built in 1995 on the eastern edge of the park. The park offers many hiking, biking and equestrian trails, as well as technical rock climbing. Living history exhibits and restored pioneer structures help make Garden of the Gods a very popular park.

To learn more: Garden of the Gods Visitor Center, 185 N. 30th St., Colorado Springs 80904; (719) 634-6666.

Gays and Lesbians

Colorado gained national attention in 1992 by passing Proposition 2, which refused to extend civil rights to gays. Although the Colorado Supreme Court later rejected this amendment to the Colorado Constitution as unconstitutional, gay organizations have worked to improve relations between the estimated 10 percent of the population who are gay and other Coloradans.

In response to ridicule, if not discrimination, Colorado gays generally stayed in the closet, usually meeting in gay bars, until the 1970s. The Denver Gay Coalition formed in 1973 and worked with the police department to end entrapment and harassment. In 1974, the coalition organized Denver's first gay pride week with a public festival and parade.

Denver holds this Gay PrideFest Parade on the last Sunday of June. It has grown to include more than 100 parade groups and 225 vendors, artists and community organizations, talks from the mayor of Denver and other prominent politicians, live entertainment in Cheesman and Civic Center Parks and some 90,000 spectators.

Denver, Aspen and Boulder have passed gay rights ordinances, but voters statewide have been less tolerant, as were the legislature and Gov. Bill Owens who, in 2000, collaborated on a law to ban gay marriages in Colorado.

To learn more

Newspaper *Out Front*, published as "Colorado's Gay Community Forum."

Parents, Families and Friends of Lesbians and Gays; (303) 333-0286.

Gay Colorado AIDS Project; (303) 830-2437.

Geology (SEE ALSO FRONT RANGE)

The geology of Colorado has been under construction for billions of years, shaping the state's plains, peaks and plateaus. Each of these landforms occupies roughly a third of the state. Glaciers (see entry), volcanoes, marine shorelines and two mountain building episodes have been major forces in shaping Colorado.

Close to Denver, the Dakota Hogback roadcut along Interstate 70 displays the colorful Dakota and Morrison rock formations. The Hogback also includes the Dinosaur Ridge interpretive trail near the town of Morrison, explaining fossils and geology of the area. Just west of the Dakota Hogback, the Pennsylvanian age (280–325 million years ago) is represented at Red Rocks Amphitheater (see entry). These great monoliths were formed on the flanks of the ancestral Rockies and uplifted 45 to 65 million years ago when the present Rockies were formed.

The spectacular pinnacles and towers of the Garden of the Gods (see entry) in Colorado Springs were created by the more recent mountain building phase. These almost vertical layers are remnants of Lyons sandstone which has been used extensively in buildings throughout the Front Range, most notably for the Boulder campus of the University of Colorado.

What tectonic forces push up, water and wind begin tearing down. The rugged cliffs of Glenwood Canyon, Black Canyon of the Gunnison and the Royal Gorge were all created through the combined efforts of uplift and water erosion in the late Tertiary Period (3–20 million years ago).

The Colorado National Monument on the northern side of the Uncompahgre Plateau in western Colorado offers an excellent presentation of red rocks formed from the erosion of the ancestral Rockies. Southwestern Colorado features the San Juan volcanic area and the Wheeler Geologic Area National Monument, where more than 100 feet of volcanic tuff and ash is eroding into unique rock sculptures.

To learn more: The U.S. Geological Survey office at the Federal Center in Lakewood, a Denver suburb, contains a geologic library, topographic and geologic maps, and information on public lands where rock and mineral collecting is permitted. (303) 236-1000; www.usgs.gov.

Members of German singing societies once traveled by wagon to their Denver performances. Colorado Historical Society.

German Americans

Of Colorado's immigrants, the most prominent, prosperous and populous were the Germans. Typically Germans arrived with more money and earned and saved more after arriving in Colorado.

Among the German movers and shakers were brewer Adolph Coors (see entry) and entrepreneur Charles Boettcher (see entry). German-born immigrants were joined by Germans from Russia. These Volga-Deutsche had been recruited by Catherine the Great to settle in Russia's Volga Valley. After the German-born czarina died, other Russian rulers revoked the tax exemption, military service exemptions and cultural autonomy she allowed the Teutons. Subsequently, thousands fled Russia. Many settled on the Great Plains of North America, including Colorado's South Platte Valley. By the 1930s, Germans from Russia dominated farming in northeastern Colorado.

Germans took a keen interest in public education, persuading the Colorado legislature to pass a law in 1877 requiring the teaching of German and of gymnastics in the public schools. The active German element led Colorado to print its laws, from 1877 to 1889, in German, as well as in

English and Spanish. By 1880, a fourth of Colorado's saloons were owned by German or Austrian-born immigrants. Inside, customers spoke and sang in German, read German newspapers and magazines, consumed sauerkraut and strudel, and quaffed beer.

Although Germans had a happier life in 19th-century Colorado than most ethnic groups, the 20th century changed that. The swelling Prohibition movement tended to blame all evil on drink. Breweries and saloons, according to this movement, were un-American bastions where people spoke German and plotted against the established order. Prohibition passed partly because of a desire to punish "foreign" immigrants, especially Germans.

The mining town of Animas Forks, seen here in 1893, is now one of the ghost towns of the San Juan Mountains. Photo by Joseph Collier; Library of Congress.

An even heavier blow came with the outbreak of World War I. Germans became the target of widespread hate campaigns. Regardless of their professed and proven patriotism, Germans lost their jobs and were physically and verbally abused. School districts outlawed German language classes. Restaurants renamed sauerkraut "liberty cabbage" and hamburgers became "liberty steaks." After Prohibition and two World Wars, this group that had contributed so much to Colorado's cultural, educational and social life never fully reemerged as a distinctive ethnic community. Some German traditions, such as Octoberfests and auto rallies featuring German-made cars, are still a part of Colorado life.

Ghost Towns (SEE ALSO PLACE NAMES)
Colorado has almost as many dead towns (about 500) as live ones (650). Mining booms and busts left the mountains littered with more than 300 ghost towns that fascinate both locals and tourists. The eastern plains and western canyon lands are also haunted by more than 200 dead towns.

Ghosts include antique Mexican plaza towns dating back to the 1850s, pre-gold rush Anglo-American villages, stage stops, cow towns, and Utopian communities. Started with high hopes, these towns were erased by droughts, dust storms, high winds and scorching heat, as well as by shaky crop and livestock prices. Abandoned by the railroads and ignored by new highways, communities died as their people migrated to larger towns and cities in search of jobs. As towns faded, their post offices closed and they were dropped from maps. Five ghosts—Autobees, Badito, Boggsville, Latham and Ula—were once county seats.

Many Hispanic settlements have disappeared, victims perhaps of not only the usual mishaps but also the dominant Anglo culture. Crumbling adobe churches, neglected graveyards and broken-down haciendas mark the sites of vanished Hispanic towns.

Glaciers
Much of Colorado's mountain scenery has been sculpted by glaciers, which still linger in the state. From Moraine Park in Rocky Mountain National Park to the Uncompahgre Valley in the San Juan Mountains, travelers can see evidence of the power of the ice caps that

covered much of the state from 10,000 to 30,000 years ago. Glacial cirques and lakes can be found throughout the mountains.

Arapaho Glacier, Colorado's largest, is located in the Indian Peaks Wilderness Area in Boulder County. In 1930 the city of Boulder purchased the glacier, which it still uses as a water supply. Arapaho Glacier covers approximately two square miles and is between 100 and 500 feet deep. The nearby St. Vrain Glacier Group consists of six glaciers.

Rocky Mountain National Park is home to Andrews, Hallett, Taylor and Tyndall glaciers. Just as wondrous are glacial features such as Glacier Gorge, Glacier Knobs and Glacier Lake. Moraine Park in Rocky Mountain National Park is so named for the hills, or moraines, made of rocks, gravel and dirt dumped by glaciers. St. Mary's Glacier is no longer a glacier, but an ice field, as it is no longer moving under its own weight.

Colorado's glaciers are slowly retreating or becoming ice fields, but you still have 100,000 years or so left to see these ice-age relics.

To learn more: Colorado Avalanche Information Center, 1313 Sherman St., Denver 80203; (303) 499-9650.

Gold (SEE ALSO LOST TREASURE; MINING)

Golden rumors drifted out of the Rockies for two centuries before the Colorado gold rush, thanks to reported discoveries by Spanish and French prospectors as well as Anglo mountain men. But not until 1858 and the William Green Russell discovery in Cherry Creek and the South Platte River did the gold rush begin.

Gold fever spread quickly to the Missouri River frontier towns such as Kansas City and Omaha, which outfitted the argonauts and encouraged them with guidebooks that prescribed supplies and routes and described the fabulous fortunes to be made in Colorado. An estimated 100,000 set out in 1859 for the vaguely labeled "Pike's Peak Diggings." Two-thirds

Gold-seekers flocked to Colorado in 1859, heading for what was called the Pike's Peak Diggings. Tom Noel Collection.

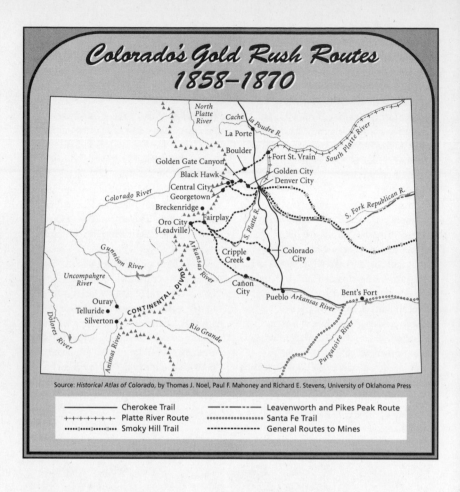

Colorado's Gold Rush Routes 1858–1870

Source: *Historical Atlas of Colorado*, by Thomas J. Noel, Paul F. Mahoney and Richard E. Stevens, University of Oklahoma Press

——————— Cherokee Trail   —————— Leavenworth and Pikes Peak Route
++++++++ Platte River Route   ∘∘∘∘∘∘∘∘∘∘∘∘ Santa Fe Trail
•••••|•••••|•••••|••• Smoky Hill Trail   ————————— General Routes to Mines

of this mass migration would become disappointed "go-backs."

In 1860, the census takers found 34,277 residents, enough to justify creation of Colorado Territory in 1861. Although very little additional gold was found in Cherry Creek and the Denver area, richer discoveries on Boulder Creek, Clear Creek and the upper South Platte and Arkansas Rivers led to permanent settlements. Black Hawk, where John Gregory found gold in 1859, and nearby Central City made Gilpin County the largest producer until the 1890 Cripple Creek discovery. Cripple Creek outproduced all other Colorado gold

regions and briefly led the world in production during the early 1900s.

As placer (surface) mining played out, Coloradans concentrated on lode (underground) mining, which transformed Central City, Leadville, Breckenridge, Ouray, Telluride and Cripple Creek into multimillion-dollar jackpots. Colorado is second only to California in total gold production over the years. Among the 505 major gold districts in the United States, 46 are in Colorado. Cripple Creek ranks second nationally; Central City, 11th; Telluride, 14th; and Leadville, 16th.

Gold production set a post World War II record in 1996, when the three surviving Colorado gold mines produced 250,000 ounces. Exhaustion of the ore body shut down the San Luis Mine in Costilla County in 1996 and the Black Cloud Mine in Leadville in 1999. The sole remaining major producing mine is the Cresson pit mine of the Cripple Creek and Victor Gold Mining Co., which produced 231,000 ounces in 1999.

Although gold no longer dominates the state's economy as it did before 1917, Colorado remains the home of the nation's largest gold mining firm, Newmont Gold Co., which had worldwide reserves in 2000 of 66.5 million ounces. Newmont is headquartered in the Denver suburb of Englewood, where the Russell Party made the initial 1858 strike.

The gold-domed state Capitol and the U.S. Mint in Denver, as well as mining towns, ghost towns and many picturesque ruins, are legacies of Colorado's golden origins.

To learn more

Western Museum of Mining and Industry, 125 Gleneagle Drive, Colorado Springs; (719) 488-0880; www.wmmi.org.

National Mining Hall of Fame and Museum, 120 W. Ninth St., Leadville; (719) 486-1229; www.leadville.com/miningmuseum.

Golf

Championship courses such as those at the Broadmoor, Castle Pines and Cherry Hills have put Colorado on the golf map. Cherry Hills twice hosted American golf's most prestigious tournament, the U.S. Open, while the Broadmoor hosted the 50th U.S. Women's Open in 1995.

Ski and mountain resorts boast scenic and challenging golf courses. High-altitude golfing is different, with the difficult break in mountain greens and with balls traveling 10 to 15 percent farther than at sea level because of the thin air. Although mountain courses are open only in summer and early fall, many lower courses, including those along the Front Range from Fort Collins to Trinidad, are open year-round.

To learn more: Colorado Golf Association, 7465 E. First Ave., Denver 80220; (303) 366-4653.

Governors

(SEE ALSO ELECTED OFFICIALS) Jefferson Territory, an extra-legal predecessor of Colorado Territory, was never recognized by the federal government. Robert W. Steele served as its governor from 1859 to 1861. The federal government created Colorado Territory in 1861 and the U.S. president began appointing territorial governors for two-year terms. With statehood in 1876, Coloradans began electing their own executive to serve two-year terms, later expanded to four-year terms. Since 1990, each governor is limited to two terms in office.

Colorado's first territorial governor, William Gilpin, was forced to resign in 1862 after Washington refused to back his federal expenditures to raise and equip Civil War troops. Gilpin's successor, John Evans (see entry), had to resign in 1865 because, being also in charge of Indian affairs, he was found ultimately responsible for the

---

End of a Dream

In an 1859 article for Harper's Weekly about a trip to Colorado along the South Platte River route, artist Alfred Bierdstadt tells of encountering "thousands of the deluded and suffering gold seekers, retracing their step ... many of them were in starving condition, barefooted, ragged and penniless....We have probably passed four thousand desponding and disappointed men returning to the states." ✲

atrocities Colorado troops committed at the Sand Creek Massacre (see entry).

Territorial Governors

William Gilpin, 1861–1862
John Evans, 1862–1865
Alexander Cummings, 1865–1867
A. Cameron Hunt, 1867–1869
Edward McCook, 1869–1873
Samuel H. Elbert, 1873–1874
Edward McCook, 1874–1875
John L. Routt, 1875–1876

State Governors

John L. Routt (R), 1876–1879
Frederick W. Pitkin (R), 1879–1883
James B. Grant (D), 1883–1885
Benjamin H. Eaton (R), 1885–1887
Alva Adams (D), 1887–1889
Job A. Cooper (R), 1889–1891
John L. Routt (R), 1891–1893
Davis H. Waite (Populist), 1893–1895
Albert W. McIntire (R), 1895–1897
Alva Adams (D), 1897–1899
Charles S. Thomas (D), 1899–1901
James B. Orman (D), 1901–1903
James H. Peabody (R), 1903–1905
Jesse F. McDonald (R), 1905–1907
Henry A. Buchtel (R), 1907–1909
John F. Shafroth (D), 1909–1913
Elias M. Ammons (D), 1913–1915
George A. Carlson (R), 1915–1917
Julius C. Gunter (D), 1917–1919
Oliver H. Shoup (R), 1919–1923
William E. Sweet (D), 1923–1925
Clarence J. Morley (R), 1925–1927
William H. Adams (D), 1927–1933
Edwin C. Johnson (D), 1933–1937
Teller Ammons (D), 1937–1939
Ralph Carr (R), 1939–1943
John Vivian (R), 1943–1947
Lee Knous (D), 1947–1949
Walter Johnson (D), 1949–1951
Dan Thornton (R), 1951–1955
Edwin C. Johnson (D), 1955–1957
Stephen McNichols (D), 1957–1963
John A. Love (R), 1963–1973
John Vanderhoof (R), 1973–1975
Richard D. Lamm (D), 1975–1987
Roy Romer (D), 1987–1999
Bill Owens (R), 1999–

A Political Pileup

The state's most bizarre election gave Colorado three governors in one day.

In the fall of 1904, Democrat Alva Adams defeated the incumbent Republican, James Peabody, by about 10,000 votes. The Republican-controlled Supreme Court and the legislature, however, declared Adams' election void due to alleged vote frauds and installed Peabody.

Widespread protest from Democrats, independents and moderate Republicans led to a compromise. Peabody resigned and his Republican lieutenant governor, Jesse F. McDonald, was given the office, becoming Colorado's third governor in one day on March 17, 1905. ✻

Grand Junction

The largest city in western Colorado, Grand Junction, is the Mesa County seat. Founded in 1881 just after the Ute Indians were removed to reservations, it was named for its site at the confluence of the Grand River (renamed the Colorado River between Grand Junction and Dotsero in 1921) and Gunnison River. This site is rimmed by three large plateaus: Grand Mesa on the southeast, Colorado National Monument of the Uncompahgre Plateau on the southwest and the Book Cliffs on the north.

George A. Crawford and others founded Grand Junction as a rail hub for the Denver & Rio Grande Railroad. The earliest pioneers lived in tents before constructing log cabins from cottonwoods growing along the river banks. Grand Junction

Ferries took people across the Colorado River at Grand Junction before bridges were built. Museum of Western Colorado.

blossomed as the regional rail supply center for a farming, ranching and orchard region.

Colorado's first sugar beet factory, opened in Grand Junction in 1899, was revamped as a uranium mill in the 1950s and has since been demolished. The Prinster brothers' City Market grocery store, opened in the 1920s, is now a major regional chain, epitomizing Grand Junction's reign over a large western Colorado hinterland. Among Colorado cities, Grand Junction is second only to Denver in wholesale business.

Irrigation canals enabled Grand Junction, which boasts 354 days of sunshine a year, to become an oasis of green lawns, trees and gardens, of apple, cherry and peach orchards, and since the 1990s, of vineyards. The city's pioneer 1881 plat established Emerson, Hawthorne, Washington and Whitman parks. Newer parks include a riverfront greenway and Lincoln Park, with its 351-foot water slide, swimming pool and golf course. The region's oil shale boom of the 1970s is reflected in the new office buildings and hotels along Horizon Drive, which leads to Walker Field Airport.

Grand Junction is sustained by a diverse regional economic base, the railroad, the *Grand Junction Sentinel*, the Museum of Western Colorado, Mesa State College, three hospitals, and outdoor recreation at Grand Mesa and Colorado National Monument. Now a city of more 42,000 people, Grand Junction has doubled its population since the mid-1970s.

Grand Mesa Grand Mesa,

southeast of Grand Junction in western Colorado, is promoted as "the world's largest flat-topped mountain." The mesa covers 380,000 acres and has more than 300 lakes at a cool average elevation of around 10,000 feet.

Information on this huge plateau, which is mostly within Grand Mesa National Forest, is provided at Grand Mesa Visitor Center, at State Hwy. 65 and Forest Road 121, and Land's End Observatory, on Forest Road 100; (970) 242-8211.

Griffith, Emily

In 1947, the most celebrated of Colorado's many superb teachers was found shot to death in her summer cabin in Pinecliffe. This still unsolved case may have been a suicide pact between the 79-year-old teacher, her developmentally disabled sister and their caretaker. Despite uncertainties about her death, no doubts shadow Emily K. Griffith's contributions to Colorado. This tiny, mild-mannered lady made a huge difference.

At a time when many Americans joined organizations such as the Ku Klux Klan to persecute poor immigrants, Emily Griffith came up with a radical alternative—to offer newcomers a free public education in English and job skills. Born in Cincinnati, Ohio, in 1868, the blue-eyed, auburn-haired maiden began teaching in a sod schoolhouse in Broken Bow, Neb., when she was still a teenager. She moved to Denver in 1895 to teach at the 24th Street School.

Griffith grew convinced that adults needed education as much as their children. She dreamed of making Denver the first city in the world with free universal adult education. Her dream came true in 1916, when the Denver Public Schools converted Longfellow School to Opportunity School.

This adult education center has evolved into the full-block complex of the Emily Griffith Opportunity School, as it was renamed when she retired in 1933. The school has educated more than 2 million people who wanted to learn how to read and write, improve their English, and gain marketable job skills.

Hard Rock Cafe

The original Hard Rock Cafe, in the tiny town of Empire about 55 miles west of Denver, celebrates Empire's mining heritage. Residents prided themselves upon being hard rock miners who dug through granite looking for gold, silver and, in recent years, molybdenum at the nearby Henderson Mine.

The owner of the Hard Rock Cafe was astonished a few years ago when the international Hard Rock Cafe chain demanded he give up the name. The global chain of trendy clubs glorifying hard-rock music lost the case. After all, the Hard Rock Cafe in Empire got its name in 1932, while the Hard Rock chain did not start until 1971 in London. The chain has opened its shrines to rock music all over the globe, including Aspen and Denver. These tourist dens could hardly be confused with the quiet cafe in Empire, which is known for good, inexpensive food and friendly service, not for loud music.

The cafe's two-story frame building, constructed in 1898 and restored in 2000–2001, is on the State Register of Historic Places. The cafe is on the ground floor and the tiny Empire town hall is upstairs under a rooftop cupola containing the town bell and fire siren. Instead of rock music icons, the cafe has a mineral specimen display case.

Rather than toady to tourists, the cafe has posted a homemade sign: "Miners will be served first."

Highways

(SEE ALSO MILEAGE CHART; MOTOR VEHICLES; PASSES; SCENIC AND HISTORIC BYWAYS) Coloradans measure highway travel in time rather than in miles because traffic congestion and terrain are as important as distance. Mountain miles are winding and slow, while isolated flat prairie roads are straight and fast.

Colorado's rugged terrain and long distances between settlements led private entrepreneurs to construct toll roads as early as the 1860s. During the early 1900s, bicyclists and automobilists began promoting public paved roads. The Colorado Auto Club and the Colorado Good Roads Association helped persuade the legislature to establish the Colorado Highway Commission in 1909. Responding to the Federal Highway Act of 1916 and 50-50 federal matching funds for building highways, the Colorado Highway Department was formed. By the 1920s it was spending $2.5 million a year on roads.

Colorado highway construction accelerated with the use of convict labor beginning in 1905. Convicts built many early paved roads, including scenic highways in the Arkansas, Big Thompson, Boulder, Colorado and St. Vrain canyons, as well as Cañon City's 1905 Skyline Drive, now a narrow, twisty relic of pioneer motoring. Colorado led the country in prisoner-built roads until the practice was abandoned in 1926. In 1919, Colorado became one of the first four states to tax gasoline to help finance road construction. The penny-per-gallon tax was doubled in 1923, was raised to 3 cents in 1927, and has been 22 cents since 1993.

U.S. 160 is the longest Colorado highway, meandering from the Kansas border to the Four Corners area where Colorado, Utah, Arizona and New Mexico meet. The shortest highway, Colorado 187, is seven-tenths of a mile long, from downtown Paonia to Colorado 133 on the north edge of town.

Colorado's first limited-access auto freeway, West Sixth Avenue, was built during World War II from downtown Denver to the federal war-production plant near Golden. The Denver–Boulder Turnpike, opened in 1952, proved so popular that tolls were removed in 1967 after the turnpike paid for itself ahead of schedule.

Although 1-25, Colorado's north-south interstate highway, was completed in 1967, the east-west 1-70 took much longer. Five

years (1968–1973) were spent blasting and burrowing under the Continental Divide for the Eisenhower–Johnson Tunnel. It took another 20 years to complete 1-70 through

> **Potatoes, as well as gold and silver, are the nuggets that gave Colorado its fast start. As many prospectors found, you cannot eat precious metals. Potatoes, on the other hand, could be eaten raw, boiled or baked, mashed or hashed.**

the Glenwood Canyon of the Colorado River. Not only the deep, narrow canyon, but also protests from environmentalists, delayed the project, inspiring engineers to design that stretch of 1-70 as Colorado's most beautiful highway.

Metro Denver is completing Interstate 76/270/225/470 as a belt-loop freeway with tolls on the I-470 portion. Coloradans, with one of the nation's highest per capita car ownership and use figures, have made I-25 one of America's 10 most congested freeways. Major widening of I-25 between Denver and Castle Rock during the early 2000s will include a light rail line. Railroads, which were often ripped out and replaced by highways, have reemerged as a proposed alternative to congested Colorado roads.

To learn more: The Colorado Department of Transportation issues free state, county and bicycle maps (303) 757-9313, and reports on road conditions (303) 639-1111. It also runs an Adopt-A-Highway volunteer cleanup program (303) 757-9713.

Colorado Highway and Road Ownership (1999)

Owner	Miles
Federal	6,969
State	9,071
County	55,447
Municipal	12,363
Other	1,299
Total	85,149

Hispanics (*See also* Peña,

Federico) Hispanics—both full-blooded Spaniards and people carrying Spanish and Native American blood—were the first Euro-Americans to settle in Colorado. They named the region for the muddy red color of its major river, the *Colorado* (Spanish for "red," "ruddy" or "colorful"). Hispanic missionaries, soldiers and adventurers explored parts of southern Colorado during the Spanish colonial period that began with the 1598 conquest by Don Juan de Oñate of the lower Rio Grande River valley.

Two Franciscan friars, Fray Silvestre Vélez de Escalante and Fray Francisco Atanasio Domínguez, made a most important expedition in 1776 and mapped Colorado for the first time. Discouraged by hostile Indians, the arid plains and canyon lands and forbidding mountains, the Spanish did not attempt to colonize what is now Colorado.

Only after the Mexican Revolution of 1821 did Hispanic pioneers settle the upper Rio Grande Valley of Colorado. To encourage agricultural settlement, the Mexican government made five large land grants in and near the San Luis Valley. Small adobe plaza towns were established first along the *Culebra* (Spanish for "snake") River, where San Luis (1851) is Colorado's oldest permanent town.

The 1848 Treaty of Guadalupe Hidalgo, which ended the Mexican–American War, promised U.S. citizenship and property rights to Mexican Americans. In spite of the treaty, much of their property ended up in Anglo hands. Frequently, Anglo settlers ignored existing Hispanic communities. Denver, for instance, dates its origins to an 1858 gold strike by U.S. citizens rather than to an 1857 claim known as Mexican Diggings.

Hispanics now make up 17 percent of Colorado's population and are the largest, and fastest growing, ethnic group in a region where they were the first non-Natives to explore, claim and settle. During the 1990s, the Hispanic population of Colorado increased by 77 percent, according to the 2000 census.

Historical Preservation (*See also*

Endangered Places; National Register of Historic Places) Most of Colorado's 19th-century buildings have been lost, and some entire communities have vanished. More than 300 former post office towns have been removed from the Colorado map. The state's post-World War II energy boom, an echo of the 1870–1893 mining bonanza years, led to the alteration or demolition of many old buildings.

Continuing threats to Colorado's architectural heritage sparked a grass-roots preservation movement in the 1970s. One result was the formation of private advocacy groups such as Colorado Preservation Inc., Historic Denver Inc. and Historic Boulder Inc.

Passage of the National Historic Preservation Act in 1966 created a federally funded state historic preservation office in each state to designate and preserve buildings of architectural and historical significance. The 1976 national bicentennial and Colorado statehood centennial inspired many communities to inventory surviving historic buildings and begin preservation efforts.

In 1991, Colorado enacted a program of state income tax credits for rehabilitation of designated national or local landmarks. This financial incentive, along with the State Historical Fund, has encouraged a proliferation of designated historic sites and districts. Colorado has 17 National Historic Landmark sites, more than 180 State and National Register Historic Districts, and more than 1,100 individual sites on the National Register of Historic Places. The State Register (which includes all National Register sites) has more than 1,400 listings.

Colorado spends more state money on preservation than any state except Florida, ever since a 1991 law allowed limited gambling in Black Hawk, Central City and Cripple Creek with a proviso that taxes generated go to, among other things, historical preservation. This gaming fund has allowed the Colorado Historical Society to spend, as of 2001, more than $80 million in gambling tax revenue on more than 1,100 preservation projects in all 64 counties.

Many cities and towns have passed local preservation ordinances, including Aspen, Aurora, Boulder, Breckenridge, Central City, Crested Butte, Cripple Creek, Denver, Durango, Fort Collins, Georgetown, Golden, Grand Junction, Longmont, Manitou Springs, Ouray and Telluride. Local preservation ordinances often regulate the demolition or abuse of landmarks. Some counties, such as Boulder, Ouray and Park, have also enacted countywide preservation measures.

History Documented human
habitation in what is now Colorado dates back at least 13,000 years. Native Americans have hunted, gathered and planted as well as fought over this land for millennia. Over the ages, different tribal groups inhabited Colorado, moving in and out of the area as lifestyle or survival needs required. In recorded history, claims to all or part of Colorado have been made by Native Americans and by England, France, Spain, Mexico, the Republic of Texas and the United States.

Although the 17th-century English colonies along the Atlantic seaboard made territorial claims stretching to the Pacific, they never pressed serious efforts to enforce such an extravagant vision.

French explorers penetrated Colorado in the 1700s, claiming it as part of Louisiana. While Robert Cavelier, Sieur de La Salle, never visited Colorado, his claim of the entire Mississippi River drainage for France was strengthened by French trappers and traders who explored northeastern Colorado. French claims were quieted by the 1803 Louisiana Purchase.

Spain did not settle its Colorado claims, but Mexico, which gained its independence from Spain in 1821, did make land grants in the region. No permanent Hispanic

Looking Back

November 1860

The *Leavenworth Republican,* of Leavenworth, Kan., reported: "Denver City is the wonder of the age! No city on the American continent has grown with such a rapidity."

settlement came, however, until 1851 at San Luis, three years after Mexico transferred all of its Colorado claims to the United States by the Treaty of Guadalupe Hidalgo, which ended the Mexican War.

The Republic of Texas, after its 1836 establishment, claimed the land between the Arkansas and Rio Grande rivers including a broad strip of the central Colorado Rockies. This claim was disallowed by the U.S. government when Texas was admitted as a state in 1845.

The U.S. government, which gained control of all of what is now Colorado by 1848, still owns 36 percent of the state's land. Of the many Native groups that lived in Colorado during the past 13,000 years, only the Utes have territory today, consisting of two reservations in the southwestern corner of the state.

Colorado Timeline

11,000 B.C. Colorado's documented habitation begins. In the ensuing millennia, the area is home to the Clovis people and later the Folsom people. Evidence of fluted projectile points suggests that the first known Coloradans used advanced stone-age technology.

9200 B.C. Clovis people occupy Dent site (in Weld County).

8800 B.C. Folsom people occupy Lindenmeier site in northern Colorado.

A.D. 1–1300 Puebloan people build pit houses, pueblos and cliff-dweller cities in southwestern Colorado. By learning to use irrigation and cultivate corn, these prehistoric Indians, the Anasazi, establish one of the most advanced civilizations in North America, which today is commemorated at Mesa Verde National Park.

400–1200 Fremont people settle northwestern Colorado.

1275–1300 Great drought in southwestern Colorado leads to depopulation of Anasazi sites.

1300–1800s The Ute tribe prevails in Colorado. These short, dark, stocky Shoshonean people used bows and arrows, and leather clothing and shelter, to establish strongholds in the Colorado mountains.

1582 Robert Cavelier, Sieur de La Salle, explores the Mississippi River and claims all of its drainage for King Louis XIV of France. This includes all of Colorado's eastern slope drained by the Arkansas and Platte Rivers.

1706 Juan de Ulibarri follows the Rio Grande into Colorado and explores the Arkansas River Valley, officially claiming both valleys for King Philip IV of Spain.

1776 Two Franciscan priests, Fray Silvestre Vélez de Escalante and Fray Francisco Atanasio Domínguez, lead a small expedition that maps Colorado for the first time.

1803 The United States acquires northeastern Colorado through the Louisiana Purchase.

1806 Lt. Zebulon Pike leads the first official U.S. exploration of Colorado.

1819 Adams-Oñis Treaty establishes the western border between Spanish territory and the United States as the Arkansas River and a line due north from its headwaters.

1834 Bent's Fort is established on the Arkansas River in southeastern Colorado.

1839 Smallpox, the "white man's disease," rages through Plains Indian camps, killing many.

1848 Treaty of Guadalupe Hidalgo ends the Mexican–American War, giving the United States title to Colorado south of the Arkansas River and east of the Continental Divide.

1851 San Luis, oldest town still existing in Colorado, is established by Hispanics from New Mexico.

1858 William Green Russell party finds gold along Cherry Creek and the South Platte River, in present-day metro Denver, triggering the Colorado gold rush.

1860 The Pony Express begins cross-country mail service, with stops in Julesburg and Denver.

1861 Colorado Territory is created by the United States and carved out of northern New Mexico, eastern Utah and western Nebraska and Kansas territories.

1861 The treaty of Fort Wise limits Arapaho and Cheyenne tribes to a small area of southeastern Colorado along Big Sandy Creek (also known as Sand Creek).

1864 Colorado troopers attack an encampment of Arapaho and Cheyenne in southeastern Colorado in what became known as the Sand Creek Massacre. Both tribes are later removed to reservations outside Colorado.

1870 Colorado's first railroad, the Denver Pacific, completes a line from Denver to Cheyenne, Wyoming Territory.

1876 Colorado becomes the 38th state on Aug. 1.

1877 Silver is discovered at Leadville, which becomes the highest, wildest and richest silver city in the Rockies.

1879 A band of Utes kills Indian agent Nathan Meeker and others at the White River Reservation.

1880 Most Utes are removed to Utah following the Meeker killings. Two small Ute reservations are established in the southwestern corner of Colorado.

1893 Katharine Lee Bates, an English professor at Colorado College, climbs Pikes Peak, inspiring her to write the words for "America, the Beautiful."

1893 Women's suffrage is approved by male voters, making Colorado the second state (after Wyoming) with women eligible to vote and hold all public offices.

1906 Mesa Verde National Park is created; the Antiquities Act is passed to keep people from destroying or removing Indian artifacts from federal lands.

1906 The U.S. Mint in Denver produces its first coins.

1915 Rocky Mountain National Park is created.

1917 William F. "Buffalo Bill" Cody dies in Denver and is buried atop Lookout Mountain by Golden.

1920s Ku Klux Klan gains power, electing members as Colorado governor (Clarence F. Morley), U.S. senator (Rice Means) and Denver mayor (Benjamin F. Stapleton).

1936 Colorado voters approve a state income tax.

1942–45 World War II transforms Colorado with military facilities, thousands of service personnel and wartime jobs. Many newcomers stay after the war and become permanent citizens of Colorado.

1948 Walter and Elizabeth Paepcke began to transform Aspen into a cultural tourism center as well as Colorado's first commercial ski resort.

1957 Colorado Springs is selected as the site for the Air Force Academy and the North American Air Defense Command.

1960 Pro football's Denver Broncos plays its first season.

1972 Colorado voters reject the 1976 International Winter Olympics, the first statewide move to limit growth.

1973 Eisenhower–Johnson Tunnel of Interstate 70 opens under the Continental Divide.

1976 Big Thompson River flood in northern Colorado kills 145, the worst natural disaster in state history.

1978 Denver Performing Arts Center opens.

1979 Interstate 70 is completed as Colorado's east–west statewide freeway.

1982 Exxon terminates Western Slope oil shale project, ending the biggest Colorado oil boom and helping precipitate the oil bust of the 1980s.

1993 Voters pass Amendment 1 limiting state spending.

1993 Colorado gets its first major league baseball team, the Colorado Rockies.

1993 Pope John Paul II becomes the first pope to visit Colorado.

1994 The Regional Transportation District in the Denver metro area revives light rail service with a central line, adding a southwest line in 2000.

1995 Denver International Airport opens.

1996 The Colorado Avalanche wins the National Hockey League Stanley Cup,

becoming the first Colorado professional sports team to win a national championship.

1998–99 Denver Broncos win back-to-back Super Bowl championships.

1999 Two students shoot a teacher and 12 students to death at Columbine High School in a Denver suburb, then kill themselves.

1999 Black Canyon of the Gunnison is designated a national park.

2000 Great Sand Dunes is approved as Colorado's fourth national park.

2001 Broomfield becomes Colorado's 64th county.

Holidays

Colorado always has some reason to celebrate, including these official state holidays:

- New Year's Day, Jan. 1
- Martin Luther King Jr. Day, third Monday in January
- Presidents' Day, third Monday in February
- Cesar Chavez Day, March 31
- Memorial Day, last Monday in May
- Independence Day, July 4
- Colorado Day, first Monday in August
- Labor Day, first Monday in September
- Columbus Day, Monday closest to Oct. 12
- Veterans Day, Nov. 11
- Election Day, first Tuesday in November in odd-numbered years
- Thanksgiving, fourth Thursday in November
- Christmas, Dec. 25

Hospitals
Catholic nuns established many of Colorado's first hospitals, which they opened to anyone who needed care. The Sisters of Charity of Leavenworth established St. Joseph's Hospital in Denver (1873) and St. Vincent's

in Leadville (1879), while the Sisters of Mercy opened St. Joseph's Hospital in Ouray (1887), Mercy Hospital in Denver (1892) and St. Nicholas Hospital in Cripple Creek (1894).

Denver's Department of Health and Hospitals traces its origins to a short-lived 1860 hospital that was restarted in 1870. With the arrival of the railroads and the population boom after 1870, many hospitals were born around the state, many of which survive to this day.

The following list identifies members of the Colorado Hospital Association and the cities where they are located.

Hospitals and Healthcare Facilities

City	Hospital
Alamosa	San Luis Valley Regional Medical Center
Aspen	Aspen Valley Hospital
Aurora	Medical Center of Aurora North
	Medical Center of Aurora South
	Spalding Rehabilitation Hospital
Boulder	Boulder Community Hospital
Brighton	Platte Valley Medical Center
Brush	East Morgan County Hospital
Burlington	Kit Carson County Memorial Hospital
Cañon City	St. Thomas More Hospital
Cheyenne Wells	Keefe Memorial Hospital
Colorado Springs	Memorial Hospital
	Penrose-St. Francis Health Services
Cortez	Southwest Memorial Hospital
Craig	The Memorial Hospital
Delta	Delta County Memorial Hospital
Denver	Porter Adventist Hospital
	St. Anthony Central Hospital
	Children's Hospital
	Denver Health Medical Center
	Exempla Saint Joseph Hospital
	National Jewish Medical and Respiratory Center
	Presbyterian/St. Luke's Medical Center
	Rose Medical Center
	Veterans Hospital
	University of Colorado Hospital
Durango	Mercy Medical Center
Eads	Weisbrod Memorial County Hospital
Englewood	Craig Hospital
	Swedish Medical Center
Estes Park	Estes Park Medical Center
Fort Collins	Poudre Valley Hospital
Fort Morgan	Colorado Plains Medical Center
Fruita	Family Health West
Glenwood Springs	Valley View Hospital
Grand Junction	Community Hospital
	St. Mary's Hospital and Medical Center
Greeley	North Colorado Medical Center
Gunnison	Gunnison Valley Hospital
Haxtun	Haxtun Hospital District
Holyoke	Melissa Memorial Hospital
Hugo	Lincoln Community Hospital
Kremmling	Kremmling Memorial Hospital District
La Jara	Conejos County Hospital
La Junta	Arkansas Valley Regional Medical Center
Lamar	Prowers Medical Center
Leadville	Saint Vincent General Hospital
Littleton	Littleton Adventist Hospital
Longmont	Longmont United Hospital
Louisville	Avista Adventist Hospital
	Charter Behavioral Health Systems
Loveland	McKee Medical Center
Meeker	Pioneers Hospital of Rio Blanco County
Montrose	Montrose Memorial Hospital
Pueblo	Parkview Episcopal Medical Center

Hospitals and Healthcare Facilities *(continued)*

City	Hospital
Pueblo	St. Mary Corwin Regional Medical Center
Rangely	Rangely District Hospital
Rifle	Grand River Hospital District
Salida	Heart of the Rockies Regional Medical Center
Springfield	Southeast Colorado Hospital
Steamboat Springs	Yampa Valley Medical Center
Sterling	Sterling Regional Medical Center
Thornton	North Suburban Medical Center
Trinidad	Mount San Rafael Hospital
Vail	Vail Valley Medical Center
Walsenburg	Huerfano Medical Center
Westminster	Centura Health– St. Anthony Hospital North
Wheat Ridge	Exempla Lutheran MedicalCenter
Wray	Wray Community District Hospital
Yuma	Yuma District Hospital

Other Hospitals

(not members of the Colorado Hospital Association)

Colorado Springs	Cedar Springs Behavioral Health System
	Healthsouth Rehabilitation Hospital
Del Norte	Rio Grande Hospital
Denver	Colorado Mental Health Institute of Fort Logan
	Cleo Wallace Centers
	Nextcare Specialty Hospital of Denver
	SCCI Hospital–City Park
	Vencor Hospital Denver
Fort Carson	Evans Army Community Hospital
Fort Lyon	Veterans Affairs Medical Center
Grand Junction	Veterans Affairs Medical Center
Pueblo	Colorado Mental Health Institute at Pueblo

Thornton	Mediplex Specialty Hospital
USAF Academy	U.S. Air Force Academy Hospital

Source: Colorado Hospital Association

Hotels

To attract residents, investors and tourists, Colorado communities in the 19th century built grand hotels. These showcase edifices strove to prove that Colorado was no provincial backwater by exhibiting the latest technological advances, fashionable architectural styles and the newest creature comforts.

Such palaces of the public were open to all for haircuts and shoe shines, drinks and gourmet meals in sumptuous surroundings. Inside, everyone could gawk at such wonders as elevators and telephones, hot water showers and flush toilets. Architectural advances such as the steel skeleton and the skylighted lobby atrium were introduced by the Brown Palace Hotel (1892). Between the 1930s and the 1950s, the Brown Palace installed the latest marvel—central air conditioning—using the old fireplaces, smoke ducts and chimney network.

Hotels today range from the 1862 Peck House in Empire, Colorado's oldest inn, to posh new chain hotels as Colorado continues to build state-of-the art palaces to

The Broadmoor Hotel in Colorado Springs. Photo by Tom Noel.

pamper tourists and business travelers. Deluxe new hotels include the Little Nell and Ritz Carlton in Aspen, Hotel Teatro in Denver and Cordillera Lodge near Wolcott.

Dr. Colorado's List of Grand Historic Hotels Still Doing Business

- The Broadmoor (1918), Colorado Springs
- The Brown Palace (1892), Denver
- The Strater (1888), Durango
- Hotel Jerome (1889), Aspen
- Hotel Boulderado (1906), Boulder
- Hotel Colorado (1893), Glenwood Springs
- The Cliff House (1873), Manitou Springs
- The Beaumont (1887), Ouray
- The Stanley (1906), Estes Park
- The Oxford (1890), Denver

The pool at Glenwood Hot Springs. Photo by Tom Noel.

Hot Springs

Of 93 natural Colorado outdoor hot springs large enough to bath in, 32 are commercially open to the public. Native Americans first discovered and soaked in these natural hot tubs, exulting in their legendary physical and spiritual healing powers. Whereas the Indians shared the pools as sacred communal places, white entrepreneurs have privatized them. Nowadays, you pay to stew in most of these therapeutic waters.

The Water Cure

Ute Indian folklore credits the Great Spirit with creating hot springs to bring them good medicine. When a plague struck the tribe, desperate survivors danced and prayed around a huge bonfire until, exhausted, they slept. Upon awakening the Indians found, in place of the bonfire, the steaming waters of a hot spring in which they bathed and drank and were cured. ✳

The huge outdoor hot springs pool at Glenwood Springs is open 365 days a year. Other commercial hot springs include Eldorado Springs, Hot Sulphur Springs, Idaho Springs, Mount Princeton, Ouray, Pagosa Springs, Salida, Steamboat Springs and Trimble. Smaller operations include Brush Creek Well, Cement Creek Ranch, Conundrum, Cottonwood, Desert Reef Beach Clubs, Dunton, 4UR Guest Ranch, Orvis, Penny, Piedra River, Rainbow, Splashland, Strawberry Springs, Valley View and Waunita Hot Springs. Some are clothing optional pools where you can bath in your birthday suit.

Hypothermia (SEE ALSO

MOUNTAIN SICKNESS) Newcomers and visitors to Colorado should be aware that the cold climate here kills several people each year. Hypothermia is a life-threatening drop in body temperature, usually brought on by exposure to the elements. Most cases of hypothermia develop between 32°F and 50°F (0°C and 10°C), non-extreme temperatures when people often fail to take sufficient precautions to avoid exposure. Early symptoms include intense shivering, stumbling, foggy thinking and poor coordination.

Hypothermia develops as the body strives to keep core organs warm, and blood flow to the extremities is reduced, which can cause frostbite. Wind and wetness can rob the body of heat faster than it can produce it. Fatigue and dehydration add to the problem.

Victims should get to warm and dry shelter as quickly as possible and change out of wet clothing. If the person is conscious, warm liquids can be given. Build a fire or get into a sleeping bag with the victim to encourage direct body heat transfer. In severe cases of hypothermia, medical attention is advisable.

Irish Americans

In the 19th century, the Irish comprised Colorado's third-largest immigrant group after the Germans and the English. The Irish served as members of the city council and occasionally as mayors. Coloradans, however, did not elect their first Irish Catholic governor, Stephen L.R. McNichols, until 1957, three years before John F. Kennedy's election as president.

Despite prejudice against them and the highest arrest record for any 19th-century ethnic group, the Irish seemed irrepressible. Their political clout revolved around saloonkeepers, policemen and politicians, three groups attracting large numbers of gregarious, power-seeking Irishmen.

Early Denver police chiefs David J. Cook and James B. Veatch were one-time saloonkeepers, as was the pioneer marshall, "Noisy Tom" Pollock. The Irish proved to be one of the most prolific immigrant groups. Unlike Scandinavians, Italians, Greek, Chinese and many other immigrants groups, both sexes of Irish came. Starving times in Ireland due to the potato famine

led many families, however reluctantly, to send daughters as well as sons to America, their only hope for a decent life. In the new world, Irish girls found jobs as domestics, factory workers or nuns. With as many Irish women as men in the new country, the Irish tended to marry each other and raise large families.

Like the Germans, the Irish were generally acculturated by the time they reached Denver. Unlike the impoverished, Gaelic speaking, just-off-the boat Irish who flooded into Boston and New York, they usually arrived in Denver with job skills and other assets, often including a family. Most had spent time in Boston, New York or elsewhere in North America, learning American English, American ways and accumulating some capital.

Most Irish came to Colorado as miners or as *terriers*, as the Irish railroad construction crews called themselves. Irish Catholics formed considerable percentages of the population in mining towns such as Central City, Cripple Creek and Leadville. In many a town, they helped establish Catholic churches, often named for St. Patrick, while Irish nuns opened and ran schools, hospitals and orphanages.

Colorado's wealthiest Irishman, and a major employer of his countrymen, grain tycoon John K. Mullen presided over the St. Joseph's Total Abstinence Society, an effort to reform hard-drinking Celts. Other leading Irish-born Coloradans included Thomas M. Patterson, owner–editor of the *Rocky Mountain News* from 1890 to 1913 and a U.S. representative (1877–1879) and senator (1901–1907); Thomas F. Walsh, owner of Ouray County's fabulous Camp Bird gold mine; and James Archer, who in the 1870s helped found the Denver Gas Co. and the Denver Water Works.

Irishmen elected one of their own, Robert Morris, mayor of Denver in 1881. Morris rewarded his constituency by sanctioning the city's first St. Patrick's Day parade in 1883. The parade became an official city function in 1906, a practice continued until World War I. Anti-Catholic, anti-immigrant and anti-liquor interests helped suppress St. Patrick's Day parades until they were revived in the 1960s. Since then Denver's Irish parade has become one of America's largest, partly by welcoming any and all celebrants—including gays and Englishmen. Irish organizations have enjoyed a renaissance, especially with the opening of many Irish pubs, more and larger St. Patrick's Day festivities and the creation in 2000 of an Irish Cultural Center in Denver (303-320-9480).

Italian Americans

Only a sprinkling of Italian-born people settled in Colorado before 1880, when the census taker found 335. In the following decades the railroads, mining companies and other industries recruited Italian labor and the 1890 census listed 3,882 natives of Italy. Between 1910 and 1940, Italians were the largest single immigrant group reaching Colorado. By 1910, their population had climbed to 14,375 and Denver, Pueblo, Louisville and other cities had "Little Italy" neighborhoods.

Italians who came to Colorado tended to be poor and from southern Italy and Sicily. They were derided for their dark complexions, Catholicism, foreign language, different food and homemade wine. Many Coloradans called them macaroni eaters, wops (Without Official Papers) and dagos (originally *Diegos*, a derogatory term for Hispanics). Many lived in tents, shacks and shanties in the river bottoms and worked at hard, poor-paying jobs—building railroads, digging coal, toiling in smelters and doing day labor.

> ### Hardship in the Mines
>
> Mother Frances Xavier Cabrini, the Italian nun who became the first U.S. citizen to be canonized a saint, visited Colorado in 1902 and reported:
>
> "Here the hardest work is reserved for the Italian worker...they merely look upon him as an ingenious machine for work....Poor miners work uninterruptedly year in and year out, until old age and incapacity creep over them, or at least until some day a landslide or explosion or an accident of some kind ends the life of the poor worker, who does not even need a grave, being buried in the one in which he has lived all his life." ✻

Mother Frances Xavier Cabrini, the Italian nun who became a saint, helped erect Our Lady of Mount Carmel Church in the Little Italy section of Denver. With the help of Mother Cabrini's church, as well as a school and orphanage, Denver's Italian community ultimately prospered, moving out of the river bottoms to North Denver and, still later, out to suburban Adams and Jefferson counties. Many popular Italian restaurants around the state can trace their origins to two pioneer Italian taverns in 1870s' Denver—Siro Mangini's Christopher Columbus Hall and Angelo and Maria Capelli's Highland House.

Pueblo had Colorado's second-largest concentration of Italian-born residents. Many came to work in the steel mills and smelters. Italian stonemasons did much construction work, often fine stonework that survives to this day. Italians also started taverns, restaurants and other food businesses. The legendary Gus's Tavern, Colorado's most celebrated blue collar saloon, is now operated by the third generation of Gus Masciotra's family in an old Italian neighborhood near the steel mill.

Angelo Notary and other Italians persuaded Colorado to become the first state to declare Columbus Day (Oct. 12) a state holiday in 1907. Since then Italians have celebrated the day with festivities and a Denver parade. Native American protesters, who called Columbus a murderer, rapist and slave trader for his actions as governor of Española (now Haiti and the Dominican Republic) ended the parade in 1992, the 500th anniversary of Columbus' arrival in America. The parade was reinstated in 2000, when it took place despite protests from Indians and Hispanics. Marchers called the parade a celebration of Italian pride.

Jackalopes *(Lepus antilocapra)* This creature is a cross between the jackrabbit and the antelope. It is difficult to provide a precise description because the species is so rare that even the Denver Museum of Nature and Science lacks specimens or full information. Perhaps the rarest animal in North America, it might be mistaken for a large jackrabbit except for its horns. Jackalopes apparently originated in Douglas, Wyo., where a large statue of the animal sits in the middle of Main Street.

While other mammals often prefer a full moon for mating rituals, jackalopes mate only during nocturnal lightning flashes. An odd trait of the jackalope is its ability to imitate the human voice. Cowboys singing to their herds at night have been startled to hear their lonesome melodies repeated faithfully from the nearby prairies.

Jackrabbits "The jackass rabbit," as Mark Twain called them in *Roughing It*, "is from one-third to twice as large [as other rabbits and] has longer legs and the most preposterous ears that were ever mounted on any creature but a jackass."

Colorado is home to both the black-tailed jackrabbit *(Lepus californicus)* and the white-tailed jackrabbit *(Lepus townsendii)*. After black-tails entered Colorado from the south around 1900, they began displacing the once-dominant white-tail. The black-tail has a distinctive black stripe extending from the rump to the tip of the tail. Living up to stereotype, the females give birth to litters of one to seven bunnies up to five times a year. The young are born fully furred, with eyes open, and are able to breed within a year.

Jackrabbits are active at night and spend the day dozing under shrubs. They often feed on domestic crops and compete with livestock for limited grazing. Farmers and ranchers have attempted with considerable success to eradicate them, and they are also the prey of coyotes, foxes, badgers and eagles. In 21st-century Colorado, you're much more apt to see the introduced cottontail than that once-ubiquitous native jackrabbit.

Jacobs, Frances Wisebart *(See also* Charities)
Colorado's "mother of charities" helped form, in 1872, the Hebrew Ladies' Benevolent Society, of which she was the

first president. Extending her Denver work beyond the Jewish community, she helped Elizabeth Byers and Margaret Evans organize the Ladies' Relief Society in 1874.

Jacobs also launched the Tabernacle Free Dispensary to provide medication. If patients did not come to the dispensary, she went looking for them, carrying a large purse filled with food, medicine and Grandpa's Tar Soap. Of her beloved poor, Jacobs declared, "God never made a pauper in the world; children come into the world and conditions and surroundings make them either princes or paupers."

Jacobs helped raise money to fund construction in 1892 of a hospital in Denver for patients with tuberculosis, then the nation's deadliest disease. Originally named in her honor, the hospital's name later was changed to National Jewish Hospital. Now the National Jewish Medical and Research Center, it remains one of America's finest treatment centers for lung and breathing disorders.

Despite warnings from doctors, Jacobs continued to make home visits, neglecting her own health. She collapsed with pneumonia during a visit in 1892 to a stifling downtown Denver apartment and died just before the opening of the tuberculosis hospital she helped to make a reality. She is commemorated by a stained glass portrait in the dome of the Colorado Capitol, by a park named for her in southeast Denver and by a statue in the lobby of the National Jewish Medical and Research Center.

Judicial System (SEE ALSO GOVERNORS; LEGISLATURE) The four-

level Colorado judicial system consists of 64 county courts, 22 district courts, a Court of Appeals and a Supreme Court. All judges are appointed by the governor from a list of nominees selected by a nonpartisan commission (except for Denver County, where the mayor of Denver does the honors).

County judges face a retention vote after 4 years, district judges after 6 years, court of appeals judges after 8 years and Supreme Court justices after 10 years. All judges must retire at age 72.

Special courts in the City and County of Denver hear probate and juvenile matters. Denver's famous Juvenile Court, established in 1900 by Judge Benjamin Barr Lindsey (see entry), became the model for subsequent courts around the world, with its focus on rehabilitation rather than punishment.

Since its creation in 1970, the Colorado Court of Appeals has handled appeals from lower courts. The decisions of its 16 judges are final unless the state Supreme Court agrees to hear the case. The Supreme Court consists of seven judges. Chief Justice Mary J. Mullarkey is the first woman to hold that position in Colorado.

Federal courts are also active in Colorado, handling cases involving federal laws and the U.S. Constitution. Denver is home to the U.S. District Court for the state of Colorado and also to the Tenth U.S. Circuit Court of Appeals, which hears appeals from U.S. district courts in Colorado, Kansas, New Mexico, Oklahoma, Utah and Wyoming.

To learn more: The state Supreme Court and state Court of Appeals are in the State Judicial Building in the Denver

Looking Back

1876

The Legislature established the Colorado School for the Deaf and Blind in Colorado Springs after Jonathan R. Kennedy had his three deaf children demonstrate their abilities to the lawmakers.

Civic Center (East 14th Avenue between Broadway and Lincoln); www.courts.state.co.us.

The Tenth U.S. Circuit Court of Appeals is in the Byron White U.S. Courthouse, 1823 Stout St., Denver 80202; www.ck10.uscourts.gov.

Ku Klux Klan

The original KKK of the 1860s and 1870s did not infest Colorado, but the 1920s' revival did. By the mid-1920s, one out of every 10 Coloradans belonged to the KKK, giving the state the second-highest per capita membership after Indiana.

> Georgetown, which prided itself upon being more sedate than other mining towns, decreed "all tippling houses, dram shops, and saloons . . . shall be closed on the Sabbath."

The Kolorado Klan targeted Jews, Catholics and foreigners more than blacks, who were a tiny minority. Running on a platform of law and order and patriotism, members of the Klan were elected to many high offices, including Denver mayor (Benjamin F. Stapleton), state governor (Clarence Morley) and U.S. senator (Rice Means). All three men listened to Grand Dragon John Galen Locke, who insisted that Catholics, Jews and foreigners be fired and Kluxers hired.

Dressed in their white hooded robes, the Klan held rallies all over the state but rarely became violent. Rather they used economic boycotts of "un-American elements" and directed members to patronize fellow Kluxers. Various scandals began to haunt the Klan by the late 1920s, when it lost membership and power.

During the 1990s, the Colorado KKK reemerged as a small group most visible in its protests of the Martin Luther King Jr. parade in Denver. The Klan has not been noticeably active in recent years.

Labor

Colorado's organized labor history began with the 1860 formation of Denver Local No. 49 of the International Typographical Union, which 32 years later opened its national retirement haven, the Union Printers Home, in Colorado Springs.

Miners first formally organized in Erie, near Boulder, where coal diggers started a local of the Knights of Labor in 1878. Leadville silver miners organized another branch of this national union in 1880 and launched Colorado's first major strike that year. It was crushed in what became a familiar scenario: mine owners brought in strikebreakers and persuaded the governor to declare martial law and send in the state militia to protect mine owners, their mines and "scab" labor.

To champion labor, the *Denver Labor Inquirer* began publication in 1882 and promoted the Denver Trades and Labor Assembly. This assembly successfully championed creation of a Colorado Bureau of Labor Statistics and establishment of the Labor Day holiday in 1887.

In 1903 the Denver-based Western Federation of Miners (WFM) organized a statewide strike to implement a minimum daily wage of $3 for a maximum workday of eight hours. Although voters had approved these measures, they had not been implemented. The 1903–1904 strike became a bloody confrontation that culminated in the bombing deaths of 13 miners at the Independence Mine, one of Cripple Creek's richest gold mines. Mine and smelter owners crushed the WFM with the help of private guards, private detectives and the state militia.

In an effort to keep coal miners satisfied and out of unions, mine owner John Osgood built a model company town at Redstone. Josephine Roche tried another unusual strategy at her Columbine Mine, where she settled what had been deadly confrontations by going into partnership with unionists and paying the highest wages in the coal mining industry.

The United Mine Workers (UMW) organized many coal miners, whose working conditions were more dangerous and less rewarding than that of the hard-rock miners. In 1913 and 1914, many went on strike in the southern Colorado coalfields at the urging of UMW organizers. At the tent town of Ludlow, strikers and their families were fired upon April 20, 1914, by the state militia and by gunmen hired by the mine owners. Among the 19 killed were two women and nine children. This bloody labor war ended only after President Woodrow Wilson sent in federal troops.

Colorado farmers joined national organizations such as the Grange. Founded in 1867, this organization remains active, although it has evolved from an economic, educational and political organization to more of a social one. During the dark days of the Dust Bowl and the Great Depression, many agrarians joined the Colorado Farmers Union. Farm workers formed various unions over the years, including the United Farm Workers, based in California, which led strikes by workers at carnation greenhouses in Brighton in 1968 and by lettuce workers in Center in 1970.

Since the 1950s, union membership has fallen from around 25 percent to 13 percent of the nonagricultural work force in Colorado. The state's per capita union membership is about 30 percent lower than the national average. Union workers at Pueblo's steel mill and the Climax Molybdenum Mine near Leadville have all been laid off. In recent decades, management has used strikes, bankruptcy and other occasions to deunionize Continental Airlines, Coors Brewing Co., Montfort Packing Co. and other major employers. Neither the fast-growing telecommunications nor computer industries are unionized.

Lakes and Reservoirs (SEE ALSO WATER SPORTS). Although landlocked, Colorado contains more than 500 natural or artificial

Longs Peak is reflected in Bear Lake, Rocky Mountain National Park. From The Rockies; *photo by David Muench.*

lakes. Most were constructed for crop irrigation, municipal water supply and flood control. The largest natural body of water is Grand Lake, on the headwaters of the Colorado River in northcentral Colorado. The largest reservoir is Blue Mesa Reservoir on the Gunnison River, west of Gunnison.

Following is a list of some of the larger, more popular and scenic Colorado bodies of water in the eastern plains, mountains and western canyon lands.

To learn more: Colorado State Parks, 1313 Sherman St., Denver 80203; (303) 866-3437.

Lark Bunting Colorado's

state bird is a dapper jet black in the male with white wing trim, which also adorns the streaked drab female. A bit larger than the house sparrow, the lark bunting (*Calamospiza melanocorys*) thrives on the prairies, where it is a common sight along roadways and barbed wire fences. Less

Body of Water	Operator	County
Eastern Plains		
Aurora Reservoir	City of Aurora	Arapahoe
Barbour Ponds	State Park	Weld
Barr Lake	State Park	Adams
Bonny Reservoir	State Park	Yuma
Boyd Lake	State Park	Larimer
Carter Lake Reservoir	Larimer County	Larimer
Chatfield Reservoir	State Park	Douglas and Jefferson
Cherry Creek Lake	State Park	Arapahoe
Horseshoe/Lathrop Lake	State Park	Huerfano
Horsetooth Reservoir	State Park	Larimer
Jackson Reservoir	State Park	Morgan
John Martin Reservoir	State Park	Bent
Julesburg Reservoir	Julesburg Irrigation District	Logan and Sedgwick
Lake Hasty	U.S. Army Corps of Engineers	Bent
North Sterling Reservoir	State Park	Logan
Prewitt Reservoir	Private	Washington
Pueblo Reservoir	State Park	Pueblo
Quincy Reservoir	City of Aurora	Arapahoe
Trinidad Lake	State Park	Las Animas
Mountains		
Antero Reservoir	Denver Water Department	Park
Blue Mesa Reservoir	National Recreation Area	Gunnison
Cheesman Reservoir	Denver Water Department	Douglas and Jefferson
Dillon Reservoir	Denver Water Department	Summit
Eleven Mile Canyon Reservoir	Denver Water Department	Park
Grand Lake	Public and Private	Grand
Green Mountain Reservoir	Northern Colorado Water	Summit
Lake Granby	National Recreation Area	Grand

Body of Water	Operator	County
Mountains, *continued*		
McPhee Reservoir	Dolores Water Conservancy	Montezuma
Morrow Point Reservoir	National Park Service	Gunnison and Montrose
Pearl Lake	State Park	Routt
Platero Reservoir	U.S. Forest Service	Conejos
Reudi Reservoir	U.S. Forest Service	Eagle and Pitkin
San Cristobol	Private	Hinsdale
Shadow Mountain Lake	National Recreation Area	Grand
Silver Jack Reservoir	U.S. Forest Service	Gunnison
Spinney Mountain Reservoir	City of Aurora	Park
Steamboat Lake	State Park	Routt
Sylvan Lake	State Park	Eagle
Taylor Park Reservoir	U.S. Forest Service	Gunnison
Turquoise Lake	U.S. Forest Service	Lake
Twin Lakes Reservoir	U.S. Forest Service	Lake
Vallecito Reservoir	U.S. Forest Service	La Plata
Williams Fork Reservoir	Denver Water Department	Grand
Western Canyonlands		
Navajo Reservoir	State Park	Archuleta
Paonia Reservoir	State Park	Gunnison
Ridgway Reservoir	State Park	Ouray
Rifle Gap Reservoir	State Park	Garfield
Sweitzer Lake	State Park	Delta
Vega Reservoir	State Park	Mesa

frequently it is seen in the foothills up to 8,000 feet. Like other prairie birds, lark buntings nest on the ground, laying four to five pale blue eggs. They leave in September to winter in Mexico and return to Colorado in April.

The lark bunting nosed out the meadowlark, the bluebird and other more glamorous birds in the 1931 state legislative proceedings to choose a state bird. The lark bunting benefited from lobbying efforts of Fort Collins schoolchildren and *Nature* magazine's objection that all the other nominated birds had already been selected by other states.

Also known as the black-headed finch, prairie finch, white-winged blackbird and prairie bobolink, the lark bunting is noted

for traveling in large flocks, for melodious song and for swooping flight, with wings cutting dark V patterns against the prairie sky.

Leadville (SEE ALSO MINING) The

"Magic City" of Leadville sprang up overnight in 1877 to capitalize on discoveries of silver. By 1880 this two-mile-high city in the central Colorado mountains had 106 saloons and 14,820 residents. Million-dollar silver mines crowded California, Stray Horse and Evans gulches on the east side of town. Although silver was the main attraction, the rich ores here also yielded gold, lead, zinc and other metals.

By 1890, Leadville shared the headwaters of the Arkansas River with a dozen lesser mining towns. Leadville, the "mother of millionaires," enriched the Guggenheim clan, whose mining and smelting empire began there, as well as David May, the department store mogul, Molly and J. J. Brown, Charles Boettcher, and Horace and Augusta Tabor (see separate entries for Brown; Boettcher; Tabor).

Pell-mell expansion over surrounding mine tunnels left the city plagued by disappearing backyards, sinking streets and black holes that swallowed everything thrown into them. As the Lake County seat, Leadville thrived during the county's silver bonanza, then began declining after the 1893 silver crash. Molybdenum mining at nearby Climax sustained Leadville from the 1920s to the 1990s, when Climax and all other major mines closed.

Leadville lingers as Colorado's best example of a busted boomtown. Once the state's second-largest city, it is now shrunken into a town of about 2,800 residents. A business district that once sprawled in all directions has retreated to hug Harrison Street. The highest and wildest of America's silver cities, Leadville still looks like a mining town. As one of Colorado's National Historic Landmark sites, Leadville is attracting tourists with its rich history, architectural heritage and spectacular scenery.

Legislature (SEE ALSO ELECTED OFFICIALS; GOVERNORS) The Colorado General Assembly consists of a Senate with 35 members and a House of Representatives with 65 members. Boundaries of the Senate and House districts are redrawn to reflect

new population figures from the census each 10 years.

Senators are elected for four-year terms, representatives for two years. Members of both chambers are limited by a 1990 constitutional amendment to a maximum of eight years in office.

Another constitutional amendment limits the legislature to annual sessions of no more 120 days. Sessions begin no later than the second Wednesday of each year and end during the second week in May. The public is invited to watch sessions of both chambers from galleries in the state Capitol in Denver.

To learn more: www.state.co.us/gov_dir/stateleg.html.

Libraries The Colorado State Library, founded in 1862 as the territorial library, promotes the establishment, expansion and cooperation of libraries statewide. The state also operates the Colorado Supreme Court Library, the State Historical Society Library, the Legislative

The Great Hall of the Denver Public Library.
Photo courtesy Denver Public Library.

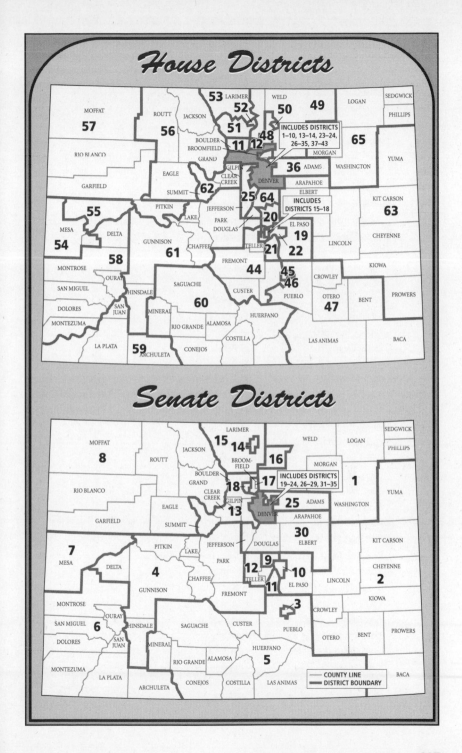

House Districts

Senate Districts

House of Representatives

District	Representative (Party)	Counties
1.	Fran Coleman (D)	Denver, Jefferson
2.	Desireé Sanchez (D)	Denver
3.	Jennifer Veiga (D)	Arapahoe, Denver
4.	Frana Mace (D)	Denver
5.	Nolbert Chavez (D)	Denver
6.	Dan Grossman (R)	Denver
7.	Peter Groff (D)	Denver
8.	Rosemary Marshall (D)	Denver
9.	Andrew Romanoff (D)	Arapahoe, Denver
10.	Alice Borodkin (D)	Arapahoe, Denver
11.	Todd Saliman (D)	Boulder
12.	Bill Swenson (R)	Boulder
13.	Tom Plant (D)	Boulder
14.	Alice Madden (D)	Boulder
15.	Bill Cadman (R)	El Paso
16.	William Sinclair (R)	El Paso
17.	Mark Cloer (R)	El Paso
18.	Doug Dean (R)	El Paso
19.	Richard Decker (R)	El Paso
20.	Lynn Hefley (R)	Douglas, El Paso
21.	Keith King (R)	El Paso
22.	David Schultheis (R)	El Paso
23.	Kelley Daniel (D)	Jefferson
24.	Cheri Jahn (D)	Jefferson
25.	John Witwer (R)	Jefferson
26.	Betty Boyd (D)	Jefferson
27.	Bill Crane (R)	Jefferson
28.	Don Lee (R)	Jefferson
29.	Mark Paschall (R)	Jefferson
30.	Rob Fairbank (R)	Jefferson
31.	Pam Rhodes (R)	Adams, Boulder, Weld
32.	Valentin Vigil (D)	Adams
33.	Shawn Mitchell (R)	Adams
34.	Lois Tochtrop (D)	Adams
35.	Ann Ragsdale (D)	Adams
36.	Mary Hodge (D)	Adams
37.	Lauri Clapp (R)	Arapahoe
38.	Joe Stengel (R)	Arapahoe, Jefferson
39.	Nancy Spence (R)	Arapahoe
40.	Debbie Stafford (R)	Arapahoe
41.	Suzanne Williams (D)	Arapahoe

House of Representatives *(continued)*

District	Representative (Party)	Counties
42.	Michael Garcia (D)	Adams
43.	Frank Weddig (D)	Arapahoe
44.	Lola Spradley (R)	Custer, Fremont, Pueblo, Teller
45.	Joyce Lawrence (R)	Pueblo
46.	Abel Tapia (D)	Pueblo
47.	Kenneth Kester (R)	Baca, Bent, Crowley, Huerfano, Las Animas, Otero
48.	W. H. Webster (R)	Weld
49.	Steve Johnson (R)	Larimer, Weld
50.	Tambor Williams (R)	Weld
51.	Timothy Fritz (R)	Larimer
52.	Bryan Jameson (D)	Larimer
53.	Bob Bacon (D)	Larimer
54.	Matt Smith (R)	Delta, Mesa
55.	Gayle Berry (R)	Mesa
56.	Al White (R)	Eagle, Garfield, Grand, Jackson, Routt
57.	Gregg Rippy (R)	Garfield, Moffat, Pitkin, Rio Blanco
58.	Kay Alexander (R)	Delta, Dolores, Montezuma, Montrose, Ouray, San Miguel
59.	Mark Larson (R)	Archuleta, La Plata, Montezuma, San Juan
60.	Jim Snook (R)	Alamosa, Conejos, Costilla, Huerfano, Pueblo, Rio Grande, Saguache
61.	Carl Miller (D)	Chaffee, Gunnison, Hinsdale, Lake, Mineral, Park, Pitkin, Rio Grande, Saguache
62.	Glenn Scott (R)	Clear Creek, Gilpin, Jefferson, Summit
63.	Brad Young (R)	Arapahoe, Cheyenne, Elbert, Kiowa, Kit Carson, Lincoln, Prowers, Yuma
64.	Joe Nuñez (R)	Douglas
65.	Diane Hoppe (R)	Logan, Morgan, Phillips, Sedgwick, Washington

Senate

District	Senator (Party)	Counties
1.	Marilyn Musgrave (R)	Loggan, Morgan, Phillips, Sedgwick, Washington, Weld, Yuma
2.	Mark Hillman (R)	Baca, Bent, Cheyenne, Crowley, El Paso, Kiowa, Kit Carson, Lincoln, Otero, Prowers
3.	Bill Thiebaut (D)	Pueblo
4.	Ken Chlouber (R)	Chaffee, Delta, Fremont, Gunnison, Hinsdale, Lake, Park, Pitkin
5.	Lewis Entz (R)	Alamosa, Conejos, Costilla, Custer, Huerfano, Las Animas, Mineral, Pueblo, Rio Grande, Saguache

continued on next page

District	Senator (Party)	Counties
6.	James Isgar (D)	Archuleta, Delta, Dolores, La Plata, Montezuma, Montrose, Ouray, San Juan, San Miguel
7.	Ronald Teck (R)	Mesa
8.	Jack Taylor (R)	Eagle, Garfield, Grand, Jackson, Moffat, Rio Blanco, Routt
9.	Doug Lamborn (R)	El Paso
10.	Ron May (R)	El Paso
11.	Mary Ellen Epps (R)	El Paso
12.	Andy McElhaney (R)	El Paso, Teller
13.	Joan Fitz-Gerald (D)	Boulder, Clear Creek, Gilpin, Jefferson, Summit
14.	Peggy Reeves (D)	Larimer
15.	Stan Matsunaka (D)	Larimer
16.	David Owen (R)	Weld
17.	Terry Phillips (D)	Boulder
18.	Ron Tupa (D)	Boulder
19.	Sue Windels (D)	Jefferson
20.	Ed Perlmutter (D)	Jefferson
21.	Deanna Hanna (D)	Jefferson
22.	Norma Anderson (R)	Jefferson
23.	Ken Arnold (R)	Adams, Boulder
24.	Alice Nichol (D)	Adams
25.	Stephanie Takis (D)	Adams
26.	Jim Dyer (R)	Arapahoe, Jefferson
27.	John Andrews (R)	Arapahoe
28.	Bruce Cairns (R)	Arapahoe
29.	Bob Hagedorn (D)	Arapahoe
30.	John Evans (R)	Arapahoe, Douglas, Elbert, Jefferson
31.	Doug Linkhart (D)	Denver
32.	Patricia Pascoe (D)	Denver
33.	Penfield Tate (D)	Denver
34.	Rob Hernandez (D)	Denver
35.	Ken Gordon (D)	Arapahoe, Denver

Library and Library Extension Agencies, including the Library for the Blind.

Beginning around 1900, library advocates gained powerful financial support from the Andrew Carnegie Foundation. Carnegie, the Pittsburgh steel tycoon turned philanthropist, required that the local government agree to a tax support of the library equal to at least one-tenth the cost of the building. Thirty-five Carnegie libraries were built in Colorado. Some in smaller, poorer communities also operated as school libraries.

Even the smallest Colorado communities pride themselves upon having a public library. Gold Hill, for instance, has a tiny public library in the attic of the town's general store, while Ward has its mini-library, complete with a rocking chair and children's nook, in back of the old town hall.

Lindsey, Benjamin Barr

During the first quarter of the 20th century, Colorado's most outspoken reformer was Denver judge Ben Lindsey. As the founding judge of Denver's Juvenile Court from 1900 to 1927, Lindsey made his rehabilitation-centered, humane treatment of youth a widely copied national model. Imprisoning youngsters with adults,

Betting on the first snowfall is no sure bet. In Denver the earliest snowstorm on record came Sept. 3, 1961, with a 4-inch thick blanket. Other years, snow doesn't fall until November.

Lindsey argued, was like sending them to a school for criminals.

Although Lindsey stood only 5 feet tall and weighed barely 100 pounds, he ranks tall among Colorado reformers. Lindsey attacked political corruption in Colorado in his book *The Beast* (with Harvey J. O'Higgins, 1910). He supported a broad spectrum of progressive causes ranging from creation of national parks to more humane treatment of miners after the 1914 labor strife in the Ludlow coal fields in southern Colorado.

Lindsey stirred even greater controversy with his book *Companionate Marriage* (with Wainright Evans, 1927), advocating cohabitation before marriage, as well as birth control and no-fault divorce. Lindsey's growing list of enemies included the powerful Colorado Ku Klux Klan as well as conservative church groups.

Ousted from his judgeship and disbarred from practicing in Colorado, he moved to California, where he was elected to the Los Angeles Superior Court. There he continued to champion humane treatment of children and youth, women's liberation, birth control, companionate marriage and juvenile justice, until his death in 1943.

Little Raven

(SEE ALSO NATIVE AMERICANS) Little Raven, chief of the Southern Arapaho, entertained white newcomers in his handsomely decorated Denver tipi in 1858 and 1859. He also visited with the white newcomers in their strange square houses. In one such house he met Albert Richardson, who described him in *Beyond the Mississippi* as "the nearest approximation I ever met to the ideal Indian," with "a fine, manly form and a human, trustworthy face."

Little Raven signed the Fort Wise Treaty of 1861 that moved his tribe from Denver and the South Platte Valley to southeastern Colorado. There, three years later, the Colorado Volunteers slaughtered many Arapaho and Cheyenne at Sand Creek. When the Arapaho were removed

Little Raven, once chief of the Southern Arapaho.
Colorado Historical Society.

from southeastern Colorado, Little Raven said: "It will be a very hard thing to leave the country that God gave us. Our friends are buried there, and we hate to leave these grounds. White Antelope, and many other chiefs lie [at Sand Creek], our women and children lie there. Our lodges were destroyed there, and our horses were taken from us."

Little Raven signed the Medicine Lodge Treaty of 1867, agreeing that the Southern Arapaho would leave Colorado for Oklahoma, and he traveled to Washington to meet President Ulysses S. Grant. Speaking before thousands of whites at the Cooper Institute in New York City, Little Raven told his audience: "The white man came to see us, and the Indians gave him buffalo meat and a horse to ride on and told him the country was big enough for the white man and the Arapahos too." But soon after the discovery of gold, "the government sent agents and soldiers out to us and both have driven us from our lands."

The Southern Arapaho leader returned to Oklahoma, where he died at Canton in 1889. In 1995, a new street in Denver's Platte Valley redevelopment area was named for Little Raven. His greatest mistake may have been to offer friendship to the prospectors who came to his camp at the confluence of the South Platte River and Cherry Creek, where Denver stands today.

Longs Peak This flat-topped, 14,255-foot mountain dominates northeastern Colorado. The name honors Major Stephen H. Long, who provided the first extensive report of the region after his 1820 U.S. Army exploration of eastern Colorado.

William N. Byers, founding editor of the *Rocky Mountain News*, and Major John Wesley Powell, the illustrious, one-armed Colorado River explorer, led the 1868 party that first officially scaled the peak. Indians may have climbed it earlier, and perhaps French trappers, who originally named the peak and its neighboring 13,911-foot high point as *Les Deux Orielles* (The Two Ears). Although appearing as a single peak from Denver, the mountain from northeastern Colorado looks like twin peaks.

Isabella Bird, one of the first women to climb the mountain, described that adventure in her classic book, *A Lady's Life in the Rockies*. Enos Mills, a celebrated naturalist and guide, led many parties up the peak and campaigned to have it and its environs designated as Rocky Mountain National Park, which was created in 1915. Mills claimed to have climbed Longs Peak 297 times.

With its 1,000-foot sheer vertical east face, known as the Diamond, and its many demanding technical routes, Longs Peak is famous among climbers. Hikers take easier routes, and an estimated 120,000 people have trekked to the summit, including a 5-year-old and an 85-year old, and a six-piece band. Yet the mountain remains notorious for sheer cliffs, steep chutes and dangerous lightning, hail and snow storms that over the years have killed more than 40 people.

A hiking party of long ago crosses a snowfield on Longs Peak. Denver Public Library, Western History Department.

Lost Treasure

Colorado abounds in legends of lost mines and buried loot. Of more than a hundred Colorado lost-mine and hidden-treasure legends, the following offer an intriguing sample.

Dr. Colorado's List of Treasure Legends

Cache la Poudre Lost Mine. Near the headwaters of the Cache la Poudre River lies, to this day, a lost lode of gold marked with the bones of a dead ox.

Caverna del Oro. The Cave of Gold once sheltered Spaniards, who marked its entrance with a Maltese cross. Treasure waits within.

Cavern of the Skulls. At the head of Deadman Creek, above Deadman Cow Camp, in what some call Deadman Cave, prospectors found human skeletons and gold. But did they get it all?

Devil's Head Treasure. Double-eagle gold pieces worth $60,000 were stolen from the U.S. Mint and hidden somewhere in the rocky Devil's Head formation, southwest of Denver in the Rampart Range, waiting to be found.

Italian's Cave. Uberto Gabello, a former miner, enlarged the natural cavern near Julesburg as a place to hide his stash, not yet recovered.

Lost Man Creek Mine. A prospector who showed up in Leadville with rich gold ore from a new find was later killed by an avalanche. His fabulous mine lies waiting to be found again along the Roaring Fork River tributary named for him.

Lost Sheepherder Lode. Sasario, a Mexican sheepherder, found an untapped gold bonanza in the Upper Lime Creek Basin of the San Juan Mountains. He died before he could mine its riches and never shared the secret of its location.

Reynolds Gang Treasure. John Reynolds and eight Rebels raided gold-carrying stages to help finance the Confederate cause—and much of the bullion remains hidden yet in Handcart Gulch in Park County.

Treasure of Trinchera Creek. A Fort Garland paymaster, pursued by Utes, threw a strongbox of gold into the creek. Look for the goldfish.

Loveland

Every St. Valentine's Day, this community east of Rocky Mountain National Park earns its nickname of America's Sweetheart City. Volunteers help the Loveland Post Office stamp valentines with its special cachet and Loveland postmark.

Loveland began offering the free service in 1947 when Ted Thompson of the Chamber of Commerce dreamed up the idea as a promotional gimmick. Other communities—Valentine, Neb.; Loveland,

Ohio; Kissimmee, Fla.—offer similar programs. But Loveland claims to send more valentines than anyplace else.

Loveland receives and remails more than 200,000 cards from all 50 states and some 110 foreign countries each year. Volunteers stamp each valentine envelope with the name Loveland, including a drawing of Cupid in cowboy hat and boots and a poem by Teresa Boynton of Loveland:

> From the Gateway to the great Rocky
> Mountains
> Under skies of magnificent blue
> Cupid sends Valentine greetings
> Directly from Loveland to you.

Lovers worldwide are welcome to put their sealed, preaddressed and prestamped valentines into a larger envelope and mail it to Loveland Postmaster, Valentine Remailing Program, Loveland 80538. Mail must be received by Feb. 9 to guarantee delivery in the United States by Valentine's Day, Feb. 14.

Magpies
Black-billed magpies (*Pica pica*) are common throughout Colorado below 10,000 feet. This easily identified member of the crow family has iridescent black plumage, a white abdomen and wing patches, and measures 17 to 22 inches in length, half of which is the tail.

Dapperly dressed in black and white with flashes of purple, bronze, green and turquoise, magpies are called vultures in tuxedos. They eat other bird's eggs and also their young. They steal food from other birds and from dog and cat dishes, and will eat newborn, sick or wounded animals.

Magpies are notoriously clever scavengers with a taste for roadkill. Their unmusical squawking sounds resemble a nasal *maag?* or *aag-aag?* and a rapid, harsh *queg queg queg queg*. Noisy, chattering birds, they have been taught in captivity to imitate some words.

Pike's Report

Zebulon Pike, in writing of his 1806 expedition, offered the first Colorado report on the black-billed western magpie. A flock of the birds landed on the sore backs of his packhorses along the Arkansas River and "picked many places quite raw." ✳

Magpies have moved into suburban and even urban areas in Colorado. They build domed nests as large as 2 feet in diameter with side entrances. These nests, although messy looking, are sturdy constructions of dried twigs, sticks and debris reinforced with mud. They are often reused by magpies, owls or herons. As with their crow and jay relatives, male and female magpies look alike.

Main Streets
Although endangered by strip malls, suburban shopping paradises and big-box stores such as Wal-Mart, old-time Main Streets are making a comeback with help from the National Trust for Historic Preservation's Main Street program and the Colorado Historical Society's preservation office.

Dr. Colorado's List
of Best-Preserved Main Streets

- Main Avenue in Durango
- Pearl Street in Boulder
- Harrison Avenue in Leadville
- Main Street in Delta
- Main Street in Grand Junction
- Business U.S. 24 in Colorado City
- Columbia Avenue in Telluride
- Union Avenue in Pueblo
- Manitou Avenue in Manitou Springs
- Main Street in Trinidad

Marmots

One of Colorado's most common, gregarious and visible mountain rodents is the yellow-bellied marmot (*Marmota flaviventris*). It is also known as a whistle-pig for its pudgy shape and loud whistling, and as a rockchuck because of its fondness for rocky talus slopes.

Living above 8,000 feet in Colorado, these rodents generally hibernate during winter. During the summer they gather seeds, leaves and flowers to store in their burrows during daylight hours. Dandelions are a favorite delicacy. They form small colonies with a  dominant male, several females and their young.

Marmots have thick, reddish brown fur with a lighter, yellowish underside, whitish noses and short legs and short tails. They are 18 to 28 inches long and weigh from 3 to 12 pounds. On Trail Ridge Road in Rocky Mountain National Park, atop Mount Evans and Pikes Peak, and in other regular Colorado tourist stops, marmots often become fairly tame.

Mileage Chart

(*see table on pages 128–129*) Mileages reflect the shortest distances between cities over state highways.

Military

As a disputed land claimed by various European, American and Native American nations, Colorado long experienced a military presence. The military is still a major factor in Colorado's economy, pumping billions each year into salaries, facilities, contracts and purchases.

Lt. Zebulon Pike's 1807 cottonwood stockade in the San Luis Valley was Colorado's first U.S. military post. Pike's Stockade is now reconstructed as a historical attraction in southern Colorado. Fort Massachusetts, built in 1852 and replaced five years later by nearby Fort Garland, protected settlers in the San Luis Valley. Fort Garland, a large adobe complex, is maintained by the Colorado Historical Society as a museum (about 25 miles east of Alamosa).

During the Civil War, Fort Sedgwick, Fort Morgan, Fort Collins, Fort Junction and Camp Weld were established along the South Platte River to ward off Native Americans and their alleged Confederate allies. While most of these installations were small and short-lived, Fort Lyon (which opened in 1860 as Fort Wise) on the Arkansas River survives as a prison.

Fort Logan opened in 1887 on the southwest outskirts of Denver, with railroads to dispatch troops quickly to wherever they might be needed. Although Fort Logan troops sporadically put down labor wars and civil disturbances, the garrison was fairly quiet until the Spanish American War and World War I, when it was Colorado's only major military post.

The outbreak of World War II led to establishment of Army camps or airfields in Denver, Colorado Springs, Pueblo and La Junta. In 1947 the Air Force became an independent branch of the military, and Army air bases become Air Force bases. After the war, Denver's vast Ordnance Plant became the even-larger Denver Federal Center.

Colorado's role as a munitions maker mushroomed with the Rocky Mountain Arsenal, operated in Adams County from 1942 until the 1990s, and the Rocky Flats Weapons Plant, operated in Jefferson County from 1953 to 1989. Both facilities are now being decontaminated and converted to wildlife areas. Army air bases at Colorado Springs, La Junta and Pueblo were purchased by those towns and converted into municipal airports.

Ready for War

In 1966 the United States and Canada built the headquarters of the North American Air Defense Command (NORAD) under Cheyenne Mountain on the southwest outskirts of Colorado Springs. This huge, subterranean fortress coordinates the monitoring of missiles and other flying objects worldwide. NORAD is a self-contained facility built to withstand nuclear Armageddon and to order the launch of missiles in response to any attack. Huge blast-proof steel gates can snap shut in 30 seconds.

This cavernous 4.5-acre-community, created by removing 693,000 tons of rock, consists of 14 metal buildings cushioned atop springs made of 3-inch-diameter steel and shock absorbers to ease vibrations from exploding warheads. ✳

Colorado Springs remains a military town, hosting the Air Force Academy (see entry) and a roster of installations: Fort Carson, Peterson Air Force Base, Ent Air Force Base and the North American Air Defense Command. A large population of retired military people, a booming high-tech military industry, military spending and defense contracts have made Colorado Springs and surrounding El Paso County the fastest-growing metropolitan area in 21st-century Colorado.

Millennial Heroes

Denver staged a year-end bash to welcome 2001 and took the occasion to honor as Millennial Heroes some individuals who have done the most to shape the city since its founding in 1858. The heroes selected by the Mayor's Millennial Awards Committee, chaired by Thomas J. Noel ("Dr. Colorado"), are:

Helen Bonfils. The daughter of *Denver Post* co-founder Frederick G. Bonfils took over the paper after his death in 1933 and ran it as the most popular and prosperous newspaper in the Rockies.

Ralph Carr. As Colorado governor, he defended the rights of Japanese Americans during World War II, although that courageous, unpopular move doomed him to never be elected to any office again.

George Ernest Cranmer. As manager of Denver parks in the late 1930s, Cranmer left a legacy of improved outdoor areas and new mountain parks, including the Winter Park ski area and Red Rocks Outdoor Amphitheater.

Dana Crawford. She spearheaded transformation of Denver's Skid Row into one of America's most vibrant, livable and profitable city neighborhoods—the Lower Downtown (LoDo) Historic District.

Bill Daniels. The "father of cable television" began installing cable in the mid-1950s to bring Denver TV stations to Wyoming, and ended up running a firm that helped develop half of the 50 largest U.S. cable companies.

Barney Ford. This pioneer black businessman established literacy classes, fought Colorado statehood until black suffrage was included and worked to improve Denver's African American community.

Emily Griffith. Her belief in education for all adults led to the founding of Denver's Opportunity School, which has brought schooling within reach of adult citizens for more than 80 years.

Frances Wisebart Jacobs. This community health worker and philanthropist helped in the 1890s to found what is now the National Jewish Medical and Research Center in Denver.

Little Raven. The head chief of the Southern Arapaho tribe welcomed whites in the mid-1800s to his camp at the

(Continued on page 130)

Mileage Table

	Alamosa	Aspen	Burlington	Cañon City	Central City	Colorado Springs	Cortez	Craig	Denver	Durango	Estes Park	Fort Collins	Fort Morgan	Georgetown	Glenwood Springs	Grand Junction	Greeley
Alamosa																	
Aspen	163																
Burlington	296	308															
Cañon City	139	145	195														
Central City	217	144	199	146													
Colorado Springs	163	157	150	45	102												
Cortez	194	277	490	302	382	347											
Craig	296	157	373	242	191	251	349										
Denver	212	162	163	115	34	70	377	208									
Durango	149	249	445	257	336	302	45	321	332								
Estes Park	280	204	230	183	63	138	445	182	71	399							
Fort Collins	274	223	224	177	82	132	439	200	65	394	42						
Fort Morgan	290	238	141	193	111	148	455	285	81	409	102	81					
Georgetown	189	116	210	132	28	112	354	153	45	309	88	106	122				
Glenwood Springs	204	41	324	187	141	198	259	116	159	231	196	220	236	114			
Grand Junction	249	130	412	248	230	287	197	152	248	169	285	308	324	202	89		
Greeley	264	212	193	166	86	122	428	233	54	384	50	30	51	96	209	298	
Gunnison	122	146	316	121	201	166	201	278	196	173	265	258	273	173	162	126	247
Julesburg	393	339	123	285	214	240	558	364	182	512	205	162	103	225	339	427	154
La Junta	147	247	159	102	207	105	341	345	175	296	243	237	181	217	290	350	227
Lamar	202	302	107	158	239	159	397	400	203	351	270	264	198	250	345	405	251
Leadville	134	59	267	117	85	129	299	162	103	254	145	164	179	57	89	178	153
Limon	228	230	77	118	122	73	421	296	86	375	153	147	83	133	246	335	134
Meeker	272	109	391	255	209	266	300	48	227	273	231	251	303	182	68	104	280
Montrose	187	141	382	186	265	231	136	213	261	108	319	323	339	238	123	61	312
Ouray	221	177	417	222	300	267	118	249	297	72	355	359	374	274	159	97	348
Pagosa Springs	89	222	385	197	277	242	105	356	272	60	341	334	350	259	264	229	323
Pueblo	122	184	191	39	144	42	316	282	112	271	180	174	190	154	227	287	164
Salida	83	88	253	57	143	102	248	222	138	202	207	200	216	115	130	193	189
Silverton	198	200	441	245	323	290	94	272	320	49	378	382	398	297	182	120	371
Springfield	233	348	153	204	285	205	427	446	249	382	315	310	244	296	391	451	296
Steamboat Springs	254	155	331	200	148	209	373	42	166	345	140	160	243	11	114	194	190
Sterling	335	281	141	227	156	182	499	304	125	454	147	102	45	167	280	379	96
Telluride	253	207	448	252	330	297	77	279	327	118	385	389	404	304	189	127	378
Trinidad	109	242	237	125	229	127	304	367	197	259	265	259	252	240	283	334	249
Vail	172	102	262	133	80	142	320	131	98	292	140	159	174	53	61	150	148
Walsenburg	73	205	223	88	192	90	267	330	160	222	228	222	238	201	247	307	212
Wray	351	324	55	251	197	206	540	370	166	495	187	167	86	207	321	410	137

Gunnison	Julesburg	La Junta	Lamar	Leadville	Limon	Meeker	Montrose	Ouray	Pagosa Springs	Pueblo	Salida	Silverton	Springfield	Steamboat Springs	Sterling	Telluride	Trinidad	Vail	Walsenburg	Wray
376																				
224	265																			
279	230	56																		
118	282	220	275																	
239	167	98	117	190																
230	412	357	413	138	314															
65	442	289	344	183	306	165														
101	477	324	380	219	340	200	36													
165	453	236	292	194	316	332	168	132												
161	280	64	119	155	114	294	226	262	211											
66	319	160	215	60	176	198	132	167	143	97										
124	501	345	400	242	364	224	59	23	109	285	191									
325	276	101	46	319	163	459	390	426	322	165	261	431								
238	322	303	371	120	254	91	237	272	314	240	180	296	416							
318	59	206	224	224	108	348	383	419	394	221	260	442	270	262						
131	508	355	410	249	372	230	66	50	178	292	198	74	456	303	449					
217	336	81	136	214	169	351	283	318	199	86	154	308	123	325	277	349				
156	278	258	319	38	185	129	184	220	232	172	98	243	336	98	219	250	310			
181	322	74	130	177	156	314	246	281	162	49	117	271	160	289	263	312	37	215		
359	67	217	163	265	133	389	424	460	435	246	301	483	209	327	85	490	292	260	279	

(Continued from page 127)

confluence of the South Platte River and Cherry Creek—now downtown Denver—in the hope that Indians and whites could coexist. He lived to see his people removed from Colorado to a reservation in Oklahoma.

Rachel B. Noel (unrelated to Thomas J. Noel). The first African American elected to the Denver School Board, she authored a board resolution, upheld by the U.S. Supreme Court, that led to the successful racial integration of the Denver Public Schools.

Federico Peña. During his two terms as mayor, from 1983 to 1991, he persuaded the people of Denver to invest billions in their city, including a new airport, libraries and a host of other improvements.

Helen Louise Peterson. As director of the Mayor's Committee on Human Relations, Peterson, a Lakota Sioux, worked tirelessly to stop repression and empower all racial minorities.

Florence Rena Sabin. Her work as a public health official for the state and for the city of Denver in the mid-20th century resulted in laws and wellness campaigns that vastly improved the health of all Coloradans.

Robert Walter Speer. As Denver mayor in the early 20th century, Speer's "City Beautiful" plan transformed the heart of the city with Civic Center Park, created boulevards and parkways, doubled the city's park space and created Denver's mountain park system.

Bernard Valdez. Born in a poor, Spanish-speaking family in New Mexico in 1912, Valdez grew into a notable Denver political and governmental role model,

serving as manager of the city's welfare department and a member of the Denver Board of Education.

Minoru Yasui. This Japanese American attorney was imprisoned for speaking out against the World War II incarceration of his people. He later became Denver's director of community relations.

(Also see individual entries for Ford; Griffith; Jacobs; Little Raven; Peña; Sabin.)

Mining *(SEE ALSO* COAL; GOLD; OIL AND NATURAL GAS; SILVER) Mining gave birth to the state of Colorado, where it was the principal occupation from 1859 until around 1910. This underground bonanza placed Colorado first among the states in total production of silver, molybdenum and vanadium, second in gold, third in tungsten, fourth in lead, sixth in zinc and eighth in copper.

Various other metallic minerals have swelled Colorado's total production over the years to more than $4 billion. Of this jackpot, molybdenum accounts for about 40 percent, gold for roughly 20 percent, silver 15 percent, zinc 10 percent and lead 10 percent.

In 1999 production of metallic minerals included gold ($69 million), molybdenum ($55 million), uranium ($5 million) and vanadium ($2 million). The Henderson Mine in Clear Creek County is the nation's top producer of molybdenum, a distinction held in previous decades by the now closed Climax Molybdenum Mine near Leadville. Molybdenum is used primarily as an alloy for hardening steel.

Colorado is second only to California in mineral variety and total production.

Looking Back

1882

British investors paid $555,000 to build the 88-mile-long "English Ditch," which diverted water from the South Platte River in Waterton Canyon to the southern and eastern outskirts of Denver.

Colorado's mineral treasure chest also contains manganese, bismuth, cobalt, nickel, arsenic, antimony and cadmium.

Mineral fuels (coal, oil, natural gas and carbon dioxide)—as distinct from metallic minerals—accounted for most of Colorado's $2.8 billion mineral production in 1999. Natural gas led with $1.5 billion, followed by coal with $360 million, oil with $326 million and carbon dioxide with $83 million.

The Colorado earth yields even more treasures. The Kelsey Lake Mine in Larimer County in northern Colorado has become North America's first large-scale, commercial diamond mine. Sand and gravel and crushed stone—all used in construction—has become a $325-million-a-year industry. The Colorado Yule marble quarry at Marble in Gunnison County is a source of building stone. And Colorado is well known for its sidewalk stone from sandstone quarries at Lyons in Boulder County.

In 1999 the gypsum mine in Gypsum, east of Glenwood Springs, produced 450,000 tons of the material used for wallboard and other products. Cement plants that opened in the early 1900s near Florence and Laporte are being expanded. Although Colorado produced about 2.5 billion tons of cement in 1999, the state remains a net importer because of its building boom.

Severance taxes on mineral production are divided equally between local governments and a state trust fund to administer natural resources. Colorado collected 1999 mineral severance taxes of $34 million and local property taxes of $112 million. In 1999, metallic mineral and mineral fuel industries employed 13,700 Coloradans at an average annual wage of $58,835, compared with a state per capita income of $22,821.

To learn more: Colorado Geological Survey, Department of Natural Resources, 1313 Sherman St., Denver 80203; (303) 866-2611.

Dr. Colorado's List of Big Bonanzas

Denver, 1858. William Green Russell discovers gold in Cherry Creek and the South Platte River. The Colorado gold rush is on.

Black Hawk, 1859. John H. Gregory discovers the mother lode that makes Black Hawk and nearby Central City major gold producers for 50 years.

Leadville, 1880s. Horace Tabor and many others find the silver source that gives birth to Leadville, Colorado's richest silver city.

Cripple Creek, 1891. Bob Womack, a cowboy chasing strays, stumbles upon gold that triggers Colorado's greatest gold rush.

Motor Vehicles

Coloradans are required to register motor vehicles in the county where they live within 30 days of establishing residency. To register your car, you need a valid title, current odometer test, bill of sale and—for metro Denver, Weld and El Paso counties—proof of emissions testing. You can order from 72 different types of license plates,

The First Auto

David Brunton, a mining engineer and inventor of the Brunton compass that is still used by engineers, acquired Colorado's first automobile in 1899. Brunton spent a day assembling his Columbia Electric runabout, then took it for a spin on the streets of Denver, terrifying horses and pedestrians. ✷

These early motorists had to pull and push after the motor conked out on a drive in 1907. Colorado Historical Society.

including regular, designer, pioneer, special interest and personalized.

Denver first began registering and licensing vehicles in 1902, when drivers were required to hang from their rear axle homemade license plates "eight inches long and four inches wide" with their registration number. An accelerating total of speeding violations and wrecks led Denver in 1909 to require that numbers be carried on the front as well as the back of vehicles. The State Department of Motor Vehicles was formed in 1913 to oversee registration, licensing and license plates, which are made by prisoners at the Colorado State Penitentiary in Cañon City.

Mountain Sickness

(*SEE ALSO* HYPOTHERMIA) At altitudes above 8,000 feet, throbbing temples, nausea, headaches, lethargy and shortness of breath are symptoms of acute mountain sickness (AMS). Reduced oxygen and humidity causes acute mountain sickness, or high altitude sickness. If the attack is mild, a quick descent will cure it immediately. Other common high-altitude health hazards in Colorado, where trails and highways routinely take travelers to elevations of 10,000 feet and above, include sunburn and hypothermia.

"Mountain fever," a widely reported disorder among early pioneers living in high elevations, may have been typhoid or a typhoid-like disorder. Physicians reported that this mysterious disease caused high fevers and serious intestinal problems and could be fatal. Some doctors successfully prescribed moving to lower altitudes and not drinking water that had passed through human and mining waste.

Mount Evans

This 14,264-foot peak, with its distinctive dimple-like cirque, dominates Denver's western skyline as the centerpiece of Colorado's Front Range.

The first recorded ascent was made in 1863 by artist Albert Bierstadt, for whom the adjacent mountain is named. Bierstadt named the peak Mount Rosalie for his sweetheart and immortalized it in his large 1866 painting "Storm in the Rocky Mountains." Coloradans renamed it in 1895 for John Evans (see entry), the second territorial governor and pioneer church, college and railroad builder. A lesser peak on the south flank of Mount Evans was named Mount Rosalie.

America's highest auto road, first opened in 1927, makes the peak accessible to all during the summer. Even in July and August, chilly winds and snow often welcome tourists at the summit. The stone ruins of a burned Summit House (1941), rest rooms, the University of Denver's high altitude observatory (1936) and sociable Rocky Mountain goats lie atop the peak.

The mountain, which is surrounded and protected by the Mount Evans Wilderness Area, offers many spectacular stops. Echo Lake, a 617-acre Denver Mountain Park, features the two-story log and stone Echo Lake Lodge, while the Mount Goliath Natural Area features an ancient bristlecone pine forest and the Denver Botanic Gardens' Alpine Gardens.

Mount of the Holy Cross

This 14,005-foot granite peak in the Elk Mountains near Vail displays the natural image of a gigantic cross, created by snow lingering in depressions. The cross was immortalized by photographer William Henry Jackson, painter Thomas Moran and poet Henry Wadsworth Longfellow, who wrote the lines:

There is a mountain in the distant west
That, sun-defying, in its deep ravines
Reveals a cross of snow upon its side.

A hut to shelter pilgrims to the mountain is a relic of various never-realized plans to erect a shrine and pilgrimage center to commercialize the Mount of the Holy Cross. President Herbert Hoover declared the mountain a national monument in 1929, but in 1950 it was demoted to again become simply part of White River National Forest.

Notch Mountain offers the best view of Holy Cross, which can also be seen from the top of the gondola at Vail, which operates

My grandma, who grew up on top of Grand Mesa at an elevation of some 10,000 feet, always bragged that Colorado has air that only the angels have breathed before.

year-round. Due to natural erosion, one arm of the cross has diminished since the 1870s when Jackson and Moran created the celebrated images that made Mount of the Holy Cross world famous.

Mule Deer

Colorado's most ubiquitous large wild animal is common throughout most of the state, including suburbs where they browse on gardens as well as native plants. The species is generally migratory, summering at higher elevations and moving downslope to winter range.

This medium- to large-size deer (*Odocoileus hemionus*) has long mulelike ears and a ropelike, black-tipped tail. The coarse coat is reddish tan in summer and a blackish gray in winter, with a white rump, tail and belly year-round.

These deer are usually nocturnal, spending the middle of the day sleeping or resting at the base of trees or rocks. They generally mate in October and November,

Mule deer. From *The Great Rocky Mountain Nature Factbook*; illustration by Marjorie C. Leggitt.

and one or two fawns are born in the spring. Adult males have antlers and weigh as much as 440 pounds but average closer to 150, while females are smaller.

Mule deer are hunted extensively, and Colorado is among the top three states for mule deer harvested, with more than 80,000 bagged annually. Growing populations of the mule deer have led to an increase in their predators, notably coyotes and mountain lions. Coyote killings of mule deer prompted the Colorado Division of Wildlife to begin a controversial program in 2001 of shooting coyotes from aircraft so that deer hunters will not be disappointed. Chronic wasting disease has become a major killer of mule deer in recent years.

The smaller white-tailed deer (*Odocoileus virginianus*), with their rather long tail that is white on the undersurface, are less common than mule deer and are seen mostly along the lower Arkansas, South Platte and White River valleys.

Mules *(Equus asinus)* This usually

sterile hybrid of a male burro (a.k.a. ass, donkey or jackass) and a female horse resembles its sire in appearance and its dam in size. Surefooted, strong pack animals, mules are cheaper to maintain and better adapted to hot weather than horses. Introduced to the United States by George Washington, they were particularly valuable in Colorado mining towns as the major beast of burden.

Although called asinine and stupid, mules often smartly saved human lives. They made better sentinels than dogs or human beings, smelling Indians a mile away and yeehawing and pointing their long ears in the direction of the threat. Mules also refused to take human riders where they shouldn't go, sensing unstable ground, bears, rattlesnakes and other dangers.

Harriet Fish Bacchus, in *Tomboy Bride*, described Colorado mining town mules as "large, genteel, patient pictures of dejection, trudging along, heads sagging, ears flopping to shake out the needle sharp particles of ice driven in by howling winds." Often packed with far more weight than their own, mules tackled mountainous routes where railroads and horses could not go.

Museums *(See also* Art and Music; Botanical Gardens; Zoos*)* The

first museums in Colorado were short-lived private businesses that often sold their artifacts. The first professional public museum was developed in 1881 by the State Historical and Natural History Society, which set up exhibit cases of birds, mammals and prehistoric artifacts in the state Capitol. The society evolved into today's Colorado Historical Society (see entry) and the modern Denver Museum of Nature and Science (see entry). In 1913 the society moved into the Colorado State Museum building on the south side of the Capitol. In 1977 it moved into its current home at 1300 Broadway.

Colorado is home to more than 150 history museums, more than

50 art galleries and museums, 32 house museums and some 50 other museums. Most Colorado museums deal with history, art or science, although others specialize in bells, boxing, buttons, cable TV, carousels, dolls, figure skating, firefighting, horses, jails, mental health, mining, money, pewter, women—and some 30 other niche interests. Among the total are seven children's museums, six dinosaur museums, five archaeology centers, four halls of fame, three energy museums and two race-car museums.

Dr. Colorado's List of Favorite Museums

Littleton Historical Museum. Offers superb exhibits, programs and living history agricultural exhibits. It includes historic homes, barnyard animals, a blacksmith shop and relics of small-town life. Founded 1969. 6028 S. Gallup St., Littleton 80120; (303) 797-5649.

Cañon City Municipal Museum. Showcases dinosaur and wild game artifacts. Founded 1928. 612 Royal Gorge Blvd., Cañon City 81215; (719) 269-9018.

Colorado Springs Fine Arts Center. Displays fine Southwestern, Spanish Colonial and Native American art. Founded 1936. 30 W. Dale St., Colorado Springs 80903; (719) 634-5881.

Museum of the American Numismatic Association. Has the country's largest collections of coins, currency, tokens and medals, plus an 11,000-volume library. Founded 1891. 818 N. Cascade Ave., Colorado Springs 80903; (719) 632-2646.

Colorado Springs Museum. Features local history, artifacts and paintings. Founded 1937. 215 S. Tejon St., Colorado Springs 80903; (719) 578-6718.

Hamill House Museum. The former mansion of English-born silver tycoon William A. Hamill, who built the home complete with a six-hole outhouse and company office in the backyard. Founded 1971. 305 Argentine St., Georgetown 80444; (303) 569-2840.

Colorado Railroad Museum. Largest rail museum in the Rockies, offers rolling stock, research archives, exhibits and live steam excursions. Founded 1958 (see entry). 17155 W. 44th Ave., Golden 80402; (303) 279-4591.

Museum of Western Colorado. Maintains a downtown observation tower and several branches specializing in dinosaurs, agriculture and local history. Founded 1965. 233 S. Fifth St., Grand Junction 81502; (970) 242-0971; www.mwc.mus.co.us.

Centennial Village. Includes 24 structures that showcase Greeley's history, high-plains agriculture and various ethnic groups. Founded 1976. 1475 A St., Greeley 80631; (970) 350-9220.

National Mining Hall of Fame and Museum. Offers mineral specimens, dioramas, murals, tools and exhibits, plus a walk-in model of a working mine. Founded 1988. 120 W. Ninth St., Leadville 80461; (719) 486-1229.

National Forests and Grasslands

During the 1890s, Americans began to question the U.S. government policy of selling land cheaply or giving it away to promote settlement and exploitation of natural resources. Conservationists urged that some lands be saved for future generations and for public recreation. This conservation crusade led to the establishment of national forests, parks, monuments and grasslands.

In 1891, President Benjamin Harrison created in central Colorado the nation's second forest reserve, White River National Forest. Despite protests from some users of public lands, President Harrison in 1892 designated additional reserves, including Grand Mesa and Pike national forests.

President Theodore Roosevelt set aside San Isabel National Forest in 1902 and, in 1905, established Gunnison, Holy Cross, Routt, San Juan, and Uncompahgre national forests, then added Arapaho National Forest in 1907. President Herbert Hoover added Roosevelt National Forest during the 1920s. Holy Cross National Forest was later made a part of White River National Forest.

Colorado's 10 national forests constitute about one-fifth of the state's terrain. The 15 million Colorado acres managed by the U.S. Forest Service are put to multiple uses. They remain a source of timber, through controlled cuts. Approximately one-third of the state's cattle and sheep graze on leased national forest sites. Nearly all of Colorado's 33 ski areas operate on leased national forest property.

Two national grasslands—Comanche National Grassland in southeastern Colorado and Pawnee National Grassland in northeastern Colorado—were created during the Dust Bowl era of the 1930s to reclaim overgrazed and plowed-over farmland and allow the return of natural

Looking Back

Feb. 28, 1861

Congress declared Colorado an official U.S. territory. Before that it was also known as Jefferson Territory and Pikes Peak Territory.

vegetation and wildlife. (See map on pages 138–139)

National Forests
(with area in square miles)
Arapaho (1,602)
Grand Mesa (541)
Gunnison (2,598)
Pike (1,729)
Roosevelt (1,232)
Routt (1,760)
San Isabel (1,736)
San Juan (2,918)
Uncompahgre (1,473)
White River (3,064)

National Grasslands
Comanche (655)
Pawnee (302)

To learn more: U.S. Forest Service, P.O. Box 25127, Denver 80225; (303) 275-5350; www.fs.fed.us/recreation/states/co.

National Historic Sites
Colorado has one long-established National Historic Site, with two other sites now being developed to memorialize a pair of difficult periods in American history. (See separate entries for Amache Japanese Relocation Camp, Bent's Fort and Sand Creek Massacre.) All three are in southeastern Colorado.

Bent's Old Fort National Historic Site.
Brothers Charles and William Bent built this imposing post on the Arkansas River in the mid-1830s, making it the trading center for the conglomeration of Natives, Euro-Americans, Mexicans and French who peopled the region. The National Park Service reconstructed the fort in 1976. Along U.S. Hwy. 50 between La Junta and Las Animas.

Amache National Historic Site.
More than 7,600 Japanese Americans from

the U.S. west coast were sent to the Amache relocation camp during World War II. Federal legislation has been introduced to designate Amache and other internment camps as National Historic Sites. Near U.S. Hwy. 50, about 17 miles east of Lamar.

Sand Creek National Historic Site. An encampment of Arapaho and Cheyenne were attacked Nov. 29, 1864, by a contingent of Colorado troopers, who slaughtered men, women and children. The National Park Service has been authorized to acquire the 7,680-acre site, which was added to the National Register of Historic Places in 2001. The remote site is near the intersection of Kiowa County Roads W and 54, about 40 miles north of Lamar. (See map on pages 138–139)

To learn more: National Park Service; (303) 969-2000; www.nps.gov.

National Monuments

Whereas both Congress and the president must approve a national park, the president can unilaterally designate a national monument. Presidents took this action with Colorado National Monument (1911), Dinosaur National Monument (1915), Hovenweep National Monument (1923), Great Sand Dunes National Monument (1932; now a national park), Black Canyon of the Gunnison National Monument (1933; now a national park), and Florissant Fossil Beds National Monument (1969).

President Clinton in 2000 designated Canyon of the Ancients National

Picture Rock at Yellow Jacket Canyon is among the features protected by the Canyon of the Ancients National Monument. Denver Public Library, Western History Department.

Monument near Cortez. He also proposed creation of Vermillion National Monument in northwestern Colorado.

Canyon of the Ancients National Monument. The monument designation is designed to provide more protection and interpretive programs for the area's many scattered prehistoric Indian villages, pit houses and cliff dwellings. In southwestern Colorado, it stretches along McElmo, Hovenweep and Yellow Jacket canyons from around the towns of Cortez and Dove Creek westward to the Utah border.

Colorado National Monument. Steep-walled canyons and sculpted spires and columns are the handiwork of wind and water at this site. The 32-square-mile monument offers spectacular drives, hikes and views. In western Colorado near Grand Junction; Rim Rock Drive, Fruita 81521; (970) 858-3617.

Dinosaur National Monument. A fossil quarry and magnificent sandstone canyon scenery highlight this 211,000-acre monument. In northwestern Colorado

Colorado National Lands

Parks, Monuments, Historic Sites, Forests, Wilderness Areas, Recreation Areas, Wildlife Refuges, Grasslands

National Parks, Monuments, and Historic Sites

1 Black Canyon of the Gunnison National Park
2 Great Sand Dunes National Park
3 Mesa Verde National Park
4 Rocky Mountain National Park
5 Canyon of the Ancients National Monument
6 Hovenweep National Monument
   (within Canyon of the Ancients
   National Monument)
7 Colorado National Monument
8 Dinosaur National Monument
9 Florissant Fossil Beds National Monument
10 Amache National Historic Site
11 Bent's Old Fort National Historic Site
12 Sand Creek National Historic Site

National Wilderness Areas

13 Black Canyon of the Gunnison
14 Black Ridge Canyons
15 Buffalo Peaks
16 Byers Peak
17 Cache la Poudre
18 Collegiate Peaks
19 Comanche Peak
20 Eagles Nest
21 Flat Tops
22 Fossil Ridge
23 Great Sand Dunes
24 Greenhorn Mountain
25 Gunnison Gorge
26 Holy Cross
27 Hunter-Fryingpan
28 Indians Peaks
29 La Garita
30 Lizard Head
31 Lost Creek
32 Maroon Bells-Snowmass
33 Mesa Verde
34 Mount Evans
35 Mount Massive
36 Mount Sneffels
37 Mount Zirkel
38 Neota
39 Never Summer
40 Platte River
41 Powderhorn
42 Ptarmigan Peak
43 Raggeds
44 Rawah
45 Sangre de Cristo
46 Sarvis Creek
47 South San Juan
48 Uncompahgre
49 Vasquez Peak
50 Weminuche
51 West Elk

National Recreation Areas

52 Arapaho National Recreation Area
53 Curecanti National Recreation Area

National Wildlife Refuges

54 Alamosa National Wildlife Refuge
55 Arapaho National Wildlife Refuge
56 Browns Park National Wildlife Refuge
57 Monte Vista National Wildlife Refuge
58 Rocky Mountain Arsenal National
   Wildlife Refuge
59 Two Ponds National Wildlife Refuge

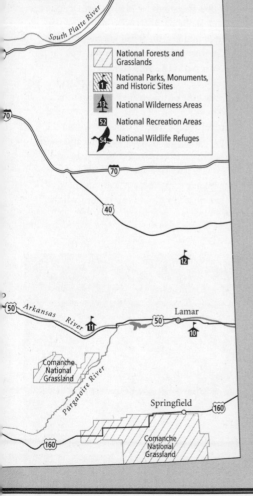

Pawnee National Grassland

South Platte River

	National Forests and Grasslands
	National Parks, Monuments, and Historic Sites
	National Wilderness Areas
	National Recreation Areas
	National Wildlife Refuges

70

70

40

12

Arkansas River

Lamar

50

50

10

Comanche National Grassland

Purgatoire River

Springfield

160

160

Comanche National Grassland

near Dinosaur; 4545 U.S. Hwy. 40, Dinosaur 81610; (970) 374-3000.

Florissant Fossil Beds National Monument. Well-preserved fossils of fish, insects, trees and plants are the product of a volcanic eruption that buried this area 35 million years ago. This nine-square-mile site includes giant sequoia tree stumps. In central Colorado, about 40 miles west of Colorado Springs; 15807 Teller County Road 1, Florissant 80816; (719) 748-3253.

Hovenweep National Monument. Hovenweep consists of widely scattered prehistoric Anasazi structures in Colorado and Utah, including square, round and oval masonry towers. The structures are reminiscent of medieval European fortifications, but openings in the Hovenweep towers may have been for astronomical observation rather than for defensive purposes. *Hovenweep* (Ute for "deserted valley") also harbors many petroglyphs and pictographs. In southwestern Colorado, 25 miles west of Cortez. The visitor center is across the state line, 16 miles east of Hatch, Utah. The original monument is now part of the larger Canyon of the Ancients National Monument created in 2000.

Vermillion National Monument. Proposed in northwestern Colorado, northeast of Dinosaur National Monument.

National Parks

Colorado's first national park, Mesa Verde, was created in 1906 to preserve ancient Native American cliff dwellings and pit houses and keep them from being plundered. Rocky Mountain National Park was founded in 1915. Black Canyon of the Gunnison became Colorado's third national park, in 1999; Great Sand Dunes was designated a national park the following year.

Black Canyon of the Gunnison National Park. Designated a national monument in 1933, this spectacular natural area is now greeting visitors in its new status as a national park. Thanks to sheer 2,000-foot-high walls and difficult access, as well as the national monument and park designations, the lower gorge cut by the Gunnison River has been preserved for the most part in its wild state.

The river drops an average of 95 feet per mile, one of the steepest fall rates for a North American river. The deepest and most spectacular 12 miles lie within the park's dark gray walls of gneiss and schist with pinkish crystalline granite bands.

The river is named for U.S. Army explorer Capt. John W. Gunnison, who led an 1853 railroad survey through the

Cliff Palace is the largest of more than 400 cliff dwellings in Mesa Verde National Park. Photo by Tom Noel.

canyon. He was killed by Paiutes west of the canyon. Embracing 21 square miles, Black Canyon is named for its dark, shadowy Precambrian rocks. Since becoming a national park, the site is being considerably expanded.

To learn more: The visitor center at Gunnison Point on the south rim is open daily 8 A.M.–6 P.M. May–Oct. and 9:00 A.M.–3:30 P.M. Wed.–Sun. the rest of the year. Lookout pavilions, camping and picnic areas are available. State Hwy. 347 via U.S. Hwy. 50, 15 miles east of Montrose; (970) 249-1914; www.nps.gov/blca.

Great Sand Dunes National Park. America's highest sand pile, designated a national monument in 1932, became a national park Nov. 22, 2000. With its elevation to national park status, Great Sand Dunes is scheduled to add 100,000 acres to the 39,000-acre site in southern Colorado, including parts of the neighboring Zapata and Baca ranches. The park hopes to include not only the dunes, but also adjacent historic ranches, foothills, mountain meadows and 14,165-foot Kit Carson Peak.

For thousands of years, prevailing westerlies have blown sand into this natural trap on the west edge of the Sangre de Cristo Mountains, creating approximately 39 square miles of dunes that rise 750 feet above the valley floor. Although the sands usually look white or tan, under a microscope they are multicolored.

Some grains are volcanic, from the San Juan Mountains across the valley; others have been formed by streams tumbling out of the mountains. The high water table helps to keep the sand moist and stable.

The Petit Grepon is one of many climbing destinations in Rocky Mountain National Park. From *The Rockies*; photo by David Muench.

Legend populates this giant sandbox with lost sheepherders, Spanish suits of armor and web-footed horses.

Archaeological exploration has found evidence of habitation 10,000 years ago by hunters of the prehistoric Folsom culture, named for archaeological discoveries in Folsom, N.M. Ute Indians once occupied the area. An astonished Zebulon Pike described these dunes in the journal of his 1806–1807 expedition as looking "like the sea in a storm."

To learn more: The park's visitor center is at 11500 State Hwy. 10, Mosca 81146; (719) 378-2356; www.nps.gov.grsa.

Mesa Verde National Park. North America's best-preserved site of prehistoric Native American cliff dwellings, pueblos and pit houses includes artifacts ranging from distinctive black-on-white pottery and baskets to *metates* (corn-grinding tables), *manos* (corn-grinding stones) and miniature ears of dried corn.

The site in southwestern Colorado was designated a national park in 1906, becoming the first U.S. park dedicated to preserving the culture of prehistoric peoples. In 1978, UNESCO designated Mesa Verde as the first U.S. World Heritage Site.

Colorado is twice the size of Old England—or of New England, for that matter. It has the highest average elevation of any state, and no point is lower than 3,333 feet; if we could iron it out flat, it would be the largest state.

Between about A.D. 1 and A.D. 1300, Native Americans known as the Anasazi built mud and stone towns atop the mesa and, late in that period, cliff dwellings in recesses eroded into canyon walls. These stone cities sometimes sheltered several hundred people in structures as high as four stories. Irrigation ditches and dams supported an intensive cultivation of corn, squash and beans.

Their remarkably stable and long-lived culture rested on their building and agricultural abilities. The prolonged drought of 1275–1300 is generally seen as the cause of the eventual exodus of the Anasazi from their cliff cities. Controversial recent discoveries of ritualistic cannibalism suggests that desperation or terrorism preceded their abandonment of southwestern Colorado. The Natives of Mesa Verde moved to, among other places, the Rio Grande Valley to build the pueblos still occupied by their descendants. Today's Pueblo Indians of New Mexico and Hopi villages of Arizona trace their history back to Mesa Verde.

Wildfires at Mesa Verde in the summer of 2000, caused by lightning, closed the park for several weeks but revealed new archaeological sites.

To learn more: The park entrance is about eight miles east of Cortez via U.S. Hwy. 160; 970-529-4465; www.nps.gov/meve.

Rocky Mountain National Park. Lying astride 40 miles of the Continental Divide in northern Colorado, Rocky Mountain National Park is one of Colorado's most popular outdoor playgrounds. More than 3 million campers, hikers, naturalists, skiers and sightseers visit the park each year. Among its attractions are Bear Lake, the restored Never Summer Dude Ranch, Trail Ridge Road and 14,255-foot Longs Peak (see entry).

The history of the park goes back to the 1890s and to Enos Mills, a naturalist, author and wilderness guide who lived at the base of Longs Peak and ran an inn there. Mills crusaded for creation of the park, working with the Colorado Federation of Women's Clubs, chambers of commerce and public officials. Even with Colorado's national forests, Mills contended that only 20 percent of the state's forests remained unspoiled. He lectured across the United States on the need to preserve some of the Rockies as a national park, as "a picturesque remnant and melancholy ruin of its former grandeur."

On Sept. 4, 1915, his dream came true when Mills presided over the dedication of Rocky Mountain National Park. Of course he had wanted a bigger park: His proposed 1,000-square-mile park had been whittled down to 358 square miles.

However, some lands were added later, and in 1978 the Indian Peaks on the southern edge of the park received protection as a wilderness area.

To learn more: The Park Headquarters Visitor Center is at the eastern Estes Park entrance, while the western entrance near Grand Lake offers Kawuneeche Visitor Center. Other informative stops include the Alpine Visitor Center atop Trail Ridge Road and the Moraine Park Museum. Rocky Mountain National Park, Estes Park 80517; (970) 586-1206; www.nps.gov.

(See map on pages 138–139)

National Recreation Areas

Colorado is home to two National Recreation Areas, one next to Rocky Mountain National Park and the other adjoining Black Canyon of the Gunnison National Park.

Arapaho National Recreation Area. The Arapaho recreation area is just outside the southwest corner of Rocky Mountain National Park. This 53-square-mile mountain haven borders the headwaters of the Colorado River including Lake Granby and Shadow Mountain Lake. Created by Congress in 1978, the area is a favorite with hikers, anglers, cross-country skiers and snowmobilers.

Curecanti National Recreation Area. The name of the Ute chief Curecanti is commemorated by a creek flowing into the Gunnison River and by Curecanti National Recreation Area in that part of Colorado. Created after the 1965 completion of 342-foot-high Blue Mesa Dam, the recreation area occupies about 65 square miles.

Fishing (including ice fishing), boating, windsurfing, swimming, camping and hunting are among the recreational possibilities. The Elk Creek Visitor Center includes a prairie dog colony.

The Cimarron Visitor Center, on U.S. 50 in the recreation area, showcases rolling stock of the Denver & Rio Grande Railroad. D&RG Locomotive 278, a narrow-gauge steam engine, is exhibited atop an 1880s' Cimarron Creek trestle, remnant of a 119-foot, four-span railroad bridge. Other bridges, as well as most of the railbed, were displaced by the reservoirs of the Blue Mesa, Crystal and Morrow Point dams. This pioneer rail remnant in a rugged, remote canyon speaks of the larger search for a rail route west beginning with the epic 1853 railroad survey of Capt. John W. Gunnison.

The Curecanti Recreation Area is west of Gunnison. It stretches for some 30 miles along the shores and tributaries of Blue Mesa Reservoir and abuts Black Canyon of the Gunnison National Park.

To learn more: www.nps.gov/cur.

National Register of Historic Places (SEE ALSO ENDANGERED PLACES; HISTORICAL PRESERVATION)

The National Register is a list of significant historical resources in each state. All National Register listings for Colorado are also included on the State Register of Historic Properties maintained by the Colorado Historical Society. The State Register includes additional landmarks and historic districts of state significance.

Colorado has more than 1,100 listings on the National Register and more than 160 National Historic Districts. Colorado also has 17 sites in the most important and exclusive National Register category: National Historic Landmarks. (See map on pages 138–139)

National Historic Landmarks

Bent's Old Fort National Historic Site, 6 miles north of La Junta.

Burlington, Kit Carson County Fairground Carousel.

Central City–Black Hawk Historic District, Colorado Hwy. 119.

Cripple Creek Historic Mining District, Colorado Hwy. 67.

Durango & Silverton Narrow Gauge Railroad.

Georgetown–Silver Plume Historic District, including the Lebanon Mine and Georgetown Loop Railroad.

Leadville Historic Mining District.

Lindenmeier Archaeological Site near Fort Collins.

Lowry Archaeological Ruin, 30 miles northwest of Cortez.

Mesa Verde National Park Administrative District, 8 miles east of Cortez.

Pikes Peak in Pike National Forest, 15 miles west of Colorado Springs.

Pikes Stockade, about 20 miles south of Alamosa.

Raton Pass, 12 miles south of Trinidad.

Rocky Mountain National Park Headquarters, 4 miles west of Estes Park.

Shenandoah–Dives Mill near Silverton.

Silverton Historic Mining District.

Telluride Historic Mining District.

To learn more: For a list of Colorado National Register sites or information on obtaining National Register designation, contact the Colorado Office of Archaeology and Historic Preservation, 1300 Broadway, Denver 80203; (303) 866-3302; www.coloradohistory-oahp.org.

National Wilderness Areas
Colorado's roster of federally designated wilderness areas come under the management of four agencies of the national government: Forest Service, Bureau of Land Management, National

Devil's Causeway, in Flat Tops Wilderness. Photo by Susan Dupere.

Park Service, and Fish and Wildlife Service.

Colorado's wilderness areas are all within the mountainous region of the western two-thirds of the state, evenly distributed from the Wyoming state line in the north to the New Mexico state line in the south. Part of the Black Ridge Canyons Wilderness Area is in Utah. Colorado shares the Platte River Wilderness Area with Wyoming.

The Forest Service and Bureau of Land Management are the principal caretakers of the wilderness areas. The wilderness areas managed by the Park Service are adjacent to national parks and serve as buffers against development, protecting flora, fauna and archaeological resources. The Fish and Wildlife Service manages a small portion of the Mount Massive Wilderness Area where a fish hatchery is located.

National Wilderness Areas in Colorado

Wilderness Area	Managing Agency	Acreage
Black Canyon of the Gunnison	NPS	15,599
Black Ridge Canyons	BLM	70,370

Buffalo Peaks	FS	43,410
Byers Peak	FS	8,913
Cache la Poudre	FS	9,238
Collegiate Peaks	FS	166,938
Comanche Peak	FS	66,791
Eagles Nest	FS	132,906
Flat Tops	FS	235,035
Fossil Ridge	FS	31,534
Great Sand Dunes	NPS	33,450
Greenhorn Mountain	FS	22,040
Gunnison Gorge	BLM	17,700
Holy Cross	FS	122,797
Hunter–Fryingpan	FS	81,866
Indians Peaks	NPS, FS	73,291
La Garita	FS	128,858
Lizard Head	FS	41,193
Lost Creek	FS	119,790
Maroon Bells– Snowmass	FS	181,117
Mesa Verde	NPS	8,100
Mount Evans	FS	74,401
Mount. Massive	FS, FWS	30,540
Mount Sneffels	FS	16,565
Mount Zirkel	FS	159,935
Neota	FS	9,924
Never Summer	FS	20,747
Platte River	FS	743
Powderhorn	BLM, FS	61,510
Ptarmigan Peak	FS	12,594
Raggeds Wilderness	FS	64,992
Rawah Wilderness	FS	73,068
Sangre de Cristo	FS	226,420
Sarvis Creek	FS	45,190
South San Juan	FS	158,790
Uncompahgre	FS, BLM	102,721
Vasquez Peak	FS	12,986
Weminuche	FS	488,200
West Elk	FS	176,172

FS: Forest Service
NPS: National Park Service
BLM: Bureau of Land Management
FWS: Fish and Wildlife Service

Trappers Lake in Rio Blanco County, once scheduled for development as a private resort, became a national prototype for a roadless wilderness area, thanks to the efforts of Arthur Carhart of the Forest Service. Carhart in 1919 persuaded his agency to deny a proposal for a road and waterfront cabins. Instead the Forest Service recommended that Trappers Lake be kept roadless and wild. Forty-five years later, Congress passed the Wilderness Act to create preserves within national forests where roads, vehicles and permanent human fixtures are banned.

Trappers Lake was included in one of the first wilderness areas, Flat Tops.

Conservation efforts have led to designation of many more of these special places where, as the Wilderness Act puts it, "the earth and its community of life are untrammeled by man; where man himself is a visitor who does not remain."

(See map on pages 138–139)

To learn more

Bureau of Land Management; (303) 239-3600; www.blm.gov.

U.S. Forest Service; (303) 275-5350; www.fs.fed.us/recreation/states/co.

National Wildlife Refuges

For animals, the nation's wildlife refuges are homes where they can thrive in protected habitats. For humans, the refuges often serve as windows into a natural world, a place where people can tiptoe in for a quiet look at wildlife.

Alamosa NWR, just east of Alamosa, is a good place to spot greater sandhill cranes and rare whooping cranes.

Arapaho NWR in remote, sparsely populated North Park, in northern Colorado, features diverse wildlife ranging from moose to sage grouse and rosy finches.

Browns Park NWR is hidden away in the northwest corner of Colorado on the Green River, where migratory waterfowl and songbirds abound.

Monte Vista NWR, between Alamosa and Monte Vista, is another place to sight greater sandhill cranes and whooping cranes.

Rocky Mountain Arsenal NWR is a former Army chemical weapons site near Denver, now in the lengthy, $1 billion process of being rehabilitated as a home for 300 wildlife species, including nesting bald eagles.

Two Ponds NWR along Clear Creek in Arvada is a place to discover wildlife within the Denver metro area.

(See map on pages 138–139)

To learn more: U.S. Fish and Wildlife Service, 134 Union Blvd., Lakewood; (303) 236-7904; www.r6.fws.gov.

Native Americans

(*SEE ALSO* ARCHAEOLOGY; LITTLE RAVEN; OURAY, CHIEF; SAND CREEK MASSACRE)
During the 1700s the eastern plains of Colorado sustained such tribes as the Apache, the Pawnee and the Comanche. All fought with the Spanish, from whom they obtained horses. The Spanish retaliated against the Apache in 1779 when New Mexico governor Juan Bautista de Anza and his troops defeated an Apache band and killed their leader, Cuerno Verde (Green Horn), along the creek in Pueblo County carrying that name.

Before becoming horseback hunters, the Apache had farmed in the Arkansas River Valley of Colorado, raising corn, squash, beans, melons and sunflowers. After acquiring horses, they became buffalo hunters and expanded their territory south and west. As Euro-American settlement pushed eastern tribes west, the Apache, Comanche and Pawnee were shoved out of Colorado and replaced by the Arapaho and Cheyenne, allied tribes who moved into Colorado during the early 1800s.

Initially the Arapaho and Cheyenne were friendly to whites. Both tribes traded at Forts Jackson, Lupton, St. Vrain and Vasquez, as well as at Bent's Fort, where William Bent married a Cheyenne, Owl Woman.

Following the Minnesota Sioux uprising of 1862, warfare swept across the Great Plains. Colorado, where gold seekers sought to dispossess Native Americans of their lands, did not escape the conflict.

Plains Indians had agreed to the 1851 Treaty of Fort Laramie, which promised the land between the Platte and Arkansas rivers at the eastern base of the Rockies to the Southern Arapaho and Southern Cheyenne. Ten years later those two tribes, or their supposed representatives, agreed to the Treaty of Fort Wise, which gave them a much smaller area.

Many Native Americans did not sign the treaties and resisted white advances. Increasingly hostile incidents culminated in the 1864 Sand Creek Massacre in southeastern Colorado, where Colorado troopers slaughtered an estimated 163 Arapaho and Cheyenne, mostly women, children and old men. In retaliation, Natives raided and burned Julesburg in 1865, but were defeated at Summit Springs

As this historical photo of a Ute mother and child suggests, that tribe excelled in leather work. Colorado Historical Society.

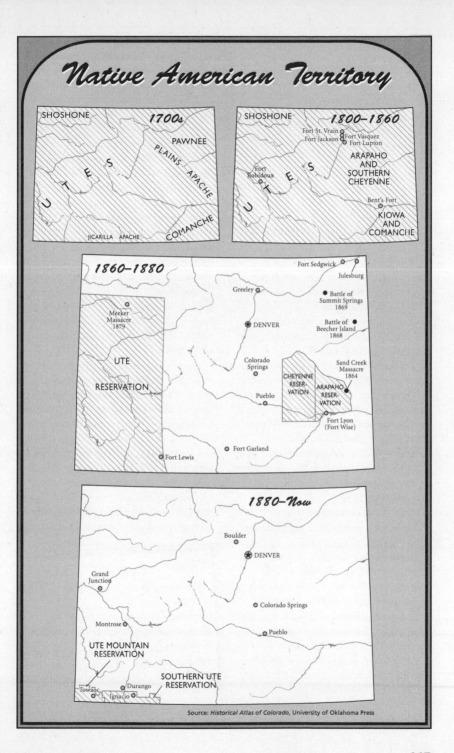

Native American Territory

SHOSHONE · *1700s*

PAWNEE

PLAINS APACHE

U T E S

JICARILLA APACHE · COMANCHE

SHOSHONE · *1800–1860*

Fort St. Vrain
Fort Jackson · Fort Vasquez
Fort Lupton

ARAPAHO AND SOUTHERN CHEYENNE

Fort Robidoux

U T E S

Bent's Fort

KIOWA AND COMANCHE

1860–1880

Fort Sedgwick
Julesburg

Greeley

Battle of Summit Springs 1869

Meeker Massacre 1879

DENVER

Battle of Beecher Island 1868

UTE RESERVATION

Colorado Springs

CHEYENNE RESERVATION

Sand Creek Massacre 1864

ARAPAHO RESERVATION

Pueblo

Fort Lyon (Fort Wise)

Fort Lewis · Fort Garland

1880–Now

Boulder

DENVER

Grand Junction

Colorado Springs

Montrose

Pueblo

UTE MOUNTAIN RESERVATION

SOUTHERN UTE RESERVATION

Towaoc · Durango
Ignacio

Source: *Historical Atlas of Colorado*, University of Oklahoma Press

147

in 1869, the last Colorado battle for the Plains Indians. The Arapaho were forced to move again, with the Southern Arapaho sent to an Oklahoma reservation, the Northern Arapaho to one in Wyoming. The Cheyenne also were eventually removed to reservations outside Colorado.

Colorado's Ute Indians, unlike Plains tribes such as the Arapaho and Cheyenne, had been in Colorado for hundreds of years. After the Domínguez–Escalante Expedition of 1776, Father Escalante described the Utes as "all of good features and very friendly." The Utes guided the Spanish party through the Uncompahgre Plateau and gave them deer meat jerky, dried berries and other delicacies.

The Utes once occupied most of present-day Colorado, but were gradually forced onto smaller and smaller reservations after the 1858–1859 gold rush drew swarms of white fortune seekers. Some say the Utes' revenge on whites has been the difficult names they left on the land: Uncompahgre, Tabeguache, Saguache, Weminuche. Only two Ute enclaves survive today in Colorado, both in the southwestern corner of the state: the Ute Mountain Ute Reservation and the Southern Ute Reservation.

Native Americans make up about 1 percent of the population of Colorado.

The Native American population declined until the 1940s, when it began increasing, apparently because of somewhat better conditions on the reservations and because of the migration of many out-of-state Indians into metro Denver.

About 18,000 Native Americans now live in the metropolitan Denver area. Denver alone has more than 7,000 Native American residents compared with just over 2,100 on the Ute Mountain Ute Reservation and 1,600 on the Southern Ute Reservation. Colorado's urban Indian population has been growing since the 1950s. To help newcomers in their adjustment to urban life, Marvin Prue, a Rosebud Lakota, and other Indians in Denver formed the White Buffalo Council of American Indians in 1955. After Prue's death in 1962, others continued his work and the White Buffalo Council remains active to this day.

American Indians in Colorado have enjoyed a cultural renaissance since the 1980s, reflected in an increasing number of Indian powwows held throughout the state. Indian dancing, music, art, culture and food are showcased at these festivals, which generally welcome non-Indians. Denver's annual January Indian Market has become a major trade show, celebrating Indian art and crafts.

Glenn Morris, a Pawnee Indian with a Harvard Law School degree, has helped make the American Indian Movement of Colorado

The First Man and Woman

An Arapaho creation myth says the earth originally lay mostly under water. A pipe floated on top as a boat for the Great Spirit. In the boat with the Great Spirit were a duck, a beaver and a turtle.

The Great Spirit knew that clay was at the bottom of the water so he asked the turtle to go down and bring him some. But the turtle came back, unable to reach the bottom. The beaver was also unsuccessful. The duck went next. He stayed longer and returned with some clay in his bill.

The Great Spirit took the clay and threw it to the four winds to form a vast area of dry ground. He made the moon and after that the man and woman from whom the People descended. The sacred peace pipe was given to the man and woman and they were instructed as to its care. The pipe was made of wood so hard and so shiny that many thought it stone. ✷

active since the Second Battle of Wounded Knee in Pine Ridge, S.D., in 1990. Morris, a professor of political science at the University of Colorado at Denver, has helped organize Native American demonstrations, including protests against Denver's Columbus Day Parade. Such protests, including the activism of Ben Nighthorse Campbell, a Northern Cheyenne, one of Colorado's two U.S. senators, and are highlighting modern issues of concern to Native Americans.

To learn more: Colorado Commission of Indian Affairs, 200 E. Colfax Ave., Room 130, Denver 80203; (303) 866-3027; www.state.co.us/indian.

Arapaho. The name *Arapaho* may be derived from the Pawnee word meaning "buyer" or "trader." The Arapaho called themselves "bison path people," "our people" or "tattooed people" (for their chest tattoos).

These Plains Indians have light skin and prominent noses. Members of the Algonquin family, they once lived in the Great Lakes area. After crossing the Missouri River, the tribe split. The Northern Arapaho headed for what would become Wyoming, the Southern Arapaho for Colorado.

During the 1840s and 1850s, as many as 5,000 Arapaho lived in Colorado, camping along the South Platte River and its tributaries. At first the Indians accepted the palefaced gold seekers who trespassed on what the federal government had recognized as Arapaho land. Little Raven, the principal Southern Arapaho chief, plus Niwot (Left Hand), chief in the Boulder area, and Chief Friday on the Cache la Poudre River, were receptive to the newcomers.

When whites found gold and began to settle, the Arapaho were doomed. They called whites "spider people" but learned too late the significance of the web of roads, survey lines and fences with which palefaces were measuring and seizing the land. As thousands settled along rivers and creeks that had been Arapaho campsites, hostilities arose.

Deteriorating relations between Indians and whites culminated in the Sand Creek Massacre, at an encampment of Arapaho and Cheyenne in southeastern Colorado. There, on Nov. 29, 1864, men, women and children of both tribes were cut down by Col. John M. Chivington and his Colorado troopers.

Arapaho survivors of the Sand Creek Massacre remained in Colorado until the 1867 Medicine Lodge Treaty assigned them to a reservation in Oklahoma. Northern

Arapaho were confined to the Wind River Reservation in Wyoming.

Cheyenne. The Cheyenne are a Plains Indian tribe of the Algonquin linguistic stock. The name *Cheyenne* is a French version of the Sioux word for "people who speak a strange tongue."

According to Cheyenne legend, they were once fishermen living around the Great Lakes, then moved west to Minnesota, where they lived in earth-lodge villages and raised crops. After acquiring horses around 1760, the Cheyenne became nomadic buffalo hunters. Ultimately the Cheyenne had 27 different words for buffalo, the beast around which their lives revolved.

The tribe split around 1830 when the Southern Cheyenne went to live along the Arkansas River and trade at Bent's Fort in southeastern Colorado, where William Bent promoted trade and friendly relations. The Northern Cheyenne settled along the upper Platte River in northeastern Colorado and southeastern Wyoming.

After the 1859 Colorado gold rush, the Cheyenne agreed by the Treaty of Fort Wise to live on a reservation, but the U.S. government failed to fulfill its promises. Many Cheyenne, facing starvation, began robbing ranchers of their livestock. Hostilities increased, culminating in the Sand Creek Massacre of Cheyenne and Arapaho in 1864.

Northern Cheyenne joined with the Sioux in defeating General George A. Custer and his Seventh Cavalry at the Little Big Horn in 1876. Forced to surrender in 1877, the Northern Cheyenne were sent to a reservation in Montana. The Southern Cheyenne were assigned a reservation in Oklahoma.

Ute Creation Myth

In the beginning, there was nothing but sky and clouds, sunshine and rain. The Great Spirit lived alone in the middle of the sky. After a while he grew lonesome and wanted to make something new. So he poked a hole in the heavens and poured dirt and water through it to make the mountains.

Then he came down to Earth and touched it with his magic stick. Where he touched the land, flowers and bushes and trees grew. When leaves turned bright colors and fell off the trees he gathered them up. He took the prettiest leaves into his hand and blew on them and they grew wings and feathers and became birds.

The Great Spirit made antelope, buffalo, bighorn goats, rabbits, squirrels and coyotes. They lived happily until the coyote began stealing things and causing fights. The Great Spirit became disgusted with his fighting creatures. So he decided to make one big, wise animal to rule the rest—the bear.

No people lived on Earth until the Great Spirit cut sticks and put them in a bag. Coyote waited until the Great Spirit left, and then he pawed the bag to see what was inside. Many, many people came running out, dashing in every direction and speaking many different languages.

The Great Spirit became very angry. He had planned to give each group of people its own place on Earth so they would not fight. Their fighting, and that of the animals, stained the land and the river red with blood.

The Great Spirit grabbed the bag and saw that only one group of people remained. He set them down in the mountains and said: "These people will be very brave and very strong. They will be called Ute." ❧

Ute. Colorado's oldest modern residents are the Utes, a mountain tribe that has been here for hundreds of years. They are physically shorter, darker and stockier than the Plains Indians and also differ from the Plains tribes in that they belong to the Shoshonean linguistic family centered in Utah and the Great Basin. They may be descendants of such cultures as the Fremont people who occupied Colorado about 500 to 1,000 years ago.

Seven different Ute bands—the Capote, Grand River, Mouache, Tabeguache, Uintah, Weminuche and Yampa—occupied central and western Colorado and eastern Utah. The Utes used deer, elk and rabbit skins to make shirts, leggings, dresses and blankets. They excelled at making leather garments to keep them comfortable during long, windy, cold winters. Ute women made beautiful leather clothing decorated with fringes, porcupine quills, elk teeth and trade items ranging from Pacific coast shells to glass beads from Venice, Italy.

After the Utes acquired horses in the 1600s, they became buffalo hunters and built tipis out of buffalo hides. With horses, they ranged into New Mexico and Arizona, raiding Pueblo and Hispanic settlements.

When the U.S. Army built Fort Garland in the San Luis Valley in the 1850s, the United States began to both fight and make treaties with the Utes. During the 1860s, the tribe agreed to a reservation consisting of the western third of Colorado. After whites found silver and gold on that reservation, the Utes were persuaded to sign the 1873 Brunot Agreement opening up the San Juan Mountains to prospectors.

In 1879 a rebellious band of Utes killed White River Indian agent Nathan Meeker and others at the White River Reservation in northwestern Colorado. Meeker's wife and daughter were captured by the Utes. Shortly before the Meeker Massacre, Utes slaughtered Major Tom Thornburgh and 13 troopers at Milk Creek. White Coloradans rose up in a demand that the Utes must go.

After that episode, the Utes were moved to reservations: the Uintah, Tabeguache, Grand River and Yampa bands to the Uintah Reservation in northeastern Utah; the Weminuche, Capote and Mouache bands to the Southern Ute and Ute Mountain Ute reservations in the southwestern corner of Colorado.

The Southern Utes welcome visitors today at tribal headquarters in Ignacio, where they own and operate a motel and restaurant, the Sky Ute Casino, the Southern Ute Cultural Center and Red Willow Production Co., a natural gas producer. At headquarters of the Ute Mountain Utes in Towaoc, the tribe maintains a trading post, a casino, and a tribal park where tours are available to historic and prehistoric Native sites.

To learn more

The Southern Ute Cultural Center Museum in Ignacio; State Hwy. 172 North, P.O. Box 737, Ignacio 81137. Open year-round Mon.–Fri. 10 A.M.–5:30 P.M.; also Sat.–Sun. 10 A.M.–3 P.M. in summer. (970) 563-9583.

Ute Mountain Ute Tribal Park in Towaoc; P.O. Box 109, Towaoc 81334. Open

March–Oct. daily, 8:30 A.M.–4:30 P.M., and by appointment. (800) 847-5485.

Newspapers (SEE ALSO BYERS, WILLIAM NEWTON; DAY, DAVID FRAKES)

A British visitor touring 19th-century Colorado marveled that even the smallest towns had a newspaper, if not two or three. "Well," he was told, "it takes a newspaper or two to keep the town alive." Newspapers with their unbridled boosterism were the main sources of promotion and information to attract settlers and capital. A town without such a voice was doomed.

More than 90 percent of all newspapers ever published in Colorado are defunct. The average life span was less than a year and the majority disappeared without a trace, leaving not even a single copy at the Colorado Historical Society Library, repository for all Colorado newspapers. Some notable newspapers have survived, however, including the first one, the *Rocky Mountain News*. Notable surviving journals include the following:

Rocky Mountain News. Founded April 23, 1859. Originally a weekly, it became a daily and has been first or second in circulation among Colorado newspapers, depending on its seesaw battle with its rival, *The Denver Post*. In 2001 the *News* and *Post* inaugurated a joint operating agreement under which they issue joint Saturday and Sunday editions while continuing separate competitive newspapers Monday through Friday.

The Denver Post. Founded 1894. This daily became the most sensational and successful of all Rocky Mountain newspapers. The *Post* agreed to the joint operating agreement with  the *News* that took effect in 2001 in a deal designed to share revenues and keep both papers profitable.

Colorado Springs Gazette Telegraph. Founded Jan. 3, 1873. The merger of the *Colorado Springs Gazette* and the younger *Colorado Springs Telegraph* gave Colorado Springs a single, strong newspaper.

Pueblo Chieftain. Founded June 1, 1868. Dr. Michael Breshoar, a pioneer physician and community leader, founded this weekly, which became a daily in 1872. The *Chieftain* has been the leading newspaper voice for southern Colorado and the Arkansas River Valley.

Grand Junction Daily Sentinel. Founded 1893. It followed the *Grand Junction News*, founded in 1882.

Durango Herald. Founded 1881. Begun as a weekly, it has been a daily since 1892. The *Herald* bought out Durango's pioneer paper, *The Record*, founded in 1880.

Greeley Tribune. Founded Nov. 16, 1870. Town founder Horace Greeley of the *New York Tribune* sent his agricultural editor Nathan Meeker west to set up this agricultural colony and its weekly, which later became a daily.

Golden Transcript. Founded November 1866. Started by Golden pioneer George West, who seven years earlier had founded Golden's first newspaper, the short-lived *Western Mountaineer.*

Fort Collins Coloradoan. Founded 1977. The *Coloradoan* traces its lineage to the *Larimer County Express* (founded 1873).

Saguache Crescent. Founded Oct. 10, 1874, as the *Saguache Chronicle*, this small-town weekly is still printed on a handset press.

Other long-established daily newspapers include the *Boulder Camera, Breckenridge–Dillon Summit News, Craig Press, Fort Morgan Times, Glenwood Springs Post, La Junta Tribune–Democrat, Lamar News, Longmont Times–Call, Loveland Reporter–Herald, Montrose Press, Salida Mail* and *Vail Daily.*

Non-daily newspapers in Colorado include the *Aspen Times, Aurora Sentinel, Bailey Park County Republican, Bayfield Pine River Times, Broomfield Enterprise, Carbondale Valley Journal, Castle Rock Douglas County News Press, Colorado Springs Independent, Cortez Journal, Crested Butte Chronicle & Pilot, Delta County Independent, Eads Kiowa County Press, Estes Park Trail–Gazette, Evergreen Canyon Courier* and *Fairplay Flume.*

Among other non-dailies are the *Gunnison Country Times, Haxtun–Fleming Herald, Idaho Springs Clear Creek Courant, Lakewood Jefferson Sentinel, Leadville Herald Democrat, Littleton Columbine Community Courier, Monument Tribune, Nederland Mountain–Ear, Pagosa Springs Sun, Rifle Citizen Telegram, Snowmass Village Sun, Steamboat Springs Pilot, Telluride Planet, Vail Valley Times* and *Windsor Beacon*

Alternative and specialty newspapers include the *Boulder Planet,* (Central City) *Little Kingdom Come,* (Denver) *Westword, Eagle Valley Enterprise, Ridgway Horseshoe, Denver Catholic Register,* (Denver) *Intermountain Jewish News* and (Paonia) *High Country News.* The B*loomsbury Review,* a bimontly published since 1981 in Denver, is Colorado's oldest, largest and only surviving literary and book review periodical.

Nudist Resorts

Colorado boasts one major haven for nudists, Mountain Air Ranch, which was voted North America's friendliest naturist resort in 1998 by the American Association for Nude Recreation. Mountain Air Ranch is in Jefferson County near Indian Hills in a forested foothills retreat on upper Deer Creek.

Founded in 1935 as the Colorado Sunshine Club, Mountain Air is a 160-acre ranch whose founders, John and Alice Garrison, were once jailed for their nudist ways. Their primitive campground has evolved into a club of almost 500 members, with a large clubhouse, pool, the Lost Bikini Grill, paddle tennis courts, 10 miles of hiking trails, cottages and mobile home sites. Mountain Air is at 8796 S. Mica Mine Road, Indian Hills 80454; (303) 697-4083.

When 100,000 fortune-seekers swarmed into Colorado with the gold rush, the Arapaho held a counsel fire to discuss moving to the East. They reckoned it must be empty after the mass migration of palefaces to the West.

Other Colorado naturist organizations include:

- Rocky Mountain Bares, Arvada; (303) 420-4565
- Desert Reef Beach Club, P.O. Box 503, Penrose 81240; (719) 784-6134
- The Well, 1 Malibu Blvd., Penrose 81240; (800) 898-9355
- Cottonwood Hot Springs, 18999 Highway 305, Buena Vista 81211; (719) 395-6434
- Orvis Hot Springs, 1585 County Road 3, Ridgway 81432 (303) 5324
- Strawberry Park Hot Springs, P.O. Box 77332, Steamboat Springs 80477; (303) 879-0342

Oil and Natural Gas

(*See also* Mining) Colorado, the second state to produce oil commercially, has been among the top 10 producers nationally. Commercial use began when Alexander M. Cassidy developed an "oil spring" in 1862 near Florence, west of Pueblo, just three years after the first U.S. oil well was dug at Titusville, Pa.

To exploit the Florence Field, Cassidy formed a firm that evolved into Continental Oil Co., or Conoco, which was headquartered in Denver until the 1930s. Big oil corporations converged on Colorado after the 1901 discovery of rich fields near Boulder and Rangely. By the 1920s oil wells had become more profitable than gold and silver mining combined.

Discovery and development accelerated during the 1920s after openings of the Wellington Field near Fort Collins and the Moffat Field south of Craig. In 1925 annual Colorado crude-oil production exceeded 1 million barrels for the first time. Production soared after World War II, climbing from 1.7 million barrels in 1940 to a record 58 million barrels in 1956.

Another boom in oil drilling, production and refining came after the 1973 Arab oil embargo pushed gasoline prices over a dollar a gallon. The 1970s' spurt in domestic oil drilling and production pumped up many subsidiary businesses ranging from law firms and geology consultants to wildcat drillers like Marvin Davis and Philip Anschutz, who became Colorado's first home-grown billionaires. Denver began to dream of eclipsing Houston as America's oil hub. Oil refineries thrived in Commerce City, a Denver suburb, and in Florence. Big oil firms either were headquartered in Denver or maintained offices there, fueling an eruption of high-rise office towers downtown.

Colorado's Most Productive Oil Fields

Oil Field	Total Production (barrels)
Rangely, Rio Blanco County	824 million
Wilison Creek, Rio Blanco County	85 million
Adena, Morgan County	65 million
Spindle, Weld County	55 million
Iles, Moffat County	19 million

Colorado's Most Productive Natural Gas Fields

Gas Field	Total Production (cubic feet)
Ignacio Basin, La Plata County	2.1 trillion
Wattenberg, Weld County	1.4 trillion
Powder Wash, Moffat County	251.5 billion
Piceance Creek, Rio Blanco County	238.3 billion
Dragon Trail, Rio Blanco County	237.6 billion

Colorado Oil and Natural Gas Production

Year	Oil (barrels)	Natural Gas (cubic feet)
1960	47.5 million	130 billion
1970	24.7 million	113 billion
1980	29.8 million	188 billion
1990	30.8 million	267 billion
1996	25.6 million	583 billion
1999	29.9 million	701 billion

Source: Colorado Department of Natural Resources

During the 1970s, Exxon and several partners began a $5 billion program to extract oil from western Colorado shale. The state supposedly contains enough oil embedded in shale to satisfy all of America's energy needs.

Boom turned to bust on Black Sunday, May 2, 1982, when Exxon abruptly abandoned the project. Exxon's exit exacerbated a statewide recession as crude-oil prices dropped from $42 per barrel in 1979 to $9 in 1983 after Middle Eastern oil exporters flooded the world market.

Oil's sister resource, natural gas, usually lies trapped in rock formations above oil deposits. Natural gas had replaced coal for heating Colorado homes and businesses by the mid-20th century. By the 1990s, gas pipelines reached most parts of Colorado.

Despite ups and downs since the original oil boom, it seems safe to say that as long as America remains addicted to gasoline-powered engines and natural-gas energy, oil and natural gas will remain Colorado's most lucrative natural resources. In 1999, Colorado oil production was worth $326 million and natural gas totaled $1.5 billion.

Opera Houses
Gilded-age Colorado cities aspired to affluence and culture, as epitomized by an opera house.

The Central City Opera House, built in 1878, was restored in 1932. Central City Opera House Association.

Even small towns often boasted an opera house, although formal opera may have rarely or never been presented there. Opera houses routinely became movie theaters and meeting places for everything from boxing matches to high school graduations.

Central City opened its opera house with a dynamite blast in 1878. Robert S. Roeschlaub, Colorado's first licensed architect, designed the handsome stone edifice. Restored and reopened on July 16, 1932, with Lillian Gish in *Camille,* it has staged summer opera ever since. In 1956, Central City offered the world premier of the great American opera *The Ballad of Baby Doe.*

Rise and Fall of the Tabor Grand

The Tabor Grand Opera House in Denver opened Sept. 15, 1881. On opening night, Horace Tabor and his mistress, Baby Doe, kept curtains drawn in their private box, too absorbed in each other to appreciate Colorado's most fabulous architectural gem. From its marble floors to its slate roof, Tabor spared no expense on this domed hall for 1,500 guests. A huge chandelier suspended 65 feet above the parquet floor shimmered with the light of 144 gas jets.

The curtain was inscribed with a stanza from a Charles Kingsley poem: "So fleet the works of man, Back to the earth again, Ancient and Holy things Fade Like a Dream." The Tabor Grand faded slowly before falling to the wrecking ball in 1964. The Denver branch of the Federal Reserve Bank now occupies the site at 16th and Curtis Streets. ✻

Inspired by Central City, Aspen has restored its Wheeler Opera House for summer performances. The Tabor Opera House in Leadville is open for tours and occasional productions. Telluride's opera house is used as a movie theater.

It's been a mixed fate for other old opera houses. Ouray's elegant Wright Opera House has been converted to a jeep rental. Golden's Opera House is now the Ace High Bar, noted for cheap beer and rowdy behavior. Colorado City's Waycott Opera House is now a bar and restaurant. Longmont's Dickens Opera House has a tavern downstairs, but there's still an opera hall upstairs. The Butte Opera House in Cripple Creek is now the fire station. The Fort Collins Opera House has been renovated and enlarged to become a retail and office complex.

Cañon City, Colorado City, Gunnison, Mancos, Montrose, Trinidad and other towns have opera halls used for various functions, but not for opera. Denver demolished the most elegant of all Colorado opera houses, the Tabor Grand. Denverites now watch traveling musicals and regular performances of the Colorado Opera in the Buell Theater of the Denver Center for Performing Arts.

Ouray, Chief (SEE ALSO

NATIVE AMERICANS) Son of a Jicarilla Apache father and a Tabeguache Ute mother, Ouray was born in 1833 in Abiquiú, N.M. He spoke various Indian languages, Spanish and English. Ouray became renowned not as a brave warrior but as a realistic peacekeeper, who once said, "The agreement an Indian makes to a United States treaty is like a buffalo makes with his hunter when he is pierced with arrows. All he can do is lie down and give in."

Chief Ouray served as interpreter and a signer of the 1868 treaty, the "Kit Carson treaty," by which the Utes surrendered central Colorado, and of the Brunot

Agreement of 1873, whereby the Utes turned over the gold- and silver-rich San Juan Mountains to whites.

After White River Utes slaughtered Indian agent Nathan Meeker and others in 1880, Ouray skillfully softened white retribution. Some Utes were removed to Utah, but Ouray—although deathly ill—helped negotiate establishment of the Southern Ute and Ute Mountain Ute reservations in southwestern Colorado.

Ever a diplomat, Ouray joined both Catholic and Protestant churches. In death, he received traditional Ute, Catholic and Presbyterian services, and his body lies straddling the Catholic and Protestant sections of the cemetery in Ignacio on the Southern Ute reservation.

Following his death in 1880, his wife Chipeta lived another 40 years in a tipi in Utah on Bitter Creek, where she returned to Ute ways. She is buried just south of Montrose, Colo., on the old farm where she

Chief Ouray, of the Ute Indian tribe. Colorado Historical Society.

and Ouray once lived, now the site of Ute Memorial Park and the Ute Museum.

Outdoor Recreation

Outdoor recreation brings many tourists and new residents to Colorado. Thanks to a dry, sunny climate and winters that can be surprisingly mild, many forms of recreation are possible year-round—even golf in January and skiing in June.

While skiing and snowboarding are best known and most popular, mountain biking, river rafting and climbed have soared in popularity since 1990. Traditional outdoor activities—bicycling, hiking, aerobics, fishing, golf, hunting, tennis, snowshoeing, running and yoga—remain popular.

See the following separate entries: Fish and Fishing; Golf; National Forests; National Parks; Skiing and Snowboarding; State Parks; Trails; Waterfalls; Water Sports.

Passes *(SEE ALSO HIGHWAYS)*

Colorado's Rocky Mountain barrier left explorers and travelers preoccupied with finding passes—the lowest and easiest places to cross high country dividing two watersheds. Native Americans first found many of these gateways, a fact commemorated by names such as Arapahoe Pass and Ute Pass.

Early Spanish explorers such as Juan de Ulibarri probed Colorado for passages through the southern Rockies. Zebulon Pike in 1806 became the first U.S. citizen of record to cross a Colorado pass when he entered South Park, possibly via Kenosha Pass. The next major U.S. explorer to traverse Colorado divides was John C.

Looking Back

1862

Oil bubbling to the surface led Alexander Cassidy to develop an oil well in Florence, Colo., along the Arkansas River. It was only the second oil well to be developed on U.S. territory.

Frémont, who publicized numerous mountain crossings. He is remembered with Fremont Pass near Leadville.

The Denver, South Park, & Pacific became the first railroad to tunnel under the Continental Divide, via the 1881 Alpine Tunnel near Williams Pass, some 30 miles east of Gunnison.

The Denver & Salt Lake (Moffat Road) first built over Rollins Pass before finally burrowing under it through the Moffat Tunnel, between Tolland and Winter Park. This tunnel is still used as the major rail route through the Rockies. The Colorado Midland first traveled over and then dug two tunnels under what is today Hagerman Pass, 15 miles west of Leadville.

Colorado history flowed over such historic divides as Raton Pass, which straddles the New Mexico border. This "Pass of the Rat" served as Colorado's southern gateway on the Mountain Branch of the Santa Fe Trail, the first Goodnight–Loving Cattle Trail, the Santa Fe and Amtrak passenger railroads and Interstate 25.

Since its 1973 opening, the most important "pass" through Colorado is not a pass at all. It is the Eisenhower–Johnson Tunnel beneath the Continental Divide on Interstate 70 west of Denver, which allows most traffic to avoid the much longer route, steeper grades, and tighter curves of the Loveland Pass road.

Colorado has at least 500 passes, ranging from railroad routes to four-lane highways to faint hiking trails. Some have no name, and others have two or more. Multiple strands of a route passing over a high divide may all bear the same name or separate names. At least a hundred passes remain unnamed.

Many highway passes are closed in winter, unless you travel on snowshoes, skis or a snowmobile. Any pass may be closed at any time by natural or unnatural happenings. These include avalanches, flash floods, mud slides, rockslides, snowstorms, traffic accidents or the apprehensions of the Colorado Highway Patrol.

Elevation and weather determine when mountain passes are open to motor vehicles. Imogene Pass in the San Juans, at 13,365 feet, is sometimes blocked by snow all year. On the other hand, 6,100-foot Gypsum Gap in the canyon country between Dove Creek and Naturita is so gentle that few notice that it really is a pass.

To learn more: Colorado Department of Transportation, road information; (303) 639-1111; www.dot.state.co.us/public/public.htm.

Principal Highway Passes

Pass	Elevation	Highway
Berthoud Pass	11,315	U.S. 40
Cameron Pass	10,276	CO 14
Cucharas Pass	9,941	CO 12
Cumbres Pass	10,022	CO 17
Dallas Divide	8,970	CO 62
Douglas Pass	8,268	CO 139
Fremont Pass	11,318	CO 91
Gore Pass	9,527	CO 134
Hoosier Pass	11,541	CO 9
Independence Pass	12,095	CO 82
Kenosha Pass	10,001	U.S. 285
La Manga Pass	10,230	CO 17
Lizard Head Pass	10,222	CO 145
Loveland Pass	11,992	U.S. 6
McClure Pass	8,755	CO 133
Milner Pass	10,758	U.S. 34
Molas Pass	10,910	U.S. 550
Monarch Pass	11,312	U.S. 50
Muddy Pass	8,772	U.S. 40
North La Veta Pass	9,413	U.S. 160
North Pass	10,149	CO 114
Poncha Pass	9,010	U.S. 285
Rabbit Ears Pass	9,426	U.S. 40
Red Hill Pass	9,993	U.S. 285
Red Mountain Pass	11,018	U.S. 550
Slumgullion Pass	11,361	CO 149
Spring Creek Pass	10,901	CO 149
Squaw Pass	9,807	CO 103
Tennessee Pass	10,424	U.S. 24
Trail Ridge High Point	12,183	U.S. 34
Trout Creek Pass	9,346	U.S. 24/285
Ute Pass	9,165	U.S. 24
Vail Pass	10,666	I-70
Wilkerson Pass	9,507	U.S. 24
Willow Creek Pass	9,621	CO 125

Peña, Federico

Born in Laredo, Texas, in 1947, Peña arrived in Denver in 1973 as a young attorney, wearing his long hair in a ponytail. He worked for the Mexican American Legal Defense Fund, then moved to a private law practice. In 1979 Peña successfully ran for the Colorado House of Representatives, where he became minority (Democratic) leader during his second term. His ponytail disappeared, and he set about becoming mayor of Denver.

"Imagine a Great City" was Peña's campaign slogan. Critics called the short, wiry Mexican American "Feddy" and his allies "the Dreamers." Despite the criticism and jokes, Feddy and the Dreamers made many of their dreams come true.

Federico Peña, former Denver mayor who went on to national prominence. Denver Mayor's Office.

Peña built a power base among white liberals, minorities and labor. He was the first mayor to solicit support from groups such as gays and historic preservationists, who both found in Peña their first city hall champion. These diverse backers, combined with newfound allies in the business and booster community, enabled Peña to do more that just imagine a great city.

During two terms as mayor, from 1983 to 1991, Peña persuaded Denverites to invest billions in their city, even though the city was then in the worst recession since the 1930s. In 1989, voters approved a $4 billion airport and a $242 million bond issue to rebuild streets, provide infrastructure for redevelopment of the South Platte Valley, improve parks, plant 30,000 trees, expand the National Western Stock Show Grounds, update Denver General Hospital and restore Civic Center Park and the City and County Building.

In 1990, Denver completed the $126 million Colorado Convention Center, with almost a million square feet on a 25-acre site between Cherry Creek and the central business district. That same year, the electorate approved a $200 million bond issue for the Denver Public Schools. Another $95 million bond issue won overwhelming support to enlarge the central library and support branch libraries. Voters narrowly approved a 0.1 per cent sales tax to build a new baseball stadium for the Colorado Rockies.

Peña declined to run for a third term in 1991. President Clinton selected him to serve as U.S. Secretary of Commerce, and then Secretary of Transportation. Peña resigned in 1998 and returned to Denver and the private sector.

Pikas
These small, rabbit-like rodents are common in all Colorado mountain areas above 9,000 feet, especially around rock slides. The pika (*Ochotona princeps*) is also known as a cony, chief

Pika. From *The Great Rocky Mountain Nature Factbook*; illustration by Marjorie C. Leggitt.

hare, calling hare, rock rabbit and rock farmer. The animal has short, rounded ears, small eyes, grayish brown fur and no visible tail.

During the short alpine summers, pikas cut leaves, stems and grasses to store under rocks as winter hay. They are often identified by their squeaky, distinctive *yank-yank* calls. They breed from late March through August and may produce more than one litter per season with an average litter of three young.

Harold M. Dunning, who made a lifelong study of pikas in Rocky Mountain National Park, describes the pika in *Over Hill and Vale*, Vol. 1, as a "small squeaky voice [and] a tiny bunch of fur skipping along the rocks. . . . The cony is always in a hurry. He never seems to go on a walk, but always on a run. Perhaps he is afraid winter will set in and he won't have any hay for his family."

Pikas do not hibernate but stay active all winter. Colorado is the state where they are most common, although they also appear elsewhere around the world and even in the Bible: "The high hills are a refuge for the wild goats; and the rocks for the conies."

Pikes Peak
Pikes Peak stands as a solitary sentinel overlooking the eastern plains, the easternmost North American peak over 14,000 feet. Native Americans probably climbed the majestic 14,100-foot-

high landmark, and perhaps the Spanish, who called it El Capitan.

The first recorded ascent was in 1820 by Dr. Edwin James, the Long Expedition botanist and physician. Major Long named the peak for James, noting that Zebulon Pike, who provided the first detailed report, had failed to reach the summit in 1806. In 1843, however, John C. Frémont used the name Pikes Peak on one of his maps and the designation stuck.

As Colorado's best-known landmark, Pikes Peak gave its name to the gold regions and to the territory itself before Colorado became the official name in 1861. Katharine Lee Bates, an English teacher, rode to the top, where she drew inspiration to write the words for "America, the Beautiful," celebrating "purple mountain's majesty above the fruited plain."

Although Zeb Pike estimated its height at 18,581 feet and pronounced the peak unclimbable, millions of people have been to the top via the Manitou & Pikes Peak Cog Railway (1891) and auto road (1915), which now whisk some 500,000 people to the top every year. The Pikes Peak Hill Climb, America's highest automobile race, has been held every July 4 since 1916.

To learn more: Weather permitting, the cog railway and auto road to the top of the mountain just west of Colorado Springs are open late April through early November. A Summit House with refreshments and curios crowns the top of the peak, which offers spectacular views.

Place Names

Many peoples contributed to the place names of Colorado. Colorado's Plains Indians are recognized in Arapaho, Cheyenne and Kiowa counties, Arapaho National Forest and Comanche National Grasslands. Ute Indian names, with their tricky pronunciations, appear on maps: Uncompahgre (un-kum-PAHG-ray)

Plateau, the town of Ouray (U-ray), Weminuche (women-OOCH) Wilderness Area, Cochetopa (kohch-i-TOH-puh) Pass, and the towns of Saguache (suh-WATCH) and Towaoc (TOH-way-ahk).

Early French trappers and traders christened parts of the landscape. Among the few surviving French names are the Platte (flat, shallow) River and Cache la Poudre (hidden gunpowder) River. Colorado, the Spanish word for red or colorful, first went to the river, then to the state where the river rises.

U.S. explorers Pike, Long, Gunnison, Frémont, Hayden and Wheeler prepared

On clear mornings atop Pikes Peak, you can see three days ahead.

reports and maps that provided official names. Frémont's hungry expedition first gave the name Pound Cake to a rock formation in Douglas County, but it was later assigned the common and less tasty title of Castle Rock.

The first U.S. citizens to prowl Colorado were often prospectors who frequently named mines and mountains for the women they left behind. The Sawatch Range mountains, once bearing names such as Mount Fannie, Mount Daisy Mae and Mount Lulu, were renamed Harvard, Yale, Princeton and Columbia in 1896. Despite popular use of the name Collegiate Range for that series of mountains in central Colorado, they are officially the Sawatch Range.

Town founders often honored themselves or those they hoped to flatter. William H. Larimer named Denver City for the Kansas Territorial governor, James Denver, hoping he would make his namesake the county seat of what was then Arapahoe County, Kansas Territory. Railroad builders founded and labeled many towns. Colorado's first railroad, the Denver Pacific, named towns along the track for its officers: Evans, Carr, Pierce and Hughes. The Denver & Rio Grande founded and named Alamosa, Antonito, Colorado Springs, Durango and dozens of other trackside towns.

Local postmasters or postmistresses submitted town names to the U.S. Post Office in Washington, which sometimes rejected difficult or overused names. Many tiny, but ambitious towns originally attached the word city to their names: Boulder City, Denver City, Golden City. After they grew into sizable places, they usually felt secure enough to drop the "City."

Naming goes on. The U.S. Board on Geographic Names recently christened Mount Machebeuf in the Sawatch Range for the pioneer Catholic missionary and bishop. Mount Arps, also in the Sawatch Range, now honors the historian, mountaineer and naturalist Louisa Ward Arps. The huge stone erection near Boulder originally named for another part of Satan's anatomy is now Devil's Thumb.

Dr. Colorado's List of Memorable Town Names

Badito. Once the seat of Huerfano County, Badito is now a ghost. The name may be a corruption of the Spanish *vadito* (Little Ford), as the town straddles a crossing of the Huerfano River.

Barnum. Phineas T. Barnum of circus fame stabled his animals here and invested in what is now the Barnum neighborhood of southwest Denver. Barnum claimed that the salubrious atmosphere would bring people back from the edge of the grave and assure long, healthy lives.

Climax. This name has stuck to the former town and now abandoned molybdenum mine atop Fremont Pass, in Lake County. The Denver, South Park & Pacific Railroad, which struggled mightily to get to the top in 1884, so named its station there.

Dotsero. A Ute princess, according to some accounts, inspired the name of this town where the Colorado and Eagle rivers join, in Eagle County. A surveyor for the Denver & Rio Grande Railroad, which built through here, claimed the name came from the use of the location as "dot zero," the starting point on a railroad survey.

Great Divide. Volney Hoggatt, editor of the *Great Divide*, a literary journal, established this Moffat County ranching town in 1917. It is now a ghost town, and the term "crossing the Great Divide" is Colorado slang for dying.

Happyville. Founded by optimistic settlers in 1910, this Yuma County town soon experienced an unhappy row between the general storekeeper and other residents. Store owner

Cleve Mason subsequently moved his buildings two miles east to what he called Headstrong. Without the general store, Happyville became a ghost town by 1922.

Hardscrabble. At the junction of Hardscrabble Creek and the Arkansas River in southcentral Colorado, this tiny agricultural and trading town existed briefly during the mid-1840s. The rocky, hard soil made it difficult for the Indians, French, Mexicans and Americans who settled here. "It was rather hard scrabbling," as pioneer trader George Simpson put it, "to get in a crop."

Hygiene. This farm colony on St. Vrain Creek in Boulder County was founded by Dunkards, as Church of the Brethren members were called for their baptismal practice of immersing a person three times. The Dunkards founded the Hygiene Home, a sanitarium that gave its name to the community founded in the 1880s. It is still a clean, healthy community.

No Name. This I-70 interchange just east of Glenwood Springs is named for No Name Creek, which flows into the Colorado River there. The town founded there in 1880 supposedly returned a state questionnaire with "No Name" written in the blank reserved for the town name.

Tiny Town. George E. Turner, owner of a Denver moving and storage company, started building miniature buildings and railroads in 1919 for his children. The extensive layout of several dozen buildings subsequently became a tourist attraction. Restored in the 1990s, this Lilliputian community 15 miles southwest of Denver via U.S. 285 continues to attract life-size people.

Plants and Trees (SEE ALSO ASPEN TREES; BOTANICAL GARDENS; COLUMBINE; SPRUCE; TIMBERLINE)

Sparse moisture, temperature extremes and high winds limit plant life in Colorado. Human activities, notably stock grazing, farming, mining and town building, have further modified native plants and facilitated an invasion of nonnative species. The big picture, however, remains unchanged: Grasslands prevail on the eastern plains, woodlands in the central mountains, and brushlands on the western plateaus.

Grasslands of eastern Colorado are dominated by grasses such as buffalo grass and blue grama. Other common plants are the prickly pear, sage and wheatgrass. Those species have deep, probing roots that dig in to survive drought and high winds.

Sunflowers, yucca, snow-on-the-mountain, prairie evening primrose and other prairie flowers give the plains a subtle, underappreciated beauty. Cottonwoods are among the few trees native to the plains, along with the box elder, hackberry and willow.

Colorado wildflowers include many colorful varieties of paintbrush. Photo by Susan Dupere.

Trees are more abundant in the foothills, especially ponderosa pine, piñon pine, juniper and scrub oak. At higher elevations lie Douglas fir, blue spruce and lodgepole pine.

Between about 8,000 feet and timberline (10,500–11,500 feet), quaking aspen are common. Englemann spruce, limber pine and alpine fir predominate at the highest elevations, where stunted, wind-sculpted trees finally give way at timberline to alpine tundra. There, on that treeless terrain, wildflowers bloom gloriously during the short summer season.

Brushlands predominate in the driest parts of the state, especially on the Western Slope. Sagebrush grows best above 4,000 feet, and its mountain and plains varieties cover much of western Colorado. These brushlands, sometimes called a cold desert or a shrub steppe, also feature other woody shrubs such as rabbitbrush and saltbush. Mountain brushlands harbor wild cherry and mountain mahogany.

Population Colorado, with a

2000 population of 4.3 million, was the third-fastest-growing state during the 1990s (after Nevada and Arizona). Five Colorado counties—Archuleta, Custer, Douglas, Elbert and Park—were among the fastest-growing U.S. counties. The U.S. Census estimates that Colorado is heading toward a population of 4.9 million by 2020.

Immigration accounted for roughly 60 percent of the 1990s growth rate, while the excess of births over deaths accounted for the other 40 percent. Of the people moving to Colorado during the 1990s, Californians were the most numerous at roughly 150,000, followed by some 25,000 Texans, 20,000 New Yorkers and 19,000 from Illinois.

Ethnically, Colorado in 2000 was 76.7 percent white, 17.1 percent Hispanic, 3.8 percent African American, 2.3 percent Asian and Pacific Islander and 1 percent

Native American. Coloradans are among the best-educated state populations, ranking fourth in the percentage of college graduates and eighth in the percentage of high school graduates.

Year	Population	Economic Factors
1860	34,277	Gold Rush of 1858–1859
1870	39,629	Civil War, Indian Wars, mining bust
1880	194,327	Railroads arrive, smelters built
1890	413,249	Silver boom, building boom
1900	539,700	Depression of 1893, silver crash
1910	799,024	Cripple Creek gold, agricultural boom
1920	939,629	Agricultural boom
1930	1,035,791	Agricultural bust
1940	1,123,296	Agricultural bust, Depression
1950	1,325,089	World War II
1960	1,753,947	Postwar boom
1970	2,207,259	Oil boom
1980	2,888,834	Oil boom
1990	3,294,394	Oil bust
2000	4,301,261	Real estate, telecommunications, high-tech booms

Sources: U.S. Census and Colorado State Demographer

For a closer look at the mosaic of groups that has helped create modern Colorado, see the following entries in this book: African Americans; Anglo Americans; Archaeology; Asian Americans;

Franco Americans; Gays and Lesbians; German Americans; Hispanics; Irish Americans; Italian Americans; Native Americans; Scotish Americans; Women.

Through boom and bust over the past century and a half, Colorado's population has risen, sometimes slowly, sometimes in great leaps.

Prairie Chickens The

greater prairie chicken (*Tympanuchus cupido pinnatus*) and lesser prairie chicken (*Tympanuchus pallidicinctus*) conduct perhaps the most dramatic courtship of any Colorado species, outperforming even Homo sapiens.

To attract hens, the males began strutting about, stamping their feet and shaking their heads to inflate orange (in the greater prairie chicken) or red (in the lesser) air sacs the size of golf balls on the sides of the neck. Their blackish neck feathers become erect. The whole ritual is accompanied by a haunting low *oo-loo-woo* call, similar to the sound made by blowing across the opening of a bottle.

Chickens gather on ancestral strutting grounds for this ritual from February through May. After reaching full display, sometimes the cocks face off and jump straight up two to six feet. Only rarely do they strike at each other. Hens walk by nonchalantly, sometimes ignoring the frantic males and taking their time selecting a mate.

Hens nest on the ground in sheltered grass or vegetation. They usually produce 10 light olive-colored eggs with brown dots and incubate and raise the chicks without any help from the males.

The greater prairie chicken is a brown, henlike grouse 17 to 19 inches long. It has mottled plumage, long ornamental neck feathers and a tail tip of rounded black feathers. Formerly common, the greater chickens were almost wiped out by market hunters. They are now rare, with the majority of Colorado birds confined to Yuma County.

The lesser prairie chicken is slightly smaller, ranging from 16 to 18 inches in length, with the distinctive brown and white barred plumage. Once widely distributed throughout southeastern Colorado, they are now mostly confined to Baca County. The plowing up of the prairie, and livestock grazing, has removed much of this bird's native environment.

To learn more: The Colorado Division of Wildlife sponsors trips to watch both chickens in courtship and discourages independent spectators who may endanger the exotic mating ritual of a rare species. Colorado Division of Wildlife, 6060 Broadway, Denver 80216; (303) 291-7366; www.dnr.state.co.us.

Prairie Dogs The black-

tailed prairie dog (*Cynomys ludovicianus*) with its distinctive black tail tip inhabits Colorado's eastern plains. The white-tailed prairie dog (*Cynomys leucurus*) of northwestern Colorado has a whitish-grayish fur and white tail tip. Gunnison's prairie dog (*Cynomys gunnisoni*) of central and southwestern Colorado is the smallest of the three Colorado species and has a yellowish buff fur and grayish tail.

These chubby, short-tailed, ground-dwelling squirrels occupy many areas of Colorado except mountains above 12,000 feet. Measuring 12 to 16 inches, including the tail, and weighing 2 to 3 pounds, they are named for their barking. The barks originate with sentinel dogs posted at every colony. These watchdogs bark a warning so all can dive into their burrows at the approach of predators—borrowing owls, black-footed ferrets, eagles, hawks, coyotes, foxes, badgers, wolves, snakes and, deadliest of all, humans.

Prairie dogs live in elaborate burrows grouped in towns, ranging from small villages of a handful of dogs to cities stretching for miles with thousands of inhabitants. The entrances to the borrows are funnel-shaped mounds that keep out water and serve as lookout posts.

Prairie dogs live primarily on vegetation and are destructive to grazing land and farm crops. This fact, plus the hazard their burrows create for horses and cattle, has led humans to exterminate them by the billions. An estimated 5 billion prairie dogs populated the Great Plains in 1800; today they number about 10 million. They have been shot, poisoned, drowned and dynamited. Prairie dogs moving into suburban areas to escape angry farmers and ranchers are now being exterminated by developers, who suck 'em up with huge, deadly vacuum cleaners.

The 1999 Colorado legislature made the furry little pups a primary target by declaring that they could not be spared by moving them to another county without the support of the commissioners in the relocation county. As neither developers nor county commissioners in possible relocation counties will abide the rodents, this law amounts to a death sentence. Governor Bill Owens quickly signed the bill into law with a joke about "burrowing into the prairie dog problem."

A fierce animal rights struggle now centers on prairie dogs. Save the Prairie

Black-tailed prairie dogs. Denver Museum of Nature and Science.

Dogs protesters, including a woman in a prairie dog suit, animated the opening of the 2001 Colorado General Assembly. Activists have begun placing white wooden crosses on the silent, dogless mounds of exterminated prairie dog colonies. Despite such protests, the state of Colorado has shown little interest in planning for prairie dog survival or controlling the growth of the subdivisions and shopping malls that have destroyed animal habitat and led to most of the prairie dog wars.

To learn more

Plains Conservation Center, 21901 E. Hampden Ave., Aurora; (303) 739-6660.

National Wildlife Federation, 2260 Baseline Road, Boulder 80302; (303) 786-8001.

Ptarmigan Above timberline

in Colorado, keep a sharp eye and ear out for the state's best-camouflaged bird. White-tailed ptarmigan *(Lagopus leucurus)* are a 12- to 13-inch-long arctic grouse whose mottled brown summer plumage turns pure white in winter. With their protective coloration, the birds are often heard before they are seen. Listen for their deep, raucous calls, *go-out, go-out* or *go-back, go-back.*

Ptarmigan frequent alpine slopes and tundra where few other birds survive. Three similar-looking species may be found above timberline in Colorado: the white-tailed ptarmigan, willow ptarmigan *(Lagopus lagopus)* and rock ptarmigan *(Lagopus mutus).*

Like chickens, these birds fly very little and spend their entire lives within a small area. In winter, flocks of ptarmigan huddle together under alpine willows and burrow into snow for insulation. Feathers on their feet serve as snowshoes, enabling ptarmigan to walk in Colorado's deepest, fluffiest snow.

Pueblo

Pueblo The Pueblo County seat originated as El Pueblo, an 1842 adobe trading post destroyed in 1854 by Ute Indians, who massacred nine inhabitants and took the rest prisoner. The modern town of Pueblo, platted in 1859, was a sleepy trading post at the confluence of Fountain Creek and the Arkansas River. It awakened in 1872 to the steam whistle of the Denver & Rio Grande Railroad. By the 1880s, the railroad and its subsidiary, the Colorado Fuel and Iron Co., transformed this little outpost into the Pittsburgh of the West. The giant CF&I steel mill on the south side of Pueblo has long produced the railroad track and barbed wire that characterize western landscapes.

The steel mill, smelters and other plants made Pueblo the state's industrial giant, with many ethnic, working-class neighborhoods. Italians initially clustered around the CF&I steel mill in Bessemer, while many Slavs worked at the Philadelphia Smelting and Refining Co. and lived nearby amid the cottonwoods lining the Arkansas River in the area known as the Grove. Later, Hispanics settled in Peppersauce Bottoms and along Salt Creek. Greeks, Irish, Japanese and others also staked out turf in the Steel City.

Pueblo aspired to replace Denver as the state capital and was Colorado's second-largest city from the 1880s until the 1960s. Although it slipped to eighth largest with its 2000 census count of 102,121, Pueblo is today capturing new industry, retirees and tourists. Notable modern attractions include the downtown Arkansas Riverwalk and parks and the Sangre de Cristo Arts and Conference Center.

Quilts

Quilts Quilts emerged historically as a symbol of western women, who treasured quilts containing pieces of clothing from mothers, grandmothers and ancestors. While pioneer men searched for riches, women sought to make homes. Uprooted from family and friends to live in a wild and often brutal land, women worked hard to bring comfort and beauty to their sod houses and log cabins.

With precious scraps of fabric they brought west with them, they made quilts. These were more than bed coverings. Intricately pieced and painstaking stitched, they became art. Women quilted their homes and dreams and politics into quilts, which they sometimes named with titles such as "Suffrage" or "Hardscrabble" or "Log Cabin" or "Rocky Road to Colorado."

To learn more: Rocky Mountain Quilt Museum, 1111 Washington Ave., Golden 80401; (303) 277-0377.

Radio Stations (SEE ALSO

TELEVISION STATIONS) Colorado's first radio station, KLZ, began broadcasting in Denver in 1922. Founder William Reynolds and his wife Naomi filled the air with the sound of music: she played the piano, he tooted the saxophone.

In 1924 the General Electric Co. started KOA with elaborate downtown Denver studios and twin 150-foot broadcast towers, along what is still called Tower Road in Aurora. Since those pioneering times, Colorado's radio broadcasting industry has grown tremendously, although ownership and formats often change.

Legacy of a Flood

The 1921 flood in the town of Pueblo killed an estimated 132 people and caused $20 million in damage. Afterward, the Arkansas River was rerouted through a concrete-lined canal. In the 1990s, Pueblo restored the abandoned riverbed and filled it with water as the centerpiece of an urban park and redevelopment area. ✻

The following table lists the location, call letters, AM or FM band, frequency and format of the state's radio stations. Although the number of stations in a listening area is relatively fixed, the formats of those stations can change quickly.

Radio Stations

City/Town	Letters	Dial	Freq.	Format
Alamosa	KRZA	FM	88.7	Public/NPR
	KASF	FM	90.9	College/ Alternative
	KALQ	FM	93.5	Country
Aspen	KAJX	FM	91.5	Public/Jazz/ Classical
	KSPN	FM	97.7	Adult Rock
	KSNO	FM	103.9	Adult Rock
	KFNO	FM	106.1	News/Talk
Aurora	KRKS	AM	990	Religious
	KRKS	FM	94.7	Religious
Avon	KYZR	FM	103.1	Modern Rock
	KSKE	FM	104.7/ 99.3	Country
Boulder	KVCU	AM	1190	College/ Variety
	KWAB	AM	1490	Progressive Talk
	KGNU	FM	88.5	Community
	KBCO	FM	97.3	Adult Alternative
Breckenridge	KSMT	FM	102.3/ 102.7	Modern Rock
Breen	KLLV	AM	550	Christian
Buena Vista	KBVC	FM	104.1	Country
Burlington	KNAB	AM	1140	Country
	KNAB	FM	104.1	Adult Contemporary
Cañon City	KRLN	AM	1400	Full Service
	KSTY	FM	104.5	Country
Carbondale	KDNK	FM	90.5	Public/NPR
Colorado Springs	KTWK	AM	740	Nostalgia
	KCBR	AM	1040	Christian
	KRDO	AM	1240	News/Sports
	KVOR	AM	1300	News/Talk
	KKCS	AM	1460	News/Talk
	KCMN	AM	1530	Nostalgia
	KWYD	AM	1580	Christian Talk
	KCME	FM	88.7	Public/Jazz/ Classical
	KEPC	FM	89.7	College/ Alternative
	KTLF	FM	90.5	Christian
	KRCC	FM	91.5	College/ NPR/AAA
	KSPZ	FM	92.9	Oldies
	KILO	FM	94.3	Rock
	KRDO	FM	95.1	Adult Contemporary
	KPRZ	FM	96.1	Christian
	KKFM	FM	98.1	Classic Rock
	KKMG	FM	98.9	Top 40
	KVUU	FM	99.9	Adult Contemporary
	KGFT	FM	100.7	Christian
	KKCS	FM	101.9	Country
	KBIQ	FM	102.7	Christian
	KYSX	FM	103.9	Classic Rock
	KSKX	FM	105.5	Smooth Jazz
	KKLI	FM	106.3	Adult Contemporary
Cortez	KVFC	AM	740	Oldies
	KISZ	FM	97.9	Country
	KRTZ	FM	98.7	Country
Craig	KRAI	AM	550	Country
	KRAI	FM	93.7	Top 40
Crested Butte	KBUT	FM	93.7	Public Radio
Delta	KDTA	FM	1400	Adult Contemporary
Denver	KLZ	AM	560	Christian
	KHOW	AM	630	Talk
	KLTT	AM	670	Christian
	KNUS	AM	710	News
	KTLK	AM	760	Talk
	KLDC	AM	800	Christian
	KOA	AM	850	News/ Sports/Talk
	KKFN	AM	950	Sports
	KCUV	AM	1150	Spanish
	KVOD	AM	1280	Classical
	KCFR	AM	1340	Public/NPR
	KJME	AM	1390	Spanish
	KEZW	AM	1430	Big Band

continued on next page

City/Town	Letters	Dial	Freq.	Format
	KEZZ	AM	1470	Nostalgia
	KYGO	AM	1600	Country
	KUVO	FM	89.3	Public/Jazz
	KVOD	FM	90.1	Classical
	KDJM	FM	92.5	R&B Oldies
	KTCL	FM	93.3	Alternative
	KHIH	FM	95.7	Jazz
	KXPK	FM	96.5	New Rock
	KYGO	FM	98.5	Country
	KKHK	FM	99.5	Classic Rock
	KIMN	FM	100.3	Adult Contemporary
	KOSI	FM	101.1	Adult Contemporary
	KRFX	FM	103.5	Rock
	KCKK	FM	104.3	Classic Country
	KXKL	FM	105.1	Oldies
	KALC	FM	105.9	Hot Adult Contemporary
	KBPI	FM	106.7	Active Rock
	KQKS	FM	107.5	Christian
	KDKO	FM	1510	Urban/Soul
Dillon	KRKY	AM	930	Country
	KHTH	AM	1130	Oldies
	KRKM	FM	106.3	Country
Durango	KIUP	AM	930	Standards
	KDDZ	AM	1240	Oldies
	KDUR	FM	91.9	Community
	KPTE	FM	99.7	Country
	KRSJ	FM	100.5	Country
	KIQX	FM	101.3	Adult Contemporary
Englewood	KADZ	AM	1550	Radio Disney
	KJMN	FM	92.1	Spanish
Estes Park	KRKI	FM	102.1	Adult Rock
Fort Collins	KIIX	AM	600	Nostalgia/ Sports
	KCOL	AM	1410	News/Talk
	KCSU	FM	90.5	Alternative
	KGLL	FM	96.1	Hot Country
	KPAW	FM	107.9	Classic Hits
Fort Morgan	KSIR	AM	1010	Talk
	KFTM	AM	1400	Country
	KBRU	FM	101.7	Oldies
	KPRB	FM	106.3	Adult Contemporary
Frisco	KYSL	FM	93.9	Adult Contemporary
Glenwood Springs	KGLN	AM	980	Oldies

City/Town	Letters	Dial	Freq.	Format
	KDRH	FM	91.9	Christian
	KKCH	FM	92.7	Adult Contemporary
	KMTS	FM	99.1	Country
Grand Junction	KRDY	AM	620	Radio Disney
	KRGS	AM	690	Oldies
	KNZZ	AM	1100	News/Talk
	KEXO	AM	1230	Spanish
	KQIL	AM	1340	Sports
	KCIC	FM	88.5	Christian
	KPRN	FM	89.5	Public/NPR
	KJOL	FM	90.3	Christian
	KMSA	FM	91.3	College/ Alternative
	KJYE	FM	92.3	Soft Adult Contemporary
	KMGJ	FM	93.1	Bright Adult Contemporary
	KKNN	FM	95.1	Rock
	KSTR	FM	96.1	Classic Rock
	KEKB	FM	99.9	Country
	KSNJ	FM	100.7	Nostalgia
	KMXY	FM	104.3	Hot Adult Contemporary
	KBKL	FM	107.9	Oldies
Greeley	KFKA	AM	1310	News/Talk
	KGRE	AM	1450	Hispanic
	KUNC	FM	91.5	Public/NPR/PRI
	KSIR	FM	107.1	Easy Listening
Gunnison	KPKE	AM	1490	Oldies
	KWSB	FM	91.1	College/Variety
	KEJJ	FM	98.9	Hot Adult Contemporary
	KVLE	FM	102.3	Classic Rock
Ignacio	KSUT	FM	91.3	Public/NPR
Johnstown	KHNC	AM	1360	Talk
La Junta	KBZZ	AM	1400	Adult Contemporary
	KBJL	FM	92.1	Country
Lamar	KLMR	AM	920	Country
	KSEC	FM	93.3	Adult Contemporary
	KVAY	FM	105.7	Country

Radio Stations (continued)

City/Town	Letters	Dial	Freq.	Format
Longmont	KLMO	AM	1060	Country
	KCDC	FM	90.7	Educational
Loveland	KHPN	AM	1570	Classic Country
Mancos	KSJD	FM	91.5	Public/NPR
Monte Vista	KSLV	AM	1340	Country
	KSLV	FM	95.3	Adult Contemporary
Montrose	KUBC	AM	580	Stardust
	KKXK	FM	94.1	Country
Morrison	KWBI	FM	91.1	Christian
Ouray	KWGL	FM	105.7	Adult Contemporary
Pagosa Springs	KWUF	AM	1400	Country
	KVNF	FM	90.9	Public/NPR/ Alternative
	KWUF	FM	106.3	Oldies
Pueblo	KCSJ	AM	590	Talk
	KRMX	AM	690	Hispanic
	KFEL	AM	970	Christian
	KGHF	AM	1340	MOR
	KTSC	FM	89.5	Top 40
	KCFP	FM	91.9	Public/NPR
	KCCY	FM	96.9	Country
	KYZX	FM	103.9	Classic Rock
	KNKN	FM	107.1	Hispanic
	KDZA	FM	107.9	Oldies
Rifle	KZKS	FM	105.3	Country
Salida	KVRH	AM	1340	Adult Contemporary
	KVRH	FM	92.3	Adult Contemporary
Steamboat Springs	KBCR	AM	1230	Oldies
	KIDN	FM	95.5	Alternative
	KBCR	FM	96.9	American Country
	KFMU	FM	104.1	AAA
Sterling	KSTC	AM	1230	Oldies
	KNNG	FM	104.7	Hot Country
	KPMX	FM	105.5	Adult Contemporary
Strasburg	KAGM	FM	102.3	Country
Telluride	KOTO	FM	91.7	Public/Variety
Trinidad	KCRT	AM	1240	Country
	KCRT	FM	92.7	Classic Rock
Vail	KTUN	FM	101.5	Classic Rock
Walsenburg	KSPK	FM	102.3	Country
Westminster	KPOF	AM	910	Christian

Radio Stations (continued)

City/Town	Letters	Dial	Freq.	Format
Windsor	KVVS	AM	1170	Spanish News
	KUAD	FM	99.1	Country
	KTRR	FM	102.5	Adult Contemporary
Wray	KRDZ	AM	1440	Oldies
Yuma	KATR	FM	98.3	Hot Country
	KNEC	FM	100.9	Music of Your Life

To learn more: Colorado Broadcasters Association; www.e-cba.org.

Railroads
Approximately 175 different railroads have laid track in Colorado. Many were small mining railroads or commuter trolleys. Numerous name changes, and the common practice of building branches and extensions under a different name than the parent rail firm, help explain the large number of railroads.

As a stagecoach territory, Colorado stagnated. Slow, expensive and uncomfortable stage travel discouraged

Railroads spurred growth of the Colorado Territory.

Colorado's rich railroad heritage is enshrined at the Colorado Railroad Museum in Golden. Photo by Tom Noel.

visitors and would-be settlers. Mining also suffered; only the highest-grade ores could be shipped east by wagon for profitable refining. Coloradans tried to coax railroads across the 700 miles of sparsely settled prairie separating them from the Missouri River frontier towns.

When the Union Pacific Railroad skirted Colorado's Rocky Mountain barrier and built the first transcontinental route through Wyoming to the north, Coloradans reacted by building their own railroad. John Evans (see entry), William Byers (see entry) and other entrepreneurs incorporated the Denver Pacific Railway to complete a line between Denver and the Union Pacific tracks at Cheyenne in 1870. Several months later the Kansas Pacific Railway was completed to Denver, connecting Colorado to Kansas City and St. Louis.

Saving the Georgetown Loop

The Georgetown Loop is the railroad that kept an interstate highway out of the Clear Creek Valley in Georgetown, some 60 miles west of Denver. To avoid ripping up the valley and its historic railroad sites, I-70 was blasted out of a mountainside. This protected the ruins of the narrow-gauge railroad, an engineering marvel that connected Georgetown to Silver Plume with hairpin turns and that looped over itself in order to reduce a 6 percent grade to 3.5 percent. At the Devil's Gate Loop, a 300-foot bridge spanned the track and Clear Creek, 95 feet below. In 1939 the loop was scrapped for $450. In 1984 the Colorado Historical Society rebuilt the loop for $2 million, and a train ride on the route now attracts passengers from all over the globe. (303-670-1686). ⚹

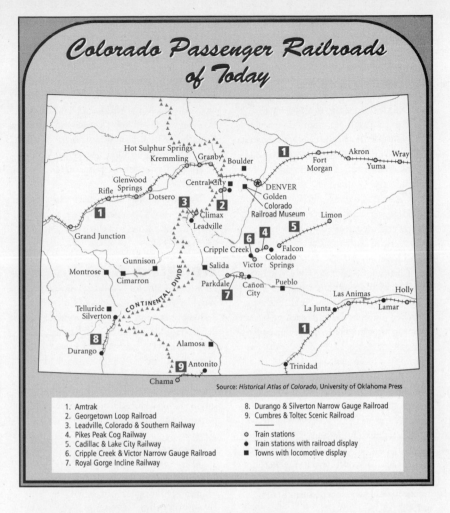

Colorado Passenger Railroads of Today

1. Amtrak
2. Georgetown Loop Railroad
3. Leadville, Colorado & Southern Railway
4. Pikes Peak Cog Railway
5. Cadillac & Lake City Railway
6. Cripple Creek & Victor Narrow Gauge Railroad
7. Royal Gorge Incline Railway
8. Durango & Silverton Narrow Gauge Railroad
9. Cumbres & Toltec Scenic Railroad

o Train stations
● Train stations with railroad display
■ Towns with locomotive display

Source: *Historical Atlas of Colorado*, University of Oklahoma Press

Railroads did more than enable existing towns to survive and prosper; they became the principal vehicle of town building. The Denver Pacific, for instance, sold the townsite for Greeley to the Union Colony promoted by Horace Greeley. Like many other rail towns, Greeley sprouted as an instant community whose pioneer buildings were carried to the town site on railroad flat cars.

Golden boasted a railroad incorporated during the 1860s, the Colorado Central. This railroad built a narrow-gauge line to Central City in the Gilpin County gold regions, then up to the early silver mining center of Georgetown. The Colorado Central, which was absorbed by the Union Pacific in 1880, also built standard-gauge branches to Denver and to Cheyenne.

In 1884 the Georgetown, Breckenridge, and Leadville Railroad completed its famous Georgetown Loop line to Silver Plume. Reconstructed in 1984, the Georgetown Loop is now a popular summer tourist line owned by the Colorado Historical Society.

The Denver & Rio Grande, biggest and best known of all Colorado railroads until the 1980s, originally used a narrow-gauge track 3 feet wide that could be built for about two-thirds the cost of standard 4-foot, 8½-inch gauge. Narrow-gauge trains could tackle tighter curves and steeper grades to reach remote mountain towns. The Denver & Rio Grande became the first railroad to cross Colorado and reach Utah, beating rivals through the Arkansas, Colorado and Gunnison river canyons.

In western Colorado, the D&RG promoted the tourist mecca of Glenwood Springs and helped establish the fruit-growing centers of Paonia, Delta and Grand Junction, as well as the coal towns of New Castle and Somerset. The D&RG was absorbed by the Southern Pacific in 1988 and then by the Union Pacific in 1997.

When automobiles and trucking became common after the 1920s, many railroads abandoned service. In the new century, as highway traffic comes to frequent standstills, some Coloradans are trying a return to rail service. The Regional Transportation District initiated Denver light rail service in 1994, opened its first suburban line to Littleton in 2000 and is planning more lines to southeastern suburbs and Denver International Airport. A light rail line to South Platte River Valley amusement centers is scheduled to open in 2002.

To learn more: Colorado Railroad Museum, 17155 W. 44th Ave., Golden 80402; (800) 365-6263; www.crrm.org.

Red Rocks Amphitheater

Colorado's most distinctive theater is a natural rock garden. Designed by Denver architect Burnham F. Hoyt, Red Rocks was completed in 1941 as a Civilian Conservation Corps project by the City of Denver. Wedged between massive red stone slabs on the northwest outskirts of Morrison, this Denver-owned outdoor theater is surrounded by 1,833-acre Denver Mountain Park.

The theater has an acoustically superb natural setting and uses native juniper trees as landscaping and native red sandstone for walls and roadways. Red Rocks has hosted many of the world's best known musicians, from the Beatles to symphony orchestras, from Judy Collins to Ray Charles, as well as an annual Easter sunrise religious celebration.

To learn more: The park and theater grounds are open and free all year. 16351 County Road 93, Morrison 80465; (303) 697-8935.

Religion

The state motto *Nil Sine Numine* is Latin for "Nothing without Providence," and a majority of Coloradans do believe in some form of providence or deity. The oldest churches in the state are the kivas used by prehistoric Indians at Mesa Verde and elsewhere to honor Mother Earth and Father Sun. Other Native Americans practiced their own religions, leaving behind sacred stone sites where they pursued vision quests and other spiritual exercises.

The first Christian rites were held by Spanish Franciscans such as Fathers Silvestre Vélez de Escalante and Francisco Atanasio Domínguez. On their 1776 expedition through Colorado, these Catholic priests converted some Ute Indians to Christianity. The oldest church still in regular use in Colorado is Our Lady Of Guadalupe, opened in 1857 in the town of Conejos in the San Luis Valley.

Settlers arriving with the mining rushes brought their own ways of worship. The oldest Protestant congregation, St. James in Central City, was started in 1859 by a group of Methodists, including Aunt Clara Brown (see entry). Other Christian denominations—Baptists, Catholics, Congregationalists, Episcopalians,

Lutherans and Presbyterians—established congregations in Denver and other larger communities.

Jewish settlers established the Hebrew Burial Society in Denver in 1860 and built Denver's Temple Emanuel in 1874. Jewish congregations also formed early synagogues in Pueblo and Trinidad, where Temple Aaron (1887) is Colorado's oldest continually operating synagogue.

Numerous immigrant groups flooded into Colorado between the 1880s and 1930s, bringing their own religions and places of worship. These ranged from the Tri State Buddhist Temple opened in Denver in 1912 to various Orthodox churches serving a large number of Russians, Greeks, Slavs and other Eastern Europeans.

Religious groups also opened schools, starting in 1864 with St. Mary's Academy, founded in Denver by the Sisters of Loretto. Episcopalians opened Wolfe Hall for girls, and a boys' school in Golden that evolved into the Colorado School of Mines. Congregationalists founded the Colorado

Papal Throng

In August 1993, John Paul II became the first pope to visit Colorado. He came for a World Youth Conference in Denver and attracted more than 400,000 participants to a Papal Mass at Cherry Creek Reservoir, the largest single gathering in Colorado history. ✻

College (1873) in Colorado Springs and Methodists founded the University of Denver with its Iliff School of Theology in 1864.

Catholic nuns opened not only schools but also hospitals, beginning with St. Joseph's in Denver in 1873. Ultimately several orders of Catholic nuns built hospitals in Colorado Springs, Durango, Georgetown, Grand Junction, Leadville, Ouray, Pueblo, Telluride and Trinidad. The Jewish Consumptive Relief Society health care center in Lakewood and National

Kivas such as this stone-lined, subterranean chamber at Mesa Verde National Park were places of religious ceremony. Photo by Tom Noel.

Jewish Hospital in Denver treated lung disease patients from all over the country.

Swedish Lutherans, Presbyterians and other religious groups opened tuberculosis sanatoria that often evolved into modern hospitals.

In the 21st century, religious organizations across Colorado continue to maintain schools and seminaries, care for the sick, hungry and homeless, and offer medical care and hospice care for the dying. Mother Teresa's Sisters of the Sacred Heart care for AIDS patients in Denver.

Charismatic Christians, conservative fundamentalists and New Age religions have found new followers in a growing Colorado population of more than 1.5 million churchgoers. Also active are the followers of the Baha'i, Muslim, Hindu and other faiths.

Restaurants Horace

Greeley, one of the many easterners to come to Colorado in 1859 looking for decent restaurants, was disappointed. Mostly he found tent taverns that specialized primarily in "wet goods" (alcohol), with little, if any, substantial food.

Except for a few resort hotels such as the Brown Palace and Broadmoor, Colorado's culinary offerings remained slim for a century. Until the 1960s, many felt the best dining in Denver was at the airport Skychef.

The emergence of Aspen, Telluride and Vail as world-class resorts for the super-rich, as well as the growing sophistication of Colorado's urban centers, has changed

the dining scene dramatically since the 1960s. The problem is no longer finding a good restaurant, but deciding among them.

Dr. Colorado's List of Notable Restaurants
(with thanks to culinary critic Bill St. John)

Ajax Tavern. Base of Ajax (Aspen Mountain) ski run, 685 E. Durant Ave., Aspen; (970) 920-9333.

Emil-lene's Steak House. Rustic, rural, down-home place where your meat will moo. 16000 Smith Road, Aurora; (303) 366-6674.

Mirabelles's. French cuisine in an old ranch house. 55 Village Road, Beaver Creek; (970) 949-7728.

Flagstaff House. Fabulous views from Flagstaff Mountain. Flagstaff Road, Boulder; (303) 442-4640.

Broadmoor Hotel Tavern. Meat, martinis and merriment in Colorado's only Aztec Deco tavern. 1 Lake Circle, Colorado Springs; (719) 634-7711.

Highlands Garden Cafe. New American food in an old cottage surrounded by lavish gardens. 3927 W. 32nd Ave., Denver; (303) 458-5920.

Tante Louise. Denver's best French food, in an old bungalow. 4900 E. Colfax Ave., Denver; (303) 355-4488.

The Fort. Great wild game in a reconstruction of Bent's Fort. Colorado Hwy. 8 just north of U.S. 285, Morrison; (303) 697-4771.

Campagna. Italian. 435 W. Pacific Ave., Telluride; (970) 728-6190.

Rivers Sitting atop the Rockies,

Colorado is the source of most of the major rivers of the American Southwest: the Arkansas, Colorado, Platte and Rio Grande. Because the rivers are just beginning in Colorado, they sometimes look more like what easterners would call creeks. They are further diminished by dams, ditches and diversions to provide water for dry areas of Colorado and also for downstream states. Since 1960, these rivers have become popular summer destinations for rapid-riding canoeists, kayakers and rafters.

Arkansas River. Flowing 1,450 miles from the high Rockies to meet the Mississippi River below Little Rock, Ark., the Arkansas River begins on the eastern slope of Fremont Pass above Leadville and flows through the Royal Gorge down to the Kansas border.

In 1806, President Thomas Jefferson asked Zebulon Pike to explore the river that soon became the boundary between the United States and Spain and later between the United States and Mexico. Traders and trappers used it as a major route into the southern Rockies and the Southwest. With the 1858–1859 gold strikes, the Arkansas became the major southern route to the Colorado gold fields. Prospectors followed the Arkansas to its headwaters and first found gold in what later became the silver city of Leadville.

The southeastern quadrant of Colorado is dry agricultural land sustained by the

Arkansas River's muddy milk. The river has only one reliable tributary, the Purgatoire. All the other streams have been known to dry up—like so many of the mining and farming towns that once lined the Arkansas.

Designation of the Arkansas between Leadville and Pueblo as a State Recreation Area has led to its recreational rebirth as America's most rafted river. Below Pueblo, it remains an agricultural mainstream on its way to join the Mississippi.

Colorado River. The Colorado starts in Rocky Mountain National Park, on whose southwestern border lies the first of many dams, ditches and diversions. Due to these obstacles, the Colorado's muddy red waters rarely reach the blue Pacific.

On its path through Colorado, the river is augmented by the Fraser, Blue, Eagle, Roaring Fork and Gunnison rivers. Strengthened by these major mountain streams, the mighty Colorado carved out the Grand Canyon and conquered the great deserts of the Southwest.

For 1,500 miles this river flows through the driest part of the United States, watering not only Colorado but also Utah, Arizona, Nevada and Southern California. In most years the river does not survive a hydraulic landscape of headgates and tunnels, of measuring stations and holding basins. Much of its water is diverted under the Continental Divide to Denver and the Eastern Slope of Colorado.

The Colorado River carries more water out of the state than the Arkansas, South Platte and Rio Grande combined—almost two-thirds of the state's total streamflow in an average year.

South Platte River. In the spring of 1739, Paul and Pierre Mallet set out from Fort des Chartres, the capital of French Illinois, on a trek to Santa Fe, N.M.. With seven other Frenchmen, the Mallets made the first recorded ascent of the Platte River.

No Respect

In his 1872 account of the mining frontier, *Roughing It*, Mark Twain wrote of the South Platte River:

"We came to the shallow, yellow, muddy South Platte, with its low banks and its scattering flat sand-bars and pygmy islands—a melancholy stream straggling through the center of the enormous flat plain.... The Platte was 'up,' they said—which made me wish I could see it when it was down, if it could look any sicker and sorrier." ✳

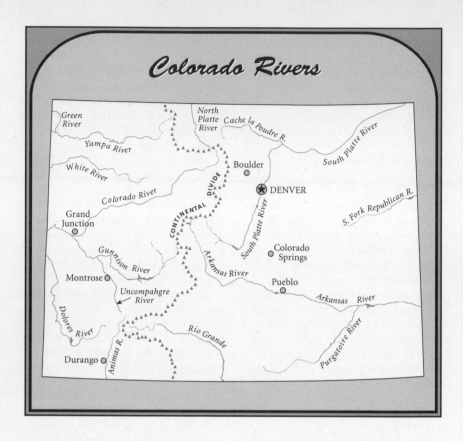

Colorado Rivers

Map labels:

Green River
North Platte River
Cache la Poudre R.
South Platte River
Yampa River
White River
Boulder
Colorado River
DENVER
CONTINENTAL DIVIDE
S. Fork Republican R.
Grand Junction
South Platte River
Gunnison River
Montrose
Colorado Springs
Uncompahgre River
Arkansas River
Pueblo
Dolores River
Arkansas River
Rio Grande
Purgatoire River
Durango
Animas R.

They gave it the name *Platte*, the French word for "flat" or "shallow."

Following gold discoveries in 1858 on the South Platte and its tributaries, settlers streamed up the river into Colorado. Many began their odyssey at Omaha, Neb., near the confluence of the Platte and the Missouri rivers. They followed the Platte to North Platte, Neb., where it divides into the North Platte and the South Platte. Both forks originate in Colorado: The North Platte rises in North Park (Jackson County) and the South Platte in South Park (Park County).

From its mountain-rimmed headwaters in South Park, the South Platte flows through Platte Canyon and then through metro Denver on its 450-mile route to North Platte, Neb. Beyond Denver, the river and its tributaries are lined by farms, ranches, gravel pits and the major towns of northeastern Colorado, Greeley and Sterling. The Platte has helped turn what was first branded the "great American desert" into Colorado's agricultural, industrial, commercial and population center.

Although generally cluttered with development, the South Platte has become recreationally prominent since 1976 with completion of much of the Platte River Trail in the Denver area, used by bikers, hikers, runners and walkers.

The South Platte watershed, with tributaries such as the Cache la Poudre and Big Thompson rivers and St. Vrain, Boulder and Cherry creeks, is home to almost three-fourths of Colorado's 4.3 million residents.

Rio Grande. The nation's third-longest river (after the Mississippi and the Missouri) guided the first Euro-American settlers into Colorado. Don Juan de Oñate in 1598 claimed the entire drainage of *El Rio Grande del Norte* for Spain, "from the leaves of the trees in the forest to the stones and sands of the river."

The Rio Grande's headwaters converge in the San Luis Valley of southern Colorado, one of the most remote reaches of Spain's former global empire. The San Juans and the Sangre de Cristos, two 14,000-foot ranges, frame the 8,000-foot-high, dusty, dry valley, which was never a priority for Spain or, after the 1821 revolution, for Mexico.

In 1848 the U.S. took possession of the valley after winning the Mexican War. In 1851, Mexican Americans established the town of San Luis. This and later Hispanic towns in the Rio Grande Valley have endured. Each community built irrigation ditches and set aside grazing fields and hunting areas that allowed poor farmers and ranchers to survive in a dry country.

On the headwaters of the Rio Grande in the San Juan Mountains, Yankees found gold and silver, which gave birth to boomtowns such as Creede. Most of those mining towns are now gone and the upper Rio Grande remains sparsely settled, a scenic and recreational delight.

Rock Art
Native Americans created rock art in the form of rock carvings (petroglyphs) and paintings (pictographs).

April 21, 1877

The oddest duel in Colorado history took place between two allegedly topless madams, Mattie Silks and Katie Fulton, in Denver along the Platte riverfront. They missed each other, but injured a spectator.

They used stone "brushes" to either peck or rub color onto rocks. Their images are usually of animals, human beings or geometric symbols. Representations are naturalistic, stylized or abstract.

Animal figures may be either celebrations of, or prayers for, successful hunting. Buffalo, deer and elk are portrayed, sometimes in large proportions, that suggest the artists were hungry. One example is the fatter-than-life buffalo painted on a cliff overlooking the Green River in Moffat County.

Ute rock art often shows bear paws and bears, perhaps connected to that tribes' distinctive bear dance. The coming of the horse is celebrated with figures of horses, sometimes with riders. Human figures often suggest fertility concerns with such detail as large phalluses. Human figures, often stick figures, frequently are wielding spears or bows and arrows. Geometric shapes, often thought to be the work of archaic or ancestral Puebloan-era artists, may be prayers, astronomical calculations or just graffiti.

Indian artists made petroglyphs either by pecking the base rock with a hard stone or using a stone to carve the surface. They often pecked or carved on basalt, a hard, dense volcanic stone with a uniformly colored, relatively smooth surface, or on sandstone.

Ancient rock art is sometimes marred by more recent graffiti, leading the State Office of Archaeology and Historic Preservation and concerned federal agencies to try to keep most sites secret. Many private property owners of rock art sites also discourage rock art tourism and potential vandalism. Consequently very few of some

300 known Colorado rock art sites are open to the public.

To learn more: One site where the public is welcome is at Cañon Pintado, on State Hwy. 139, 12 miles south of Rangely in the northwestern corner of the state. A highway sign welcomes visitors to this site inhabited by Fremont people from approximately A.D. 500 to 1150. Along the self-guided walking tour lie several pictographs and petroglyphs, rock shelters and granaries. In 1776 the Domínguez–Escalante expedition marveled at these paintings, and Father Silvestre Escalante christened the area Cañon Pintado (Painted Canyon). A central figure is Kokopelli, the humpback flute player who also appears in Arizona and New Mexico rock art.

Calf roping at the Toponas rodeo. Photo by Susan Dupere.

Rocky Mountain Spotted Fever

This infectious disease is spread by a virus harbored in rodents and other animals and carried by infected ticks that attach themselves to humans. First discovered in the Bitterroot Mountains of Montana, this fever occurs in Colorado, but is most common in the southeastern states.

Symptoms include high fever, coughing, headache, pain in the back and legs and a skin rash that first appears on the extremities and spreads to the trunk. Severe cases may lead to a drop in blood pressure, delirium, coma and death.

You can help avoid ticks by wearing long pants, boots and long-sleeve shirts in wooded or grassy areas and by wearing tick repellent. If potentially exposed to ticks, inspect the scalp, groin, armpits, behind the knees, around the waistband and other potentially moist, sheltered body parts.

Rodeos

These exhibitions display the skills of cowboys and cowgirls at riding bucking broncos and steers, bulldogging steers, lassoing, and barrel racing. Originally rodeos were held at cattle roundups, where cowboys would show what they could do. In the 1880s and 1890s, many communities began staging rodeos.

Colorado counties and towns still sponsor annual rodeos, of which the biggest and best known is a highlight of Denver's National Western Stock Show every January. The Greeley Stampede in late June, Monte Vista's Sky Hi Stampede in July, and Colorado Springs' Pikes Peak or Bust Rodeo in August are other major Colorado rodeos (see Calendar of Events).

To learn more: ProRodeo Museum Hall of Fame and Museum of the American Cowboy, 101 ProRodeo Drive, Colorado Springs 80910. Open daily 9 A.M.–5 P.M., $3–$6. (719) 528-4764.

Sabin, Florence Rena

Dr. Sabin was the first Coloradan selected for Statuary Hall in the nation's Capitol. This world-renowned medical scientist and champion of public health care succeeded in vastly improving the lives of all Coloradans.

In 1874 when she was 4 years old, her father, a Central City miner with a strong interest in medicine and healing, moved the family to Denver. Her own interest in medicine was awakened by the deaths of her two brothers in infancy and, when she was only 7 years old, by her mother's death. She excelled in school and went on to study at Smith College in Massachusetts.

As a student at Johns Hopkins Medical School in Baltimore, Md., Sabin designed a beeswax model of a newborn baby's brain stem that was used by generations of medical school neurology classes, along with her textbook *Atlas of the Midbrain and Medulla*. In 1917 she became the first female full professor at the medical school. She also became the first woman member of the National Academy of Sciences and, in 1924, the first woman physician–scientist at the Rockefeller Institute for Medical Research in New York City.

Sabin retired from the Rockefeller Institute at the age of 67 in 1938 and returned to Denver to live with her sister. In 1946, Colorado Gov. John Vivian asked

Florence Sabin became Colorado's most noted scientist and physician. Denver Public Library, Western History Department.

her to head the state health committee. Sabin found that Colorado, the home of sunshine, fresh air and health resorts, was one of America's sickest states. It had one of the nation's highest infant mortality rates, the fifth-highest incidence of diphtheria and the third-highest scarlet fever death rate.

Sabin drafted eight health bills, including laws requiring pasteurization of milk and adequate sewage treatment plants and providing for public health education. She lobbied the governor and the legislature and toured the state to promote the so-called Sabin Health Laws, which passed in 1947.

That same year, Denver Mayor Quigg Newton persuaded Sabin to become Denver's manager of health and charities. She began a citywide x-ray program to diagnose tuberculosis, cutting the Denver infection rate in half. She also launched campaigns to remove rats from alleys and dumps, teach public health, and offer vocational training for the poor.

Not until 1951 did the 80-year-old public health crusader retire. She died two years later at her Denver home.

Saloons

The first and most common public buildings in frontier Colorado—saloons—did more than serve drinks. Among other things, they often housed pioneer governments. The Colorado Territorial government and that of Denver City were conceived, born and raised in saloon halls, by pioneers reluctant to pay taxes to build more dignified homes for government. Saloons also doubled as theaters, art galleries and dance halls, and even housed church services.

Some barkeepers graduated to grander structures that sported classic mirrored back-bars, plate glass windows and elegant furnishings. The following is a sampling of some memorable old watering holes that continue to fulfill their basic mission.

Dr. Colorado's List of Favorite Saloons

Hotel Jerome Bar. Jerome B. Wheeler, whose bristly, bearded face is framed behind the front desk, built the three-story brick hotel and saloon named for him in 1889. After surviving Prohibition disguised as a soda fountain, this legendary saloon retains its mahogany doors, silver chandeliers, fans hanging from the high, pressed-tin ceiling, and an unusual Eastlake Style golden oak back-bar. 330 E. Main St., Aspen; (303) 925-5518.

Crook's Palace. In claiming to be Colorado's oldest tavern, the Palace traces its ancestry to a demolished 1860s saloon on the same site. Tom Crook opened the current establishment around 1900 with a classic storefront, chandeliers and risqué Victorian "art" that still adorn this tiny, old-time saloon, now recycled as a casino. 200 Gregory St., Black Hawk; (303) 582-5094.

Gold Pan Saloon. The Gold Pan has stoutly resisted the transformation of a ramshackle mining town into a cute ski and summer resort. Behind the swinging doors of Breckenridge's oldest saloon, raucous regulars fight off the invading armies of tourists. The dinginess of the Gold Pan also shields it from stray tourists. This tavern consists of two tipsy, clapboard buildings leaning on each other since 1879 atop wobbly log foundations. 103-05 N. Main St., Breckenridge; (970) 453-5499.

Teller House Bar. President Ulysses S. Grant stepped out of a stagecoach on April 28, 1878, to find the Teller House walkway paved with silver bricks. Presumably the cigar-chomping Civil War hero also visited the bar. Herndon Davis, a Denver artist, painted a woman's face on the barroom floor in the summer of 1936, drawing inspiration from Hugh d'Arcy's poem "The Face on the Barroom Floor." This barroom is also graced by *Apollo, Aphrodite with an Apple, Leda and the Swan* and five other life-size murals of Greek goddesses and gods. 110 Eureka St., Central City; (303) 582-3200.

Buckhorn Exchange. Denver had no Museum of Natural History until 1900, but saloons offered some astonishing natural and unnatural history. The best of the tavern/museums, the Buckhorn Exchange, still has more than 300 stuffed mammals and birds, and a menu featuring alligator, buffalo, elk, pheasant, quail and other wild game. 1000 Osage St., Denver; (303) 534-9509.

Kozy Corner Bar and Cafe. King Arthur had his round table where all were equal. So does Goodrich, Colo., where the round table fills much of the tiny Kozy Corner Bar and Cafe. In this tiny dirt-street village on the

north bank of the South Platte River, some 60 miles northeast of Denver, the Kozy Corner welcomes locals and visitors to rest atop tractor seats mounted on milk can stools. 24213 Weld County Hwy. 39, Goodrich; (970) 645-2064.

Silver Dollar Saloon. This 1879 saloon is well-preserved from its vintage front foyer to its back rooms for gaming, dancing and other activities. Named for Silver Dollar Tabor, a daughter of Horace Tabor, this museum-like tavern celebrates the silvery past of American's highest, wildest and biggest silver city. 315 Harrison Ave., Leadville; (719) 486-9914.

Gus' Place. Colorado's best-known blue-collar saloon is a small, one-story brick corner tavern that blends into a working-class neighborhood. Augusto Masciotra, an Italian immigrant, went to work at age 14 at the nearby CF&I steel mill and saved to buy the house at 1201 Elm. In 1926 he added a grocery to the front of his home and, with the end of Prohibition in 1933, converted the grocery to the tavern now operated by his grandson. 1201 Elm St., SW corner Mesa Avenue, Pueblo; (719) 542-0756.

San Isidro

The patron saint of farmers, San Isidro (St. Isidore) of Spain, is a favorite among Hispanics who do much of Colorado's agricultural work. Born in 12th-century Madrid, he often paused amid his work to pray (skeptics say he was taking siestas). While he was praying, an angel took over his plowing. Thus statues or paintings of the saint usually include an angel and a plow.

He was canonized in 1622, and his feast day is May 15. Images of San Isidro may be found in many Hispanic churches in Colorado, in the Denver Art Museum and in the Colorado Springs Fine Arts Museum.

Sand Creek Massacre

(SEE ALSO NATIVE AMERICANS) The 1861 Treaty of Fort Wise required Colorado's Cheyenne and Arapaho Indians to abandon Denver and most of the eastern plains for a small reservation in remote, arid southeastern Colorado. Hungry, angry Indians sometimes left this reservation to hunt game—and occasionally the white man's livestock and other possessions. Scattered serious incidents, including massacres of white families, led territorial governor John Evans to raise the Third Colorado Regiment in August 1864. Evans put in command a friend and political ally, a 6-foot, 4-inch Methodist preacher noted for his "muscular Christianity," John M. Chivington.

Chivington had defeated Confederate Texans intent on invading Colorado at the Battle of La Glorietta Pass in New Mexico two years earlier. Promoted to colonel and put in charge of the Third Colorado, he went hunting in November of 1864. Chivington learned that many Cheyenne and some Arapaho were winter-camped on Big Sandy Creek, 160 miles southeast of Denver. Big Sandy Creek formed the eastern boundary of the Cheyenne and Arapaho Reservation. This intermittent stream, misnamed Sand Creek in early accounts of the "battle," is now forever assigned that name as the scene of the deadliest U.S. massacre of peaceful Native Americans.

Before daybreak on Nov. 29, 1864, Chivington's troops found the Indian camp. Just before they charged in the freezing early-morning dimness, Chivington instructed his troops, which numbered about 725 men: "I don't tell you to kill all ages and sexes, but look back on the Plains of the Platte, where your mothers, fathers, brothers, sisters have been slain. . . . Nits make lice."

Chivington's attack completely surprised the 500 Natives in 103 lodges. They were awakened by gunfire and later by howitzer bombardment only to find their horses had already been captured. Assuming a mistake had been make, Chief Black Kettle of the Cheyenne raised a U.S. flag and a white flag. His gesture did no good. The camp scattered. Some fleet-footed young men escaped. Women, children and the old died.

While the hastily raised 100-day enlistees of the Third Regiment attacked, some regular army officers with the First Regiment refused to join in the slaughter of peaceful Indians camped where they had been told to camp. Capt. Silas M. Soule forbade his men to participate. When Soule was later scheduled to testify in Denver about what happened that day, he was mysteriously shot and killed.

According to George Bent, who was there, an estimated 163 Indians, mostly women, children and old men, were slain. Some Indian women were raped, scalped and mutilated.

Among Chivington's men, 10 were killed and 28 were wounded.

"All acquitted themselves well, and the Colorado soldiers once again covered themselves with glory, " reported the *Rocky Mountain News* that December. "Among the brilliant feats of arms in Indian warfare, the recent campaign of our Colorado volunteers will stand in history with few rivals." Unwittingly, the *News* was correct.

The atrocity led the federal Congress to pause during the Civil War to investigate. After considerable testimony and study, Washington pronounced Sand Creek "a

Looking Back

April 7, 1987

A sudden cold front caused Denver temperatures to plunge 50 degrees in a single afternoon.

foul and dastardly massacre." Both Chivington and Gov. John Evans were forced to resign.

In 2000, Colorado U.S. Sen. Ben Nighthorse Campbell sponsored legislation to create Sand Creek National Historic Site. President Bill Clinton signed the law, authorizing the National Park Service to begin acquiring the 7,680-acre site in Kiowa County about 40 miles north of Lamar, not far from the present-day town of Chivington. There the story of Sand Creek will be retold, with considerable input from descendant Cheyenne and Arapaho, who have not forgotten.

Scenic and Historic Byways

Colorado is a state full of fascinating backroads, and the state's Scenic and Historic Byways program has identified many of the best. The state looks for special virtues in the routes: extraordinary scenery, scientific interest, cultural or historical importance.

The byways take drivers off the main routes and onto some lesser-known wonders, ranging from Cache la Poudre Canyon to the Gold Belt Tour of Cripple Creek and Victor, from the Pawnee Buttes to the Highway of Legends where Juan Humaña and his conquistadors mysteriously disappeared in the 1800s.

Northwest

Dinosaur Diamond. Grand Junction to Rangely over Douglas Pass, through Dinosaur into Utah.

Grand Mesa. Between I-70 and Cedaredge.

Flat Tops Trail. Connects Yampa and Meeker.

Colorado River Headwaters. Between Rocky Mountain National Park and State Bridge via Granby and Kremmling.

Northcentral

Guanella Pass. Between Georgetown and Grant.

Mount Evans. From Idaho Springs to the 14,264-foot summit of Mount Evans.

Peak to Peak. Between Estes Park and Black Hawk.

Trail Ridge Road. Through Rocky Mountain National Park.

Cache la Poudre and North Park. Between Fort Collins and Walden.

Northeast

Pawnee Pioneer Trails. Links Sterling, Fort Morgan, Grover and Ault.

South Platte River Trail. Between Julesburg and Ovid.

Southwest

Unaweep/Tabeguache. Between Whitewater and Placerville.

Trail of the Ancients. From the Utah state line near Hovenweep through Cortez.

San Juan Skyway. Connects Durango, Ridgway, Telluride and Cortez.

Alpine Loop. Connects Lake City, Ouray and Silverton. Portions require four-wheel drive.

West Elk Loop. Connects Carbondale, Hotchkiss, Gunnison and Crested Butte.

Southcentral

Top of the Rockies. Connects Leadville, Minturn, Twin Lakes and Copper Mountain Resort.

Silver Thread. From South Fork to Lake City.

Los Caminos Antiguos. Between Cumbres Pass and Alamosa, via Antonito, San Luis and Great Sand Dunes.

Gold Belt Tour. Connects Florissant, Cripple Creek, Victor, Florence and Cañon City. Portions require four-wheel drive.

Frontier Pathways. Connects Pueblo, Westcliffe and Colorado City.

Southeast

Highway of Legends. Links Trinidad, La Veta and Walsenburg.

Santa Fe Trail. From the Kansas state line near Holly to the New Mexico state line at Raton Pass.

To learn more: Colorado Department of Transportation; (800) 999-4997

Scottish Americans

Although not as numerous as the English or the Irish, the Scots had a Colorado population of around 2,000 by 1890 and had organized a Caledonian Club and a St. Andrew Society.

William J. Palmer and Dr. William A. Bell of the Denver & Rio Grande Railroad laid out North Denver's Scottish Village, a tiny neighborhood of short, curving streets with Scottish names. Although some Scotch-Irish settled in that area known as Highlands, they were soon outnumbered by Irish, Italian and Hispanic residents.

Like the English, the Scots assimilated into the dominant Anglo culture and made less of their ethnicity than most other groups. One of the few traces of Denver's Scottish pioneers is a bronze statue of Robert Burns installed in City Park in 1904 by the Colorado Caledonian Club.

(Continued on page 186)

Colorado Scenic and Historic Byways

1 Dinosaur Diamond
2 Grand Mesa
3 Flat Tops Trail
4 Colorado River Headwaters
5 Guanella Pass
6 Mount Evans
7 Peak to Peak
8 Trail Ridge Road
9 Cache la Poudre and
   North Park
10 Pawnee Pioneer Trails
11 South Platte River Trail
12 Unaweep/Tabeguache
13 Trail of the Ancients
14 San Juan Skyway
15 Alpine Loop
16 West Elk Loop
17 Top of the Rockies
18 Silver Thread
19 Los Caminos Antiguos
20 Gold Belt Tour
21 Frontier Pathways
22 Highway of Legends
23 Santa Fe Trail

- - - - - Scenic and Historic
          Byways

　　　　National Forests
          and Grasslands

　　　　National Parks
          and Monuments

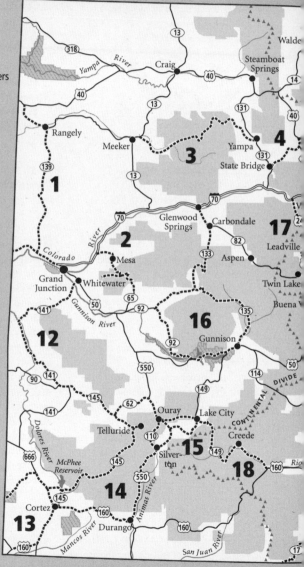

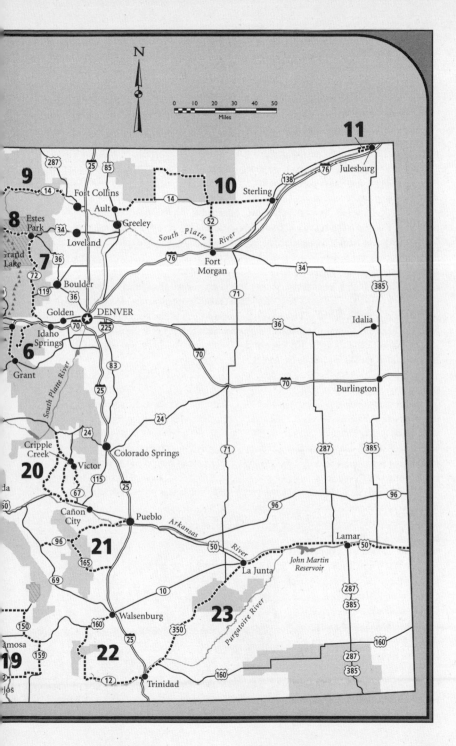

N

0 10 20 30 40 50
Miles

11
287 25 85 Julesburg
9 76
14 Fort Collins 138
Ault 10 Sterling
8 Estes 34 Greeley 14
Park 52
34 Loveland South Platte River
Grand 36 76
Lake 7 Fort 34
72 Morgan 385
119 Boulder
36 71
Golden DENVER
70 225 36 Idalia
Idaho
6 Springs 70
83
Grant 70 Burlington
25
South Platte River
24
Cripple 24
Creek Colorado Springs
20 Victor 71
115 287 385
67
25
Cañon 96 96
96 City Pueblo Arkansas Lamar
21 50 River 50
165 La Junta John Martin
69 Reservoir 287
10 385
150 Walsenburg
19 159 160 350 23 Purgatoire River 160
22 25
2 12 Trinidad 160 287
jos 385

(Continued from page 183)
Its inscription reads:

A poet, peasant born,
Who more of fame's immortal dower
Upon his country brings
Than all her kings.

Burns' statue stands close to Ferril Lake, named for the Scottish American poet, Thomas Hornsby Ferril (see entry), longtime Colorado poet laureate and premier bard of the Rocky Mountain region.

Scottish culture has been celebrated in recent years with a large autumnal festival in Estes Park, the Highland Games. The St. Andrew Society has hosted, since 1962, an annual Metro Denver Highland Games, now held in Highlands Ranch.

Silks, Mattie Colorado's

most celebrated madam ran brothels in Alaska and in Colorado at Georgetown and Jamestown, as well as houses in Denver at 1916, 1942 and 2009 Market St. The latter two are designated local landmarks.

Mattie's birthplace and birth date are uncertain. Her maid said it was in 1847 in Terre Haute, Ind., but the U.S. manuscript census said 1846 in New York. She ran away from home in her early teens. At age 19, she ran a brothel in Springfield, Ill.

Short, blonde and attractive, she was well upholstered and carried a pistol. Her marksmanship troubled her lover, Cort Thomson. She shot him in the neck during her famed April 21, 1877, duel with rival madam Katie Fulton on the banks of the South Platte in what is now Commons Park.

The 1900 U.S. manuscript census lists Mattie as a "land lady" on Denver's Market Street renting to "female borders" age 19 to 25. Mattie went east each year to recruit fresh talent, which she supposedly paraded through the streets of Denver to attract new customers and reenergize old ones. She treated her girls well, letting them keep half the high prices she charged for their favors. She served her girls two fine meals daily, breakfast at 11:30 and dinner at 5:00.

Unlike most of hell's belles, Mattie retired to respectability with Smiling Jack Ready to a ranch in Wray, Colo. There she lived to a ripe old age, becoming a plump, grandmotherly soul who never lost her wink. Mattie's House of Mirrors at 1942 Market St., the most celebrated Colorado brothel, was restored in 1998 as an elegant restaurant, bar and mini-museum.

Silver (SEE ALSO MINING) Coloradans

first mined silver from the Belmont Lode near Georgetown in 1864 and at Caribou in 1869, but the bonanza days came in the 1880s in the Leadville district, which ultimately yielded one-third of the state's silver.

The mad rush to Leadville spilled into neighboring Pitkin, Gunnison and Chaffee counties. Silver seekers swarmed over Independence Pass to establish Aspen in 1880. Aspen eventually rivaled even Leadville's silver production, and boasted the largest nugget in the world, a 1,870-pound monster from the Smuggler Mine that was 93 percent silver.

The mining town of Leadville in 1879. Colorado Historical Society.

The 1893 silver crash turned the boom to bust. The U.S. had demonetized silver in 1873, shifting from a bimetallic to a gold standard. To placate silver supporters, the federal government continued to subsidize silver mining with purchase programs, including the Sherman Silver Purchase Act of 1890. In 1893, when the Sherman Act was repealed, the price of silver sank to less than 60 cents an ounce. Silver miners turned to other pursuits, while many of the silver towns became ghosts.

Some silver continues to be mined in Colorado, primarily as a by-product of gold mining. A post World War II production record was set in 1996 with 312,000 ounces of silver, but that figure had dropped by 1999 to an estimated 81,000 ounces. Once nicknamed the Silver State, Colorado now has only a slim silver lining to a cloudy mineral future.

Silverheels

Mount Silverheels, a 13,817-foot-high mountain eight miles northwest of Fairplay in central Colorado, commemorates a legendary dance hall heroine. The belle of Bill Buck's Saloon wore silver slippers and a silver ribbon in her black hair. She said nothing about her past and welcomed the name the miners gave her: Silverheels. When Bill Buck developed smallpox, she nursed him tirelessly. He died in her arms.

A smallpox epidemic ravaged Fairplay that winter of 1863. Everything closed, even the mines and the saloons. Silverheels kept Bill's saloon open so she could nurse old customers and anyone else stricken by the epidemic. At times when no ill people came to the saloon, she went door to door looking for the sick and dying. Her bosom became many a miner's dying pillow.

By the time spring and good health returned to Fairplay, many of the residents lay in the cemetery. Survivors raised a purse of $5,000 to thank Silverheels. They took it to her cabin, but she had disappeared. Some said she went to San Francisco, some said it was to Australia. Others suspected that smallpox killed her, too, or maybe disfigured her so badly she did not want to be seen. In her memory Fairplay residents named the most prominent nearby peak for her.

A 1954 musical, *Silverheels*, by Waldo Williamson and Russell Porter of the University of Denver Theater Department, honored the legendary dance hall queen. Some say she still shows up on dark nights at the old Fairplay Cemetery, an angel once again visiting the smallpox victims resting in the boneyard.

Skiing and Snowboarding

Scandinavian immigrants introduced skiing to Colorado's gold and silver camps as early as the 1860s. Winter travelers, mail carriers and even circuit-riding preachers used skis.

One Norwegian immigrant, Carl Howelsen, fathered recreational skiing in Colorado. A stonemason who gravitated to the mountains, he spearheaded Colorado's first winter-sports carnival and ski-jump competition in 1912 at Hot Sulphur Springs. The next year "the Flying Norseman" moved to Steamboat Springs and turned that town into a winter sports center where Howelsen Hill still attracts ski jumpers.

Skiing is a sport for both young and old. From Ski the Rockies; photo by Marc Muench.

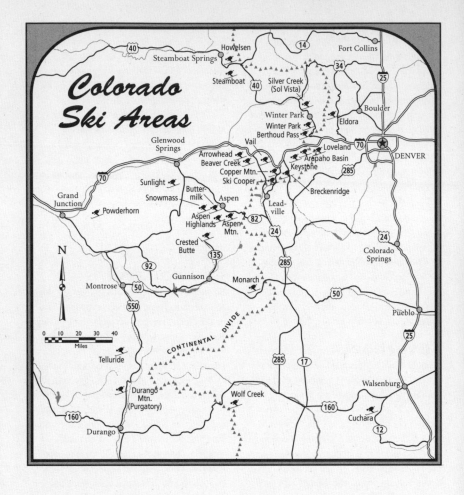

Colorado Ski Areas

In the beginning, skiers spent most of their day on long, difficult hikes up the slope. Then they descended with their feet strapped onto long, heavy skis with bindings known as bear traps. Development of cable bindings (1931), steel edges (1934), mechanical lifts and groomed slopes improved the sport tremendously.

Aspen Mountain opened as Colorado's first commercial ski area in 1937, using old mining-tram towers and cables to drag skiers uphill in a rowboat. Winter Park, a creation of the Denver Parks and Recreation Department, opened in 1938 as Colorado's second commercial area. Winter Park is still one of the most popular areas, noted for its family and handicapped ski programs.

Arapahoe Basin originated in 1941 when U.S. Forest Ranger Wilfred "Slim" Davis began a school to teach fellow rangers how to ski and patrol ski areas, which are nearly all on land leased within national forests.

Vail, opened in 1962 on a former sheep ranch, has become the largest ski area in North America. Vail spinoffs include lavish new resorts at Beaver Creek (1980) and Arrowhead (1989).

One of the devices used to pull skiers uphill during the 1940s is preserved at the base of a chairlift in Aspen. Photo by Tom Noel.

Aspen's spectacular transformation from a fading silver camp to an internationally celebrated tourist mecca with four major ski areas (Aspen Highlands, Aspen Mountain, Buttermilk and Snowmass) encouraged other declining mining towns to exploit "white gold." Breckenridge (1961), Crested Butte (1963), Keystone (1970) and Telluride (1972) got into the game.

As lift ticket prices climbed, now hitting $60 and more, and the cost of skis, boots and attire soared, many turned to cross-country skiing and snowshoeing. Cross-country touring can be done anywhere snow falls, but it became the specialty of dude ranches such as Bear Pole, Conejos, Devil's Thumb, Diamond J, Latigo, Vista Verde, Waunita Hot Springs and the YMCA's Snow Mountain Ranch.

Snowboarding is the fastest growing winter sport, particularly among those under 30. Snowboarders, whose single wide boards work well on all kinds of snow, are welcome at most ski areas.

Approximately 100 Colorado ski areas have come and gone over the decades, ranging from small-town rope tows to slick, multimillion-dollar operations with high-speed quad lifts and closed gondolas. What began as a quaint practice for a few Scandinavian miners has snowballed into an industry attracting millions of people each year. Colorado now captures a fourth of the annual U.S. total of skiing activity.

To learn more: Colorado Ski Country, 1560 Broadway, Suite 2000, Denver 80202; (303) 837-0793; www.skicolorado.org.

Smith, Jefferson Randolph "Soapy"

Jeff Smith unpacked his carpetbag near Denver's Union Station in the 1880s and began selling soap. Not just ordinary soap, he assured the crowds that gathered, as he inserted large-denomination bills between the soap and its wrapper.

People clamored to buy the soap that had the big bills under the wrapper. But only Jeff's shills ever recovered the bonanza bars. Other buyers ended up with nothing but a nickel cake of ordinary soap. Two police officers arrived a few days later as Jeff was setting up for the day's sales. He balked at giving his name, so they booked him as "Soapy" Smith.

In court, Soapy offered to convince the judge of his innocence by demonstrating his soap game. He carefully wrapped the soap in tissue paper and, after catching the judge's eye, inserted a $100 bill. At an appropriate moment the judge pocketed the bill and found Soapy innocent. Or so goes one of the many legends about this slippery character.

Soapy managed to convince Denver police that his soap sales could be profitable for them. They allowed him to operate as long as he fleeced only out-of-towners. Soapy also ran a fake mining company, complete with a gorgeous secretary and an impressive suite of offices. He worked nights as a gambler, raising capital for myriad scams.

When he moved into politics, ingratiating himself with the Republican gang who ran local politics, he enabled voting—early and often—by Denver's tramps, prostitutes and shady underworld characters. Each time they cast ballots as directed, they were rewarded with drink and dollars.

In 1893, reformers chased Soapy out of town. After notorious careers in Leadville and Creede, he headed for Skagway, Alaska, where vigilantes in 1898 gunned him down and laid him in his grave.

Snow

All Coloradans have gone to bed at night with the snowflakes flying, to awaken in the morning to a crystal blue sky with sun and snow creating a magic, sparkling landscape. Usually, Colorado snow does not last for long. Warm sun and dry air encourage quick melting and evaporation. Chinook (snow-eater) winds may also follow a storm with dry warm air and help with the disappearing act.

In Colorado, March and April are the snowiest months. The most snowfall ever recorded in a 24-hour period in the western United States fell at Silver Lake in San Juan County April 14–15, 1921—a total of 76 inches. Colorado's record blizzard to this day occurred in December 1913 when 30 to 50 inches blanketed the Front Range of eastern Colorado from Trinidad to Fort Collins. Georgetown received 86 inches and Denver reported 46 inches,

which is still the Mile High City's heaviest recorded snowfall.

The deadliest blizzard occurred in November 1946 when more than 3 feet of snow killed at least 13 people on the eastern plains. Thousands of stranded cattle were saved from starvation by the U.S. Air Force, which dropped bales of hay from airplanes.

Denver's highest one-day snowfall, on Dec. 24, 1982, brought 36 inches of the stuff. Thousands of stranded holiday motorists jammed motels and restaurants along eastern I-70. The city itself lay in frozen silence for 48 hours.

More Frigid Facts

Highest Colorado snowfall: 838 inches, Wolf Creek Pass (winter of 1978–1979).
Earliest first snow in Denver: Sept. 3, 1961.
Latest first snow in Denver: Nov. 15, 1944.
The no-snow year: 1976–1977, the winter of no major snow until March.
Fun with snow: International Snow Sculpture Championships (third week in January) and Ullr Fest honoring the Norse god of snow (fourth week in January), both in Breckenridge.

Sports, Professional

Many Coloradans pursue an active outdoor lifestyle and also are avid fans of professional sports. Denver boasts the only major league teams between Salt Lake City and Kansas City, drawing a fan base from throughout the Rockies and the High Plains. The city has major league football (Denver Broncos), baseball (Colorado Rockies), basketball (Denver Nuggets), hockey (Colorado Avalanche) and soccer (Colorado Rapids).

Denver Broncos. The Broncos have been Denver's National Football League team since 1960. The Broncos started playing in the University of Denver stadium after the university dropped football as

Holiday Surprise

Warm December sunshine smiled on Colorado in 1982, when 60-degree days made it hard to anticipate a white Christmas. But snow started falling on Christmas eve and did not stop for 24 hours, dumping 3 feet on the Front Range in a single day. Airports shut down, newspapers ceased publication for one day and mail carriers did not deliver as eastern Colorado came to a white, frozen standstill. ❋

unproductive. The Broncos soon moved to the Denver Bears baseball park, which was expanded and renamed Mile High Stadium in 1968. Following many losing seasons and four embarrassing Super Bowl losses, the team won back-to-back Super Bowl championships in 1998 and 1999.

The Broncos in 1999 persuaded taxpayers to help finance a new stadium with more luxury boxes and higher-priced seats. That $362 million stadium, Invesco Field at Mile High, opened in 2001, with a total of 76,000 seats, including 8,000 luxury seats costing $175 to $250 per game. Even when the Broncos are losing, they attract rabid fans to a sold-out stadium, and there is an immense waiting list for season tickets. Denver Metropolitan Stadium District; (303) 244-1002; www.denverbroncos.com.

Colorado Rockies. This National League baseball team began playing in 1993. The Rockies quickly became baseball's most successful franchise in terms of attendance. More than 80,000 attended the Rockies' first home game at Mile High stadium, and by year's end, attendance of 4.5 million had broken the record—by more than 400,000— set the previous year by the Toronto Blue Jays. The Rockies repaid the fans by gaining a wild card spot in the National League championship playoffs in 1995.

The Denver metro area passed a 0.1 percent sales tax to build Coors Field in Lower Downtown. Opened in 1995, with a prize-winning design by Hellmuth, Obata and Kassabaum, it resembles that firm's famous Camden Yards field for the Baltimore Orioles. This high-tech stadium complements the neighboring historic industrial-warehouse area with its red brick and red sandstone walls and old-time look. (303) 762-5437; www.coloradorockies.com.

Denver Nuggets. James Naismith, who invented basketball in 1891, once worked at the Denver YMCA, where he introduced

Coors Field in Denver, home of baseball's Colorado Rockies, opened in 1995. Photo by Tom Noel.

the game to Coloradans. Concerned about the lack of winter recreation, Naismith nailed peach baskets to opposite gymnasium walls and had youngsters try to throw in soccer balls.

In 1948, Colorado's first professional basketball team, the original Denver Nuggets, began playing. The team lasted (under various names) only three years. The Denver Rockets, an American Basketball Association team, began playing in 1967.

They were followed by the Denver Nuggets, the city's first National Basketball Association team. The Nuggets played in McNichols Arena until moving into the Pepsi Center when that modern, circular arena opened in 1999. The $190 million facility was built with private money. (303) 405-1100.

Colorado Avalanche. Denver had a series of professional ice hockey teams before the Avalanche arrived in 1995. Among them were the Colorado Rockies of the National Hockey League, which played from 1977 until they moved to New Jersey in 1982 and became the Devils. The NHL Colorado Flames lasted for only a year, 1983–1984, followed by the Colorado Rangers, 1987–1989, and the Denver Grizzlies, 1993–1994.

Since 1995 the Colorado Avalanche, a National Hockey League team previously playing as the Quebec Nordiques, have been on the ice in Denver. After they won the national championship and the Stanley Cup in 1996, a crowd of more than 300,000 celebrated Colorado's first major-league championship in any sport. The "Avs" graduated in 1999 from the old McNichols Arena to the new Pepsi Center—and in 2001, again won the Stanley Cup. (303) 405-1100.

Colorado Rapids. Since 1995, the Rapids have played soccer in Denver, using Mile High Stadium. As part of the Major League Soccer organization born in 1993, the Rapids rapidly improved, winning 16 and losing 16 in 1998 before their first winning season in 1999, when they won 20 games and lost 12. (303) 299-1599.

Colorado Springs boasts two professional minor league teams, the **Chicago Sky Sox**, AAA farm team of baseball's Colorado Rockies, and an ice hockey team, the **Colorado Gold Kings**. The Kings arrived in 1998 after Colorado Springs built the $57 million World Arena, a 9,500-seat complex with three ice rinks.

Spruce, Colorado Blue

The Colorado state tree (*Picea pungens glauca*) is native at elevations of about 7,000 to 10,000 feet, but has been grown successfully all over the state. Its bluish-silverish color and symmetrical shape make it one of the most beautiful and most widely planted evergreens, extremely popular for landscaping and as a Christmas tree.

The blue spruce is an extremely hardy tree although susceptible to the tussock moth and spruce gall aphid. The largest known specimen, located in Gunnison National Forest, is 106 feet high, with a trunk circumference of 16 feet and a lower branch span of 36 feet. Homeowners often have planted these beautiful little trees only

to have them grow into towering giants that can overwhelm their settings.

Stagecoaches

Before the arrival of the railroads, stagecoaches dominated Colorado transportation. Of the many stage lines once crisscrossing Colorado, most were short-lived due to the extreme distances, raw climate, bandits and the intense competition to capture federal mail subsidies.

In 1859, the first stages rumbled into Denver. These Concord coaches of the Leavenworth and Pike's Peak Express Co. had traveled 687 miles from "the States" to the Pikes Peak gold regions. The company was later reorganized under a new name and extended service on to California. Financial woes forced the reorganized company to go on the auction block, where it was picked up in 1863 by Ben Holladay, king of western stagecoaching. Holladay in turn sold out in 1866 to Wells Fargo and Co.

Wells Fargo, the western branch of the American Express Co., came to dominate western stagecoaching. The growing network of railroads led Wells Fargo to abandon all its Colorado stage operations in 1875—but the company returned more than a hundred years later, in 1999, to become the state's biggest bank.

Colorado's most enduring stage empire, Barlow, Sanderson, and Co., operated along the Arkansas River, with branches south to Trinidad and north to Denver. In 1876, Barlow and Sanderson opened the first major line up the Rio Grande and into the San Juan Mountain mining region of southwestern Colorado.

Railroads began replacing stages in 1870, but in areas without railroads, stages survived as late as the early 1900s and the advent of the motorcoach. Many Colorado communities still celebrate their stagecoach days, restoring old stage stops as museums and tourist accommodations.

State Capitol

This neoclassical building uses the cruciform plan of many other state capitols. Its gold dome, reaching 272 feet above the ground, is 42 feet in diameter. The capitol on a 10-acre site in Denver was begun in 1890 but not finished until 1907.

The building has exterior walls of granite quarried near Gunnison, foundations and walls of Fort Collins sandstone, floors and steps of Colorado Yule marble and wainscoting of Colorado

The State Capitol originally was to have been crowned by a female figure with an upraised lamp, indicated in this 1886 drawing. Legislators, however, ultimately chose a globular red light instead. Colorado State Archives.

onyx from Beulah, a small town 30 miles west of Pueblo. All materials are native except the steel girders and trusses and the ornamental brass.

In 1908 the dome was covered with Colorado gold leaf at the bargain price of $14,680. The first-floor rotunda walls display murals by artist Allen Tupper True, depicting the state's history, and a poem, "Here Is a Land Where Life Is Written in Water," by Colorado's premier poet, Thomas Hornsby Ferril:

> Here is a land where life is written in
>   water,
> The West is where the water was
>   and is,
> Father and son of old, mother and
>   daughter,
> Following rivers up immensities
> Of range and desert, thirsting the
>   sundown ever,
> Crossing a hill to climb a hill still drier,
> Naming tonight a city by some river
> A different name from last night's
>   camping fire.
>
> Look to the green within the mountain
>   cup,
> Look to the prairie parched for water
>   lack,
> Look to the sun that pulls the oceans up,
> Look to the cloud that gives the oceans
>   back,
> Look to your heart and may your
>   wisdom grow
> To power of lightning and peace of
>   snow. . . .

To learn more: Free tours, 200 E. Colfax Ave., Denver 80203; (303) 866-2604.

State Parks (SEE ALSO

NATIONAL PARKS) Colorado created a State Parks and Recreation Authority in 1937, but didn't give it any money until 1957.

(Continued on page 196)

Colorado State Parks

Steamboat Lake
Walden
Pearl Lake
Craig
Yampa River
318
13
125
14
14
125
Steamboat Springs
40
Stagecoach
40
13
Colorado River
9
139
Dillon Reservoir
Rifle Falls
Rifle Gap
Harvey Gap
70
24
Glenwood Springs
Sylvan Lake
Leadville
91
N
70
82
Highline
Island Acres
River
Vega
24
Colorado
Buena Vista
Grand Junction
Colorado River
50
133
Paonia
141
Gunnison River
92
Crawford
Arkansas
Sweitzer Lake
92
Gunnison
50
550
CONTINENTAL DIVIDE
141
149
145
Ridgway
62
285
141
Dolores River
McPhee Reservoir
145
149
Rio
160
666
Animas River
160
145
Mancos
San Juan River
145
Durango
160
160
Navajo
San Juan River
17

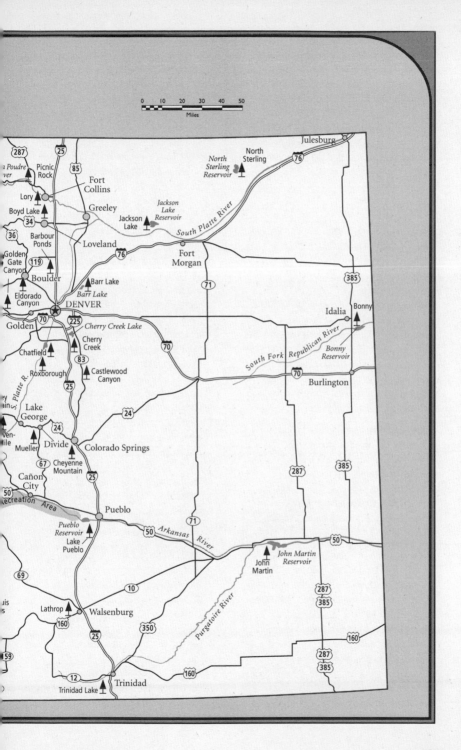

(Continued from page 193)
It was not until 1959 that Colorado's first state park, Cherry Creek Reservoir, opened to the public.

Thirty-nine additional state parks now offer a great variety of recreational activities. Cheyenne Mountain in Colorado Springs and John Martin Reservoir near Las Animas are scheduled to become the 41st and 42nd state parks. Another candidate for state park development is Lone Mesa in Dolores County.

The parks are among beneficiaries of Colorado's lottery, which assigns a bulk of its profits to parks, recreation and open space programs. The Foundation for Colorado State Parks makes grants for parks projects. Members of Volunteers for Outdoor Colorado help staff and maintain the parks. The parks welcome volunteers as naturalists, campground hosts and trail crew members.

To learn more: Colorado State Parks, 1313 Sherman St., Room 618, Denver 80203; (303) 866-3437; www.coloradoparks.org.

Dr. Colorado's List of Mighty Fine State Parks

Arkansas Headwaters State Park. The park north of Salida is in the heart of the Arkansas Headwaters Recreation Area, a 148-mile-long river playground that stretches from Leadville to Pueblo. The recreation area offers Colorado's most popular kayaking and rafting as well as fishing, hiking and scenery in deep canyons and broad valleys framed by the state's highest snow-capped peaks.

Barr Lake State Park. Only 20 miles northeast of downtown Denver, this tranquil 2,600-acre park hosts 330 different bird species, including resident bald eagles since 1986. Wooden walkways take you into various wetlands for closeup birding.

Cherry Creek State Park. Denver's only sandy, swimmable beaches lie on this 880-acre watery oasis. A prairie dog colony, horseback riding, boating, windsurfing, hunting dog training grounds and a model airplane field are among the many diversions. The park is at 4201 S. Parker Road, off I-25.

Colorado State Forest State Park. In remote mountains near Gould, Colo., and the Wyoming border, this lightly used park offers rental cabins, more than 100 campsites, a forest preserve of more than 70,000 acres, horseback riding and sand dunes open to motorized trail bikes and ATVs.

Eldorado Canyon State Park. More than 500 named rock climbing routes distinguish one of the best climbing parks in the United States. Fishing, swimming, soaking in Eldorado Warm Springs and hiking also make this park seven miles southwest of Boulder a special destination.

Eleven Mile State Park. Colorado's premier ice fishing leads anglers to the remote Eleven Mile Reservoir 50 miles west of Colorado Springs. During warmer months this 3,405-acre reservoir has yielded record-size trout, mackinaw, kokanee salmon and pike.

Lake Pueblo State Park. Interpretive features explain the local geology, history and natural history at this beachfront park on Pueblo Reservoir. The park, just west of the city of Pueblo, provides two marinas and water sports in what was once a prehistoric swamp, still rich in fossils.

Mueller State Park. About 12 miles north of Cripple Creek, Mueller State Park features a massive rock dome reminiscent of the domes of Yosemite. This 12,103-acre preserve entices visitors with mountain views, terrific trails, and wildlife viewing, plus a state-of-the-art interpretive and visitor center.

Navajo State Park. A petroglyph-covered rock guards the visitor center at Arboles on the New Mexico state line. Navajo Lake occupies 3,000 of the park's almost 5,000 acres, attracting anglers, houseboaters and water-skiers.

Rifle Falls State Park. Waterfalls, limestone caves and cliffs, and a misty spray that drenches mossy rocks and lush vegetation have given this park northwest of Glenwood Springs its nickname: Colorado's Hawaii.

State Symbols

Here are the official symbols of the state of Colorado:

 State bird: Lark bunting
 State flower: Columbine
 State fossil: Stegosaurus

State seal.

Stegosaurus, the state fossil.

 State gemstone: Aquamarine
 State grass: Blue grama
 State insect: Colorado hairstreak butterfly
 State mammal: Rocky Mountain bighorn sheep
 State tree: Colorado blue spruce
 State motto: *Nil Sine Numine* (Nothing without Providence)
 State song: "Where the Columbines Grow"

(*Also see* separate listings: Bighorn Mountain Sheep; Columbine; Dinosaurs; Lark Bunting; Spruce.)

Tabor (Horace, Augusta and Baby Doe)

Leadville's silver king, Horace Austin Warner Tabor, was a stonemason from Augusta, Maine, where he had married the boss's daughter, Augusta. The couple joined the Colorado gold rush and ultimately struck it rich in Leadville. Hard-working Augusta took in boarders, cooked, ran the Tabor General Store and served as postmistress. Her hard work helped make Horace a popular and wealthy man, but he later divorced her.

Horace built Leadville's Tabor Opera House and Vendome Hotel, then moved to Denver after his 1879 election as lieutenant governor. In Denver, he built the Tabor Grand Opera House and the Tabor Block (now replaced by the Tabor Center). In 1881 he was appointed to replace Henry M. Teller as U.S. senator after Teller became Secretary of the Interior.

In Washington, he married his mistress, Elizabeth "Baby Doe" McCourt Doe. After a 90-day appointment as senator, Tabor was not renominated because of the Baby Doe scandal. He returned to Denver and was wiped out financially by the 1893 silver crash.

After Tabor died in Denver in 1899, Baby Doe lived another 36 years, dying in her cabin at the Matchless Mine in Leadville. The Matchless and Baby Doe's cabin are now a museum, as are Leadville's Tabor Opera House and the old Tabor residence, but the Tabor Grand Opera House in Denver has been demolished. The Tabors' riches to rags story has been immortalized in the great American opera *The Ballad of Baby Doe.*

Taxes (SEE ALSO ELECTED OFFICIALS; LEGISLATURE) Colorado has a flat income tax of 5 percent. There is also a statewide sales tax of 2.9 percent.

Coloradans may make tax-deductible donations from a portion of their income tax refunds to special causes sanctioned by state law: nongame wildlife, relief of domestic abuse, homeless prevention and other causes. The Colorado Department of Revenue collects not only state taxes but also local taxes on behalf of more than 300 cities, towns, counties and special districts.

Some communities also charge their own additional sales tax: Arvada (3.21 percent), Aurora (3.75), Boulder (3.26), Brighton (3.75), Broomfield (3.75), Castle Rock (3.6), Denver (3.5), Golden (3.0), Lakewood (2), Littleton (3) and Westminster (3.25) are a few examples. Within the metro Denver area, residents also pay sales taxes of 0.6 percent for the Regional Transportation District, 0.1 percent for the Scientific and Cultural Facilities fund and 0.1 percent for the new Denver Broncos stadium—bringing the sales tax paid in the city of Denver to 7.2 percent. Other cities and towns around the state also charge varying sales taxes.

In 1993, Colorado voters approved Amendment 1, the so-called Taxpayer's Bill of Rights, that requires voter approval for any new taxes, extension of taxes or government debt. The amendment also limits increases in state revenues to the annual inflation rate plus the percentage change in state population. Excess revenue is to be returned to taxpayers unless they vote otherwise.

Income taxes provide about 55 percent of state revenue, with sales taxes generating another 29 percent. Various other taxes, fees and federal funds make up the rest.

Television Stations

(*SEE ALSO* RADIO STATIONS) Colorado's first television station, Channel 2, began broadcasting in 1952, followed by Channel 7 (CBS), Channel 4 (NBC) and Channel 9 (ABC) in 1953, all in Denver. Since the 1950s, the numbers have shuffled, with Channel 4 becoming CBS, Channel 7 ABC

Televisions Stations

City/Town	Letters	Channel	Affiliation
Arvada	KRMT	41	Christian
Colorado Springs	KKTV	11	CBS
	KRDO	13	ABC
	KXRM	21	FOX
	KXTU	57	UPN
	KOAA	5/30	NBC
Denver	KWGN	2	WB
	KCNC	4	CBS
	KRMA	6	PBS
	KMGH	7	ABC
	KDTV	8	Municipal
	KUSA	9	NBC
	KBDI	12	PBS
	KTVD	20	UPN
	KDEN	25	Independent
	KDVR	31	FOX
	KSHP	43	Shopping
	KCEC	50	Spanish
	KPXC	59	PAX
	KSBS	63/67	Telemundo
Durango	KREZ	6	CBS
Glenwood Springs	KREG	3	CBS
Grand Junction	KREX	5	CBS
	KJCT	8	ABC
	KKCO	11	NBC
	KRMJ	18	PBS
Montrose	KREY	10	CBS
Pueblo	KTSC	8	PBS
Sterling	KTVS	3	UPN

and Channel 9 NBC. Channel 6 (PBS) began broadcasting in 1956. As the continuing prominence of these pioneer channels suggests, Colorado's television broadcasting industry is more stable in terms of ownership and format than the state's radio industry.

Cable television networks are the fastest growing part of Colorado's media industry. While most of the programming on cable networks is the same nationwide, local programming is available on some. Cable network channels are numerous and generally specialized to follow niches such as movies, sports, 24-hour news, business, history, arts and entertainment.

To learn more: Colorado Broadcasters Association; www.e-cba.org.

Timberline
Between elevations of about 10,500 and 11,500 feet in Colorado, the climate becomes too cold and windy for even the hardiest evergreen trees. As the altitude increases, trees grow smaller and leaner and then disappear, giving way to alpine shrubs, plants and tundra.

Even from miles away, timberline is visible as the line between dark evergreen trees and lighter gray mountaintops of rock and sparse alpine vegetation. The sparkling glow of mountains above timberline in bright sunshine or moonlight led the Indians to call them "shining mountains." The Frenchman Pierre La Verendrye labeled them on his maps as *Les Montagnes de Pierres Brillantes*.

Tourism (_SEE ALSO_ NATIONAL PARKS; RAILROADS; STATE PARKS)

Tourism has been a major Colorado industry ever since the 1890s' decline of silver mining inspired railroads to switch from hauling ore to hauling tourists. Although some passenger railroads survive, automobile travel is now the principal method that rubberneckers use to explore Colorado.

State Welcome Centers at the major highway entry points—Burlington, Cortez, Dinosaur, Fort Collins, Fruita, Julesburg, Lamar and Trinidad—pamper tourists. Friendly local volunteers offer advice, free state maps, brochures, pamphlets and postcards. Crowded highways, fishing spots and ski lift lines, however, led Colorado voters to reject state funding for tourist ads. By 1999, Colorado had fallen from the fourth to the sixth most popular tourist destination state.

Losing ground to other states left many Coloradans relieved that they had gained more recreational ground for themselves. But tourism still remains the state's second-largest industry, after the service industry.

Information for Tourists: Where to Get It

Colorado Ski Country USA
1560 Broadway, Suite 2000
Denver 80202
(303) 837-0793
www.skicolorado.org

Colorado Springs Convention and Visitors Bureau
104 S. Cascade Ave.
Colorado Springs 80903
(719) 635-7506

Colorado State Parks
1313 Sherman St.
Denver 80203
(303) 866-3437
www.coloradoparks.org.

Colorado Travel and Tourism Authority
1672 Pennsylvania St.
Denver 80203
(800) 265-6723
(303) 832-6171
www.colorado.com

Denver Metro Convention and Visitors Bureau
1555 California St.
Denver 80202
(800) 462-5280
(303) 892-1112
www.denver.org

Dr. Colorado
www.coloradowebsites.com/dr-colorado
www.denvergov.org /aboutdenver
www.coloradohistory.org

Fort Collins Convention and Visitors Bureau
P.O. Box 1998
Fort Collins 80522
(800) 274-3678
(970) 482-5821

Grand Junction Convention and Visitors Bureau
740 Horizon Drive
Grand Junction 81506

Greeley Convention and Visitors Bureau
1407 Eighth Ave.
Greeley 80631

National Park Service
12795 W. Alameda Parkway

Lakewood 80228
(303) 969-2000
www.nps.gov

Silverton Chamber of Commerce
P.O. Box 565
Silverton 81433
(800) 752-4494
www.silverton.org

Southwest Colorado Travel Region
(970) 247-9621
www.swcolotravel.org

Summit County Tourism Division
1625 Broadway
Denver 80202
(303) 592-5510

U.S. Forest Service
P.O. Box 25127
Denver 80225
(303) 275-5350
www.fs.fed.us/recreation/states/co

**U.S. Bureau of
Land Management**
2850 Youngfield St.
Lakewood 80215
(303) 239-3600
www.blm.gov

Arch Support

On July 4, 1906, Mayor Robert Speer dedicated a 65-foot high Welcome Arch in front of Denver's Union Station. Speer promised it would stand forever to welcome tourists, but Mayor George Begole had it torn down in 1931 because it was "an impediment to the automobile." Some Denverites are now trying to reerect the Welcome Arch as "an impediment to the automobile." ✳

**Vail Valley Tourism and
Convention Bureau**
100 E. Meadow Drive
Vail. 81657
(970) 476-1000
www.visitvailvalley.com

Dr. Colorado's List of Offbeat Tourist Lures

- Fake Cliff Dwellings, Manitou Springs
- Fake Ghost Town, Colorado City
- Santa's North Pole Workshop, Cascade
- Coney Island Diner, Conifer
- Alligator Farm, Alamosa
- Tower of Genoa, Genoa
- May Bug Museum, Colorado Springs
- Big Pagosa Hot Springs, Pagosa Springs
- Fairy Caves at Glenwood Springs Caverns
- Shroud of Turin Museum, Colorado Springs

Trails (*SEE ALSO* NATIONAL FORESTS; NATIONAL PARKS; STATE PARKS; TOURISM; WATERFALLS) You can hike till you drop along the thousands of miles of public trails that wend their way throughout Colorado. The state's Division of Parks coordinates building and maintenance of trails not only for hikers, but also for bicyclists, skateboarders and inline skaters.

The Colorado Greenway Trail, inaugurated in 1976 with the opening of Denver's South Platte River and Cherry Creek trails, has expanded to include trails along much of the Platte and its tributaries, transforming once trashy urban waterways into scenic passageways and parks.

The Colorado Trail, a 470-mile footpath through the Rockies, stretches from Waterton Canyon, 20 miles south of Denver, to Durango. The Continental Divide Trail offers hikers a continuous route through Colorado from the Wyoming border to the New Mexico border along the crest of the continent. Trail opportunities are endless, with trails in state parks, national parks and other federal outdoor sites, and in and around many communities.

To learn more

Colorado State Parks; (303) 866-3437; www.coloradoparks.org.

Colorado Department of Transportation; bicycle routes (303) 757-9982.

National Park Service; (303) 969-2000; www.nps.gov.

U.S. Forest Service; (303) 275-5350; www.fs.fed.us/recreation/states/co.

Transportation *(SEE ALSO AIRPORTS; HIGHWAYS; MOTOR VEHICLES; RAILROADS)* In a large state of long distances and mountainous obstacles, transportation has always been a major concern. Denver emerged as the state capital by making itself the hub for stagecoach and rail transportation, and subsequently the junction of the state's I-25, I-70 and I-76 freeways, as well as the regional air travel hub.

As one of the most isolated inland states, Colorado has been obsessed with transportation systems. Fear of being bypassed began early when railroads and, later,  airlines originally avoided the state because of the 14,000-foot-high Rocky Mountain barrier. To secure Colorado's place on the national transportation map, Denver opened a new $5 billion airport in 1995.

Colorado's long distances, lack of public transportation and mountain obstacles have made Coloradans auto-dependent. A 1999 Denver Regional Council of Governments report found that the eight-county Denver metro area has 16.6 percent more registered vehicles than licensed drivers. A Council survey found that only 4 percent of those surveyed used buses or light rail. Fourteen percent said they sometimes walked or rode a bike instead of driving.

The Colorado Department of Highways changed its name in 1993 to the Department of Transportation, signifying a new approach to encourage not only highway motoring but also the use of buses, light rail, car pools, bicycles—and even feet.

To learn more: Colorado Department of Transportation; (800) 999-4997; www.dot.state.co.us.

Trinidad The Las Animas County seat, founded in 1859, is on the Purgatoire River at the northern base of Raton Pass, the major crossing point from southcentral Colorado into New Mexico.

The Mountain Branch of the Santa Fe Trail ran through Trinidad, as did the Goodnight-Loving Cattle Trail. Trinidad was also headquarters for the Prairie Land and Cattle Co.'s vast holdings. Trinidad grew slowly and did not incorporate until 1879, in part because litigation of Mexican land grant claims kept property ownership uncertain until the mid-1870s.

Trinidad boomed between the 1880s and the 1920s, when the thriving coal industry made it Colorado's fourth-largest city. It attracted numerous immigrants, including those of Anglo, German, Hispanic, Irish, Italian, Lebanese and Slavic heritage. When natural gas and electricity started to replace coal in the 1940s, Trinidad began losing population. From a peak of 13,223 in 1940 it has dwindled to 9,000.

The Trinidad of today retains a good bit of its antique cityscape. Although the Pueblo Revival-style Santa Fe Railroad depot and Cardenas Hotel have been lost, Trinidad still has its grand Columbian Hotel, First National Bank, Opera House, Temple Aaron, Toltec Hotel and West Theater.

Many landmarks are constructed of the distinctive local sandstone. The town's architecture is highlighted in the Corazón de Trinidad (Heart of Trinidad) Historic District.

To learn more: Trinidad History Museum, 300 E. Main St., Trinidad 81082; (719) 846-7217.

Universities and Colleges (SEE ALSO EDUCATION)

Colorado's state-supported higher-education system consists of universities, state colleges and community colleges. In addition, the state is home to several private colleges and universities and to the U.S. Air Force Academy.

The state's most popular single campus is the Auraria Higher Education Center in Denver, a novel concept in which three institutions— Denver Community College, University of Colorado at Denver and Metropolitan State College of Denver—share many facilities (such as library, recreation center and student center). The joint enrollment of the three schools at the Auraria Center is about 33,000.

Vocational-technical training for adults began with the Opportunity School established by Emily Griffith (see entry) and the Denver Public Schools in 1916. Such training now is offered at the state's regional voc-tech centers in Alamosa, Aurora, Boulder, Cortez, Delta, Fort Collins and Trinidad.

During the 1960s and 1970s, Colorado greatly expanded its higher education facilities. Federal funding, already significant with the GI Bill after World War II and the Korean War, increased as a result of the 1964 Civil Rights Act and the Higher Education Act of 1965. Colorado aspires to make higher education available to all residents and prides itself on having the country's fourth-highest education level, as measured by per capita college graduates.

Looking Back

Jan. 29, 1938

A trainload of Denverites officially opened Winter Park, a municipal ski area west of Denver in Grand County.

State Universities

University of Colorado, founded in 1876, is the largest of the state schools, with a total of more than 40,000 students on four campuses. Boulder is the main and oldest campus, with younger sisters in Colorado Springs and Denver, including the Health Sciences Center in Denver, the state's only medical school. At Boulder: Euclid Avenue and Broadway, 80309; (303) 492-1411. At Colorado Springs: 1420 Austin Bluffs Parkway, 80933; (719) 262-3500. At Denver: Speer Boulevard and Larimer Street, 80202; (303) 556-5600.

Colorado State University, founded in 1879 as the state agricultural college, has become a full-fledged university while retaining an emphasis on agricultural education and research. Administration Building, The Oval, Laurel Street and College Avenue, Fort Collins 80523; (970) 491-7600.

University of Northern Colorado, established in 1889 as the state teachers college, has evolved into a full university. Carter Hall Administration Building, Greeley 80639; (970) 351-1700.

University of Southern Colorado, founded in 1933, was first known as Pueblo Junior College, then Southern Colorado State. 2200 Bonforte Blvd. and Hwy. 47, Pueblo 81005; (719) 549-2100.

Colorado School of Mines, founded in 1874, is one of the world's foremost colleges of mineral engineering.

1500 Illinois Ave., Golden 80401; (303) 273-3000.

State Colleges

Adams State College, founded 1925. Richardson Hall, 208 Edgemount Blvd., Alamosa 81101; (719) 587-7122.

Fort Lewis College, founded 1911. 1000 Rim Drive, Durango 81301; (970) 247-7100.

Mesa State College, founded 1925. College Street and North Avenue, Grand Junction 81502; (970) 943-0120.

Metropolitan State College of Denver. Speer Boulevard and Auraria Parkway, Denver 80202; (303) 556-3058.

Western State College, founded 1911. 909 Escalante Dr., Gunnison 81230; (970) 943-0120.

Community Colleges

A system of two-year community, or junior, colleges modeled on California's pioneer efforts to democratize higher education was established in 1967.

Aims Community College, P.O. Box 69, Greeley 80632; (970) 330-8008.

Arapahoe Community College, 5900 S. Santa Fe Drive, Littleton 80160; (303) 794-1550.

Aurora Community College, 16000 Centreteck Parkway, Aurora 80011; (303) 360-4700.

Colorado Mountain College, with campuses in Aspen, Breckenridge, Glenwood Springs, Leadville and Steamboat Springs; P.O. Box 1001, Glenwood Springs 81602; (970) 945-8691.

Colorado Northwestern Community College, 500 Kennedy Drive, Rangely 81648; (970) 675-2261.

Denver Community College, 1111 West Colfax Ave., Denver 80204; (303) 556-2600.

Front Range Community College, 3645 W. 112th Ave., Westminster 80030; (303) 466-8811.

Lamar Community College, 2401 S. Main St., Lamar 81052; (719) 335-2248.

Morgan Community College, 17800 Road 20, Fort Morgan 80701; (800) 622-0216.

Northeastern Community College, 100 College Drive, Sterling 80751; (970) 522-660.

Otero Junior College, 1802 Colorado Ave., La Junta 81050; (719) 384-8721.

Pikes Peak Community College, 5675 S. Academy Blvd., Colorado Springs 80906; (719) 576-7711.

Pueblo Community College, 900 W. Orman Ave., Pueblo 81004; (719) 549-3200.

Red Rocks Community College, 13300 W. Sixth Ave., Lakewood 80228; (303) 988-6160.

Trinidad State Junior College, 600 Prospect St., Trinidad 81082; (719) 846-5011.

Air Force Academy

The Air Force Academy, which opened on the north side of Colorado Springs in 1958, enrolls some 4,000 cadets aspiring to become Air Force officers. USAF Academy 80840; (719) 333-9400.

Private Universities and Colleges

University of Denver was founded in 1864 by Territorial Governor John Evans as the Colorado Seminary. It is the state's oldest institution of higher learning and its largest private school, having absorbed Colorado Women's College during the 1980s. 2199 S. University Blvd., Denver 80210; (303) 871-2000.

Regis University developed from an institution founded in 1877 by the Catholic

teaching order of Jesuits. 3333 Regis Blvd., Denver 80221; (303) 458-4100.

Colorado College, founded in 1873, is the state's best-endowed private school, widely known for undergraduate education and for its block courses in which students focus on one subject for several weeks at a time. 930 N. Cascade Ave., Colorado Springs 80903; (719) 389-6000.

Nazarene Bible College. 1111 Academy Park Loop, Colorado Springs 80910; (719) 596-5110.

Colorado Christian University. 180 S. Garrison St., Lakewood 80226; (303) 202-0100.

Uranium
The first U.S. discovery of uranium came in Gilpin County, Colorado, in 1871. Subsequent early production for Marie Curie's radium studies made Colorado the birthplace of the U.S. uranium mining industry. Production during the first quarter of the 20th century produced radium for use in cancer treatment and in luminated paint for dials, instruments, watches and gunsights.

Widely distributed in Colorado, the most common uranium mineral is called uranite in its primary form. It is characterized by high density, black to dark brown color, pitchy or greasy luster and high radioactivity. A secondary form, carnotite, is bright yellow. Because of uranium's use in nuclear weapons, the U. S. government was for a time the only legal purchaser of uranium.

The rush for uranium accelerated after geologist Charlie Steen became an overnight millionaire by discovering a vein of uranium ore at his Mi Vida mine south of Moab, Utah, in 1952. A frenzied mineral rush, comparable to earlier gold and silver rushes, brought hordes of prospectors using Geiger counters into Colorado and Utah.

Surface prospecting quickly gave way to deeper lode mining by Homestake Mining Co., Amax and others. By 1980, $100 million worth of uranium had been extracted from the Colorado plateau. Small western Colorado towns such as Naturita, Paradox and Uravan boomed. Grand Junction became the uranium hub after the Atomic Energy Commission opened an office there and mills were built throughout the Western Slope to process uranium ore.

By the 1980s the boom was over, although a new boom began in the cleanup of hazardous radioactive waste sites. Some uranium mining continues, with Colorado's 1999 production worth $5 million.

U.S. Mint
One of Colorado's most popular free attractions commemorates the state's gold rush origins. The U.S. Mint in Denver started out as the private mint of Clark, Gruber and Co. During 1860 and 1861, that firm was one of Colorado's largest gold dust buyers, minting gold pieces in denominations of $2.50, $5, $10 and $20 as well as printing $1 and $5 bills. The original minting equipment, greenback dollars and coins may be seen at the Colorado History Museum (1300 Broadway, Denver; 303-866-3682).

Intense devotion to the Denver Broncos—Broncomania—was diagnosed by a Denver psychiatrist as "a healthy outlet for a whole variety of emotions.... Commitment, investment, fervor, and interest are always better than apathy."

When the federal government outlawed private mints in 1862, brothers Austin and Milton Clark and Emanuel H. Gruber sold their mint at 1600 Market St. to Uncle Sam. The federal government continued to assay, buy, refine and store gold in Denver, but shipped it to Philadelphia for minting until 1906. That year the government opened its long-promised Denver mint.

The splendid 1906 edifice, a two-story gray fortress architecturally inspired by the Palazzo Medici-Riccardi in Florence, Italy, celebrates the Italian Renaissance origins of banking and the modern monetary system. Architects Gordon, Tracy, and Swarthout of New York City used pink, black-flecked Pikes Peak granite for the base and Cotopaxi gray granite for the upper walls. Allegorical murals by Vincent Aderente in the main hall portray Colorado's mining, manufacturing and commerce.

The mint has not been robbed since 1922, when three burglars with shotguns got away with $200,000. With large building additions made in 1987 and 2000, the mint now occupies the full block bounded by West Colfax and West 14th avenues between Cherokee and Delaware streets in Denver's Civic Center. The Denver Mint makes 12 billion coins a year, stamping each penny, nickel, dime, quarter and dollar with the letter D. No gold coins have been minted since 1931, although the Sacagawea one-dollar coin first minted in 2000 has a golden look.

To learn more: Visitors are welcome Monday–Friday, 8 A.M.–3 P.M. The 20-minute tour is free but includes no samples. The gift shop sells commemorative coins and other souvenirs. Three subterranean floors housing the mint's stash of gold bars are not open to the public. (303) 405-4761.

Vital Statistics (SEE ALSO POPULATION) On an average day, Colorado

experiences 92 marriages, 163 births and 73 deaths.

In the decade between 1990 and 2000, Colorado's population increased by about 30 percent, to 4.3 million. The state has the third-highest birth rate and fourth-lowest death rate in the United States.

Compared with average national figures, Colorado has a lower rate of births to teenagers, a lower rate of infant deaths and of deaths from heart disease and cancer, and a lower homicide rate. Life expectancy is higher. At the same time, there is a higher death rate for suicide, and a higher rate of death related to motor vehicles, drugs or alcohol.

To learn more: Colorado Department of Public Health and Environment; www.cdphe.state.co.us.

Voting (SEE ALSO CONGRESSIONAL DELEGATION; ELECTED OFFICIALS; LEGISLATURE) To vote in Colorado, you must be a U.S. citizen at least 18 years old who is registered to vote in the state; you can't be a felon in prison or on parole.

Colorado tries to make registration easy. Coloradans can register with the county clerk or elections commission, and also at places where driver's licenses are issued. Registration can also be done by mail.

Mail-in voting is available for people who can't or don't want to go to their precinct polling place on election days, where polls are open 7 A.M. to 7 P.M.

General elections including candidates for national office are held on the Tuesday after the first Monday in November in even-numbered years. State and some local elections also are held on the Tuesday after the first Monday in November in the odd-numbered years.

Colorado holds its presidential primary election on the first Tuesday of March of each presidential election year. The state primary election is on the second Tuesday of August in even-numbered years. Only those who have declared a choice of party may vote in the primary of a particular party, although unaffiliated voters may select their party at the polling place on election day.

Selection of candidates for the two major parties begins with precinct caucuses held by Democrats and Republicans in each neighborhood precinct, a geographical area containing up to 1,000 registered voters. In each of about 3,500 Colorado precincts, the precinct captain arranges for the caucus, which is usually held in the evening in a private home.

It's like a pyramid, with the precincts at the base. Each precinct caucus selects a delegate to a county convention. The county convention selects delegates to the state convention. The state convention selects nominees to appear on the primary ballot.

Candidates can bypass the caucus system by trying to gather a certain required number of signatures, allowing them to be included on the primary ballot.

Waterfalls Colorado's

waterways tumble from the Rockies in a jubilant procession of rivulets, cascades, creeks, rivers and waterfalls. Most waterfalls are on public lands where everyone is welcome to feel the mist, enjoy the well-sprinkled vegetation and dip into the chilly, bubbly water.

Fish Creek Falls, near Steamboat Springs. Photo by Gail Brooks.

Marc and Nancy Conly in *Waterfalls of Colorado* (Pruett Publishing Co., 1993) categorize 265 named Colorado falls into different types: plumage, horsetail, fan, segmented, punchbowl, tiered, serial and cascade. Falls often dig out plunge pools ideal for bathing and swimming. Following is a look at some of the most spectacular and accessible waterfalls.

Dr. Colorado's List of Top Waterfalls

Boulder Falls. A 40-foot beauty that lies at the end of a mere tenth-of-a-mile trail as the centerpiece of a Boulder mountain park, eight miles west of Boulder on State Hwy. 119.

Bridal Veil Falls. Tallest in Colorado at 431 feet, is on the San Miguel River two miles upstream from Telluride. A short, steep hike takes you to the top.

Bridal Veil Falls. (Yes, another one.) Along the Colorado River in Glenwood Canyon. Accessible from the Hanging Lake Rest Area. Hike the steep Dead Horse Creek Trail 1 mile to Hanging Lake at the base of these falls. The falls flow into Hanging Lake over moss-hung cliffs, at one place dividing into a triplet of veils.

Cascade Falls. On the northeast edge of the amphitheater cliffs rimming Ouray. Only a half-mile walk from the center of town. The 80-foot waterfall is visible from many parts of town.

Falls Creek Falls. Makes an initial leap of 60 feet, then a separate plunge of 170 feet, and winds up with a 50-foot slide over rock. A 3.3-mile trial leads to the falls from a trailhead 10 miles north of Pagosa Springs on Archuleta County Road 400.

Fish Creek Falls. Flies through an 80-foot upper segment before reaching its 50-foot lower section. The falls, framed by rock shoulders decorated with evergreen trees, is four miles from Steamboat Springs on Fish Creek Falls Road.

Rifle Falls. Makes its show with three falls, each tumbling 60 to 70 feet. The display is northwest of Glenwood Springs at the Rifle Falls State Recreation Area.

Helen Hunt Falls. Named for a prominent Colorado author and defender of Native American rights. This 30-foot falls is within Cheyenne Canyon Park, about four miles west of the Broadmoor Hotel in Colorado Springs on North Cheyenne Creek Road.

Seven Falls. A commercial attraction on South Cheyenne Creek at Colorado Springs. Consists of a series of seven falls with a cumulative drop of 261 feet. Night lighting and observation decks, even an elevator, make this an easy treat for even the most sedentary waterfall lover.

Treasure Falls. On Falls Creek. Makes its fabulous 105-foot leap about 12 miles west of Wolf Creek Pass, near U.S. Hwy. 160. A walk of two-tenths of a mile leads to a fine view of the falls.

Water Sports (SEE ALSO LAKES AND RESERVOIRS; RIVERS; STATE PARKS)

Colorado rivers, lakes and reservoirs offer not only scenery and fishing, but also quiet rowing and paddling, sailing, water-skiing and whitewater kayaking and rafting.

Colorado rivers come in three flavors; flat water; modest Class I and II rapids; and serious Class III to V rapids providing a boisterous raft, canoe or kayak ride. The river-flows during spring runoff, when snow is melting fast, provide the wildest, fastest descents.

The many commercial outfitters in or near river towns offer possibilities ranging from half-day to multiday excursions. Rafting has transformed the Arkansas and Colorado into two of the most rafted U.S. rivers. Raft trips are also available on many other waterways, from Clear Creek to the Cache la Poudre River, even on the South Platte through metro Denver.

Most Popular for Rafting and Kayaking

Arkansas River: Browns Canyon and Royal Gorge between Buena Vista and Cañon City, in the Arkansas Headwaters Recreation Area.

Colorado River: Glenwood Canyon and Glenwood Springs.

Blue River: Silverthorn to Green Mountain Reservoir.

Roaring Fork River: Aspen to Glenwood Springs.

Most Popular for Canoeing
Colorado River: Loma to Westwater, Utah.
Gunnison River: Escalante Canyon Bridge to Whitewater.
Yampa River: Craig to Juniper Hot Springs.
Dolores River: Confluence of San Miguel and Dolores rivers to Gateway.

Most Popular for Sailing and Water-Skiing
Pueblo Reservoir, just west of Pueblo.
Chatfield Reservoir, a few miles southwest of Denver.
Cherry Creek Reservoir, southeast edge of Denver.
Dillon Reservoir, some 60 miles west of Denver.
Grand Lake, near the western entrance to Rocky Mountain National Park.

To learn more
Bureau of Land Management has information on access and river flows. (303) 239-3600; www./blm.gov.
Colorado River Outfitters Association can provide a directory of licensed rafting outfitters. (303) 280-2554; www.croa.org.
Centennial Canoe; canoe outfitter (303) 755-3501;www.centennialcanoe.co.

Wildlife Areas
Colorado has more than 100 state wildlife areas used to maintain animal habitat. They are available for hunting and other recreational uses. Most are small, and many are adjacent to other public lands. The following are among the larger and more notable state wildlife areas.
• Big Thompson Ponds SWA, Larimer County
• Bitter Brush SWA, Moffat County
• Jumbo Reservoir SWA, Logan and Sedgwick counties

Rafters ride the Colorado River through Glenwood Canyon to Glenwood Springs as an Amtrak train races by. Photo by Tom Noel.

• Overland Trail SWA, Logan County
• Tilman Bishop SWA, Mesa County
• Waunita Watchable Wildlife Area, Gunnison County
To learn more: Colorado Division of Wildlife, 6060 Broadway, Denver 80216; (303) 291-7366; www.dnr.state.co.us.

Wind
The "only flaw in the climate of Colorado," according to the *Encyclopaedia Britannica* (9th ed.) "is its violent storms of wind."

Winds of 100 miles an hour or more regularly scour the state. From the mountaintops to the plains, nothing stands in the wind's way and nothing stops it. The mountains are scarred with blowdowns of fallen trees and the plains with blowouts where high winds have destroyed vegetation and scooped holes into the earth. On Oct. 2, 1997, winds reaching 120 miles per hour flattened more than 4 million spruce and fir trees in Routt National Forest near Steamboat Springs.

Winter winds accompanying falling snow create blizzards. Even on clear days, winds can generate ground blizzards by blowing around already fallen snow. Winds also stir up dust storms and whirling dervishes. They can also be benevolent, air-conditioning hot summer days or blowing away the brown cloud of pollution that accumulates in populated river valleys.

Wineries
William N. Byers, founding editor of the *Rocky Mountain News* and Colorado's greatest promoter, experimented with wine making in Denver during the 1860s. Serious grape growing and wine making began in the Palisade-Grand Junction area after the 1884 completion of the Grand Ditch irrigation project.

Among the viticultural pioneers was George Crawford, founder of Grand Junction. By 1900, the U.S. Census of Agriculture reported Colorado produced 586,300 pounds of grapes and 1,744 gallons of wine.

Prohibition dried up the wine business between 1916 and 1933. Not until 1968 did Dr. Gerald Ivancie resurrect the activity with the winery he opened in Denver, using grapes grown in and around Palisade in Mesa County. His success led to establishment of the Colorado Wine Industry Development Board in 1990.

Palisade, in the Grand (Colorado River) Valley near Grand Junction in western Colorado, boasts a third of Colorado's 26 wineries, with others scattered around the state from Colorado Springs to Salida. In Colorado's high altitude, chardonnay and merlot grapes grow best and make up about half of the vineyards.

To learn more:
www.coloradowine.com.

Dr. Colorado's List of Selected Wineries

Colorado Springs
Pikes Peak Vineyards, 3901 Winery Road, Colorado Springs 80906; (719) 576-0075. Tasting room daily except Sun. and holidays, noon–5:30 P.M. Founded 1981; 6,000 gallons a year.

Olathe
Cottonwood Cellars, founded 1994; 3,400 gallons a year. Tasting room Wed.–Sat. 11 A.M.–6 P.M. 5482 State Hwy. 348, Olathe 81425; (970) 323-6224.

Minturn
Minturn Cellars, founded 1990; 2,000 gallons a year. Tasting room daily noon–5 P.M. 107 Williams St., Minturn 81645; (970) 827-4065.

Palisade
Carlson Vineyards, founded 1988; 12,000–15,000 gallons a year. Tasting room daily 11 A.M.–6 P.M. 461 35 Road, Palisade 81526; (970) 464-5554.

Colorado Cellars, founded 1978; 50,000 gallons a year. Tasting room Mon.–Sat. noon–4 P.M. 3553 E Road, Palisade 81526; (970) 464-7921.

Grand River Vineyards, founded 1987; 10,000–15,000 gallons a year. Tasting room daily 9 A.M.–7 P.M. 787 Elberta Ave. via I-70 exit 42, Palisade 81526; (800) 264-7696.

Plum Creek Cellars, founded 1984; 18,000–30,000 gallons a year. Tasting room daily 10 A.M.–6 P.M. 3708 G Road, Palisade 81526; (970) 464-7586.

Rocky Mountain Meadery, founded 1995. Tasting room daily 10 A.M.–5 P.M. 3701 G Road, Palisade 81526; (970) 464-7899.

Women

Colorado, according to the first census in 1860, had 20 males for each female. In 1870 and 1880, women composed roughly a third of the population. Not until the 20th century did the ratio become even.

Although a minority, 19th-century Colorado women helped make Colorado the first state where men voted yes on the specific issue of women's suffrage. When Colorado became a state in 1876, delegates considered including women's suffrage in the constitution, but only Henry Bromwell of Denver and Agapita Vigil of Huerfano County voted for it.

Women were allowed to vote only in school and library board elections. When women's suffrage was first referred to the state electorate, in 1877, it passed only in Boulder County.

"Let the women vote! They can't do any worse than the men!" became the slogan of the suffrage campaign of 1893.

With the help of national leaders such as Carrie Chapman Catt, Colorado men were persuaded to approve women's suffrage that November, by a vote of 35,798 to 29,451.

In 1894 women were first elected to the state House of Representatives. Helen Ring Robinson, a Denver Democrat, became the first female state senator in 1912. Virginia Neal Blue was the first woman state treasurer, from 1967 to 1970. Colorado's first woman lieutenant governor was Nancy Dick, 1978–1982.

In 1972 Patricia Schroeder became the first woman elected by Coloradans to the U.S. Congress. Mary Mullarkey became Colorado's first female state supreme court justice in 1998. Colorado has yet to elect a woman governor or U.S. senator.

To learn more

League of Women Voters, 1410 Grant St., Denver 80203; (303) 863-8683.

Women of the West Museum, 1536 Wynkoop St., Denver 80202; (303) 541-1000, www.wowmuseum.org.

Zip Codes

Postal zip codes were instituted in the United States in 1963, and new ones are created every year as the population increases. The U.S. Postal Service added six new codes for Colorado in 2000—one each for Boulder, Durango, Highlands Ranch and three suburban Denver communities in Adams and Weld Counties. The following list includes towns with their zip code or codes.

Agate   80101
Aguilar   81020
Akron   80720
Alamosa   81101–02
Allenspark   80510
Almont   81210
Amherst   80721
Anton   80801
Antonito   81120
Arapahoe   80802
Arboles   81121
Arlington   81021
Arriba   80804
Arvada   80002–05
Aspen   81611
Atwood   80722
Ault   80610
Aurora   80010–19, 80045
Austin   81410
Avon   81620
Avondale   81022
Bailey   80421
Basalt   81621
Bayfield   81122
Bedrock   81411
Bellvue   80512
Bennett   80102
Berthoud   80513

Bethune   80805
Beulah   81023
Black Hawk   80422
Blanca   81123
Bond   80423
Boone   81025
Boulder   80301–04
Brandon   81026
Branson   81027
Breckenridge   80424
Briggsdale   80611
Brighton   80601
Bristol   81028
Broomfield   80020–21
Brush   80723
Buena Vista   81211
Burlington   80807
Byers   80103
Cahone   81320
Calhan   80808
Campo   81029
Canon City   81212
Carbondale   81623
Carr   80612
Cascade   80809
Castle Rock   80104
Cedaredge   81413
Center   81125
Cheraw   81030
Cheyenne Wells   80810
Cimarron   81220
Clark   80428
Clifton   81520
Climax   80429
Coalmont   80430
Collbran   81624
Colorado City   81019

Colorado Springs   80903–11, 80913–22,
   80925–26, 80928–30, 80933, 80946
Commerce City   80022
Conejos   81129
Conifer   80433
Cope   80812
Cortez   81321
Cotopaxi   81223
Craig   81625
Crawford   81415
Creede   81130
Crested Butte   81224
Cripple Creek   80813
Crook   80726
Dacono   80514
De Beque   81630
Deer Trail   80105
Del Norte   81132
Delta   81416
Denver   80202–12, 80214, 80216–25, 80229,
   80231, 80233–37, 80239, 80241,
   80249–50, 80262
Dillon   80435
Dinosaur   81610, 81633
Divide   80814
Dolores   81323
Dove Creek   81324
Drake   80515
Durango   81301–02
Eads   81036
Eagle   81631
Eastlake   80614
Eaton   80615
Eckert   81418
Eckley   80727
Edwards   81632
Egnar   81325
Elbert   80106
Elizabeth   80107
Englewood   80110–12, 80150, 80155
Erie   80516
Estes Park   80517
Evans   80620
Evergreen   80439
Fairplay   80440
Flagler   80815
Fleming   80728

Florence 81226
Florissant 80816
Fort Collins 80521, 80523–26
Fort Garland 81133
Fort Lupton 80621
Fort Morgan 80701
Fountain 80817
Fowler 81039
Franktown 80116
Fraser 80442
Frederick 80530
Frisco 80443
Fruita 81521
Galeton 80622
Gardner 81040
Gateway 81522
Genoa 80818
Georgetown 80444
Gilcrest 80623
Gill 80624
Glenwood Springs 81601–02
Golden 80401, 80403
Granada 81041
Granby 80446
Grand Junction 81501–06
Grand Lake 80447
Granite 81228
Greeley 80631, 80634
Grover 80729
Guffey 80820
Gunnison 81230–31
Gypsum 81637
Hamilton 81638
Hartman 81043
Hasty 81044
Haswell 81045
Haxtun 80731
Hayden 81639
Henderson 80640
Hesperus 81326
Hillrose 80733
Hoehne 81046
Holly 81047
Holyoke 80734
Hooper 81136
Hotchkiss 81419
Howard 81233

Hudson 80642
Hugo 80821
Hygiene 80533
Idaho Springs 80452
Idalia 80735
Ignacio 81137
Iliff 80736
Indian Hills 80454
Jamestown 80455
Jefferson 80456
Joes 80822
Johnstown 80534
Julesburg 80737
Karval 80823
Keenesburg 80643
Kersey 80644
Kim 81049
Kiowa 80117
Kirk 80824
Kit Carson 80825
Kremmling 80459
La Jara 81140
La Junta 81050
La Salle 80645
La Veta 81055
Lafayette 80026
Lake City 81235
Lake George 80827
Lakewood 80215, 80226–28, 80232
Lamar 81052
Laporte 80535
Larkspur 80118
Las Animas 81054
Leadville 80461
Lewis 81327
Limon 80828
Lindon 80740
Littleton 80120–27, 80160
Livermore 80536
Loma 81524
Longmont 80501, 80503–04
Louisville 80027
Loveland 80537–38
Lowry 80230
Lyons 80540
Mack 81525
Manassa 81141

Mancos   81328
Manitou Springs   80829
Manzanola   81058
Matheson   80830
Maybell   81640
McClave   81057
McCoy   80463
Mead   80542
Meeker   81641
Meredith   81642
Merino   80741
Mesa   81643
Milliken   80543
Minturn   81645
Model   81059
Moffat   81143
Monte Vista   81144
Montrose   81401–02
Monument   80132
Morrison   80465
Mosca   81146
Nathrop   81236
Naturita   81422
Nederland   80466
New Castle   81647
New Raymer   80742
Norwood   81423
Nucla   81424
Nunn   80648
Oak Creek   80467
Olathe   81425
Olney Springs   81062
Ophir   81426
Orchard   80649
Ordway   81063
Otis   80743
Ouray   81427
Ovid   80744

Padroni   80745
Pagosa Springs   81147
Palisade   81526
Palmer Lake   80133
Paonia   81428
Parachute   81635
Paradox   81429
Parker   80134
Parlin   81239
Parshall   80468
Peetz   80747
Penrose   81240
Peyton   80831
Pierce   80650
Pine   80470
Pinecliffe   80471
Pitkin   81241
Placerville   81430
Platteville   80651
Pleasant View   81331
Powderhorn   81243
Pritchett   81064
Pueblo   81001–08
Ramah   80832
Rangely   81648
Red Feather Lakes   80545
Redvale   81431
Ridgway   81432
Rifle   81650
Rocky Ford   81067
Roggen   80652
Rollinsville   80474
Rush   80833
Rye   81069
Saguache   81149
Salida   81201
San Luis   81152
San Pablo   81153
Sanford   81151
Sedalia   80135
Sedgwick   80749
Seibert   80834
Sheridan Lake   81071
Silt   81652
Silverthorne   80498
Silverton   81433
Simla   80835

Slater   81653
Snowmass   81654
Snyder   80750
Somerset   81434
South Fork   81154
Springfield   81073
Steamboat Springs   80477, 80487
Sterling   80751
Stoneham   80754
Strasburg   80136
Stratton   80836
Sugar City   81076
Swink   81077
Telluride   81435
Timnath   80547
Toponas   80479
Towaoc   81334
Trinchera   81081
Trinidad   81082
Twin Lakes   81251
Two Buttes   81084
USAF Academy   80840
Vail   81657
Vernon   80755
Vilas   81087
Villa Grove   81155
Vona   80861
Walden   80480
Walsenburg   81089
Walsh   81090
Ward   80481
Watkins   80137
Weldona   80653
Wellington   80549
Westcliffe   81252
Westminster   80030
Weston   81091
Wetmore   81253
Wheat Ridge   80033
Whitewater   81527
Wiggins   80654
Wiley   81092
Windsor   80550
Woodland Park   80863, 80866
Woodrow   80757
Wray   80758
Yampa   80483

Yellow Jacket   81335
Yoder   80864
Yuma   80759

To learn more: www.usps.gov/ncsc/lookups/lookups.htm

Zoos
Colorado has three major zoos and one major aquarium, plus several specialized animal refuge and display sites.

Cheyenne Mountain Zoo. The Broadmoor Hotel in Colorado Springs once had a considerable menagerie of hotel pets, including a boa constrictor, an elephant and monkeys. After one of the monkeys bit a guest, hotel owner Spencer Penrose created the Cheyenne Mountain Zoo in 1926, providing a home for his animals. The zoo has grown to house more than 500 animals representing 150 species in a 75-acre mountainside park. Open daily 9 A.M.– 6 P.M.; $4.50–$7.50. 4250 Cheyenne Mountain Zoo Road, Colorado Springs 80906; (719) 389-6800; www.cmzoo.org.

Once scoffed at, Colorado wineries are gaining respectability. You really can drink their stuff.

Colorado's Ocean Journey. This $93 million, 106,00-square-foot aquarium and zoo arose along the South Platte River in central Denver in 1999. Situated near Elitch Garden's Amusement Park and the Denver Children's Museum, Ocean Journey has 15,000 animals representing more than 300 species. Thematically the main exhibit traces the Colorado River environment and wildlife from the river's origin in Rocky

Mountain National Park to Mexico's Sea of Cortez. Open daily 9 A.M.–6 P.M.; adults $15, seniors $13, children $7, under 4 free. 700 Water St., Denver 80211; (303) 561-4450; www.oceanjourney.org.

Pueblo Zoo. Founded in 1903, the Pueblo Zoo displays more than 300 animals on a 25-acre site. Open daily 9 A.M.–4 P.M., $1–$4. Goodnight Avenue and Pueblo Boulevard in City Park, Pueblo 81005; (719) 561-9664; www.pueblozoo.org.

Denver Zoological Gardens. Located in City Park next to the Denver Museum of Nature and Science, the zoo houses 3,500 animals representing 660 species, making it one of the most diverse of U.S. zoos.

Billy, a black bear cub given to Mayor Thomas S. McMurray, opened the Denver Zoo with a growl. The mayor gave the troublesome bruin to Alexander J. Graham, the keeper of City Park. After the bear gobbled up Graham's chickens and turkeys, he built the first zoo cages in 1896.

The zoo was a sad jumble of caged and chained creatures by the time Robert W. Speer became mayor in 1904. Speer had the zoo's director, Victor H. Borcherdt, design and build Bear Mountain, the high point in the zoo's history—and topography. Completed in 1918, this artificial hill 43 feet high and 185 feet long has a steel skeleton hidden under tinted and textured concrete. The mountain's natural-looking bear pits are surrounded by moats, native plants and a stream. After designation as a National Register Landmark in 1986, Bear Mountain received a $250,000 restoration benefitting the species that gave the zoo its start.

The Denver Zoo grew over the years with development of Monkey Island, then a children's zoo, a pachyderm habitat, a feline house, a giraffe house and an animal hospital. Special display and habitat areas were built for birds, mountain sheep and primates. The Northern Shores area built in

---

The Gators of Colorado

Ewing and Lynne Young moved from Florida to Alamosa in the San Luis Valley in 1987 to start a fish farm, using a natural hot springs for raising talapia and other warm-water fish. They brought along alligators to dispose of the fish remains. People began dropping in to see the gators, so the Youngs opened their large fenced lagoon to visitors.

Along with about 120 alligators, the Colorado Alligator Farm now features other reptiles, a petting zoo and fish tanks. The farm is on State Hwy. 17 in Mosca, 17 miles north of Alamosa. Open year-round, most daylight hours. 719-589-3032; www.rmii.com/gatorfarm. ✻

1987 houses sea lions and other arctic wildlife, including Klondike and Snow, polar bears rejected by their mother and raised by the zoo staff. Tropical Discovery is an $11.5 million exhibit topped by a huge glass pyramid soaring over plants, animals and a pre-Columbian temple ruin.

Some 1.6 million visitors annually come to visit creatures from all over the globe at 2300 Steele St., Denver 80205. Open daily April–Sept., 9 A.M. TO 6 P.M.; Oct.–March, 10 A.M.–5 P.M. $3–$8. (303) 376-4800.

Other Animal Centers. Several sites offer specialized animal-viewing opportunities. They include:

Big Cats of Serenity Springs. P.O. Box 112, Calhan 80808; (719) 347-9200.

Prairie Wind Animal Refuge. 2111 County Road 150, Agate 80101; (303) 763-6130.

Raptor Center. 5200 Nature Center Road, Pueblo 81003; (719) 549-2414.

Wolf Refuge. P.O. Box 211, Silver Cliff 81249; (719) 746-2919.

Buffalo preserves. See Buffalo entry.

Colorado News Highlights, 2000-2001

The following is a collection of news items from mid-2000 to mid-2001. *The Colorado Almanac*™ wishes to credit stories printed in the *Rocky Mountain News* and *The Denver Post* as the primary sources of information for Colorado News Highlights.

Colorado Goes for Bush. Coloradans went to the polls Nov. 7, 2000, and gave their state's eight electoral votes for president to Republican George W. Bush. Bush won 883,858 votes (50.7 percent of the votes cast for president), trailed by Democrat Al Gore with 738,379 (42.4 percent). Ralph Nader of the Green Party received 91,461 votes (5.3 percent); the Reform Party's Pat Buchanan picked up 10,482 votes (0.64 percent).

While Bush won a majority of votes, the traditional Democratic urban strongholds of Denver, Boulder and Pueblo went for Gore. All six Colorado U.S. representatives—Democrats Diana DeGette and Mark Udall, and Republicans Joel Hefley, Scott McInnis, Bob Schaffer and Tom Tancredo—easily won reelection.

In the state Legislature, Democrats seized control of the Senate for the first time in nearly 40 years, although Republicans maintained control of the House of Representatives.

Voters were called on to settle a potpourri of ballot questions. They said yes to the medical use of marijuana (53.6 percent voted in favor) and to additional school funding (52.7 percent).

Voters also approved participation in a multistate lottery (51.6 percent) and a property tax reduction for senior citizens (53.8 percent). They also voted to require background checks for weapons purchases at gun shows (see next item).

The affirmative mood ended when it came to ballot questions on certain other tax cuts, on a local citizen growth management plan and on a proposal to use excess state revenue for math and science education. Those initiatives lost at the polls.

Columbine Killings Prompt Gun-Law Reform. Coloradans by a two-to-one margin voted to close a gun-law loophole allowing unregulated sales at gun shows.

The measure on the November 7, 2000, ballot received approval of 70 percent of those voting. It requires background checks of purchasers at gun shows.

Voters went to the polls with the memory of April 20, 1999, when students Eric Harris, 18, and Dylan Klebold, 17, walked into Columbine High School in the Denver suburb of Jefferson County and opened fire on their classmates. Twelve students and one teacher died in the gunfire before the killers took their own lives.

According to the Jefferson County sheriff, some of the weapons used had been purchased at gun shows.

Columbine, in an affluent suburb, is a modern school of 1,900 students and 150 staff members. After the shooting, the library where some of the killings took place was demolished and rebuilt.

Colorado Gets Two New National Parks. Two Colorado treasures have joined the ranks of America's national parks. Black Canyon of the Gunnison National Park and Great Sand Dunes National Park were upgraded from their previous status as national monuments.

President Clinton in October 1999 signed the law approving the new designation for Black Canyon of the Gunnison, the deep and spectacular gorge in west-central Colorado.

Congress in October 2000 approved national park status for Great Sand Dunes, the remarkable landscape of windblown dunes rising as high as 750 feet above the valley floor in southern Colorado's San Luis Valley near Alamosa. President Clinton signed the law a month later.

Sheridan Steele, superintendent at Black Canyon of the Gunnison, said increased entrance fees will be used to improve interpretive sites such as the South Rim Visitor Center, with its spectacular view 2,200 feet down into the canyon.

The new park becomes the centerpiece of a connected family of protected lands, including Gunnison Gorge National Conservation Area, Black Canyon of the Gunnison Wilderness Area and Curecanti National Recreation Area.

Conservation efforts in the area are focusing on the Gunnison sage grouse (*Centrocercus minimus*) and Gunnison's prairie dog (*Cynomys gunnisoni*).

Denver Dedicates Commons Park.

Denver's birthplace—the confluence of the South Platte River and Cherry Creek—is the site of the city's new Commons Park. Mayor Wellington E. Webb dedicated the 26-acre, $20 million park on July 11, 2000.

Commons Park may be the shiniest new park addition, but it's not the only one during Webb's tenure, and far from the largest. Other recent acquisitions include 193 additional acres at Red Rocks Denver Mountain Park, 800 acres in the Lowry neighborhood, and 1,116 acres in the Stapleton neighborhood, former home of Denver's old airport, which closed in 1995.

The park picture also improved with transformation of the old Northside Sewage Treatment Plant into a 13-acre park with a heron pond and bird viewing blind—and relics of the old plant recycled as sculptural pieces.

Mayor Robert W. Speer, who presided from 1904 to 1918, was renowned as a park builder who doubled Denver's parklands

from about 500 acres to more than a thousand acres. Mayor Webb's administration has surpassed Speer's acquisition record by adding more than 2,300 new park acres.

Littleton Train Station Is Reborn.

Littleton emerged in the 1870s as a streetcar suburb of Denver. Streetcars and passenger trains served the town until rail service was abandoned in the 1950s. The stations of the Denver & Rio Grande Railroad and the Santa Fe Railroad closed their doors.

The Santa Fe depot has been recycled as an art gallery, and the D&RG depot was reincarnated in 2000 as the Littleton station for the first suburban light rail line of the Denver Regional Transportation District. This alternative to congested highways between Denver and Littleton mostly follows the old rail route.

Littleton celebrated the reopening with a huge welcome party at the reborn station, which once again greeted commuters. The restored stone depot displays a mural celebrating Littleton's past as a grain milling hub that became a popular, prosperous and progressive Denver suburb. With an average of 32,000 riders a day, the Littleton line was running at 42 percent over ridership projections.

Massacre Site Gets Federal Designation.

The southeastern Colorado location of the infamous Sand Creek Massacre of Native Americans has been designated a national historic site.

President Clinton signed legislation in October 2000 creating Sand Creek National Historic Site. The legislation was written and championed by Colorado U.S. Sen. Ben Nighthorse Campbell, a member of the Cheyenne tribe that was a victim of the massacre.

At the site on Nov. 29, 1864, Colorado troops under command of Col. John M. Chivington attacked an encampment of

Cheyenne and Arapaho. When the carnage ended, an estimated 163 Natives, mostly women, children and old men, lay dead. (See entry for Sand Creek Massacre.)

Colorado Loves Its SUVs. One out of every five drivers in Colorado is behind the wheel of an SUV—a sport utility vehicle—with Ford Explorers and Ford Expeditions leading the parade.

The ever-larger SUVs have been known to intimidate motorists in smaller cars who cannot see over or around the behemoths, which are noted for high gas consumption and the strength to demolish sedans that cross their path.

The SUVs of today are the grandchildren of World War II Willys Jeeps, International Harvester Scouts and AMC Jeep Commandos. The modern power-wagons proliferated in the 1990s, with sales jumping 71 percent between 1992 and 1997. Inspired initially by the popularity of Chrysler Motor Co.'s Jeep Cherokee, nearly every other car maker, even BMW, Cadillac, Lincoln and Mercedes, began making SUVs during the 1990s.

In 2000, the most popular SUVs in Colorado, listed in order of most vehicles sold, were:

1. Ford Explorer
2. Ford Expedition
3. Jeep Grand Cherokee
4. Toyota 4-Runner
5. Chevrolet Blazer
6. Dodge Durango
7. Jeep Cherokee
8. Jeep Wrangler
9. Chevrolet Tahoe
10. Nissan Pathfinder

Wildfires Ravage Colorado. Wildfires began early in the dry spring of 2000 and burned record amounts of acreage in Colorado. Among the hardest hit areas were Mesa Verde National Park and Boulder, Jefferson and Larimer counties.

On June 12, an out-of-control campfire started the Bobcat Fire in Larimer County, destroying 22 buildings and 11,000 acres. On the same day, a cigarette ignited the High Meadows Fire in Jefferson and Park counties, which consumed 58 structures and 12,000 acres. September rains finally ended Colorado's costliest fire season.

Throughout the West that year, wildfires burned nearly 7 million acres and firefighting costs approached $1 billion.

Developers Recycle Stapleton Airport Site. Stapleton International Airport is now history, but the former Denver airfield site is coming back to life as a $4 billion community development project. Only the parking garages and control tower of the airport survive as the old landmarks of a new neighborhood scheduled to begin opening in 2002. Quebec Square, the initial 750,000-square-foot commercial development, will open with a Home Depot, a Super Wal-Mart and a Starbucks.

Forest City Enterprises, the Cleveland, Ohio-based developer, is nationally noted for redevelopment projects such as the new corporate headquarters for the *New York Times* in Times Square. When completed by around 2020, the entire Stapleton community is expected to have 12,000 homes, 30,000 residents and employment for 35,000 people.

Bounded roughly by Quebec Street on the west, Montview Boulevard on the south, Rocky Mountain Arsenal National Wildlife Refuge on the north and Havana and Peoria streets on the east, the 4,700-acre development will have considerable open space, including the Sand Creek and Westerly Creek greenways.

The name "Stapleton" is causing some concern. Denver Mayor Benjamin Franklin Stapleton, who opened the airfield in 1929 as Denver Municipal Airport, was a member of the Ku Klux Klan, which endorsed him as their candidate. Consequently many people are insisting that Denver's huge new neighborhood of the future be given another name.

Number of Homeless on the Rise.

As the average price of buying a new or used home climbed to over $200,000 in Colorado, the number of homeless in metro Denver increased to 7,689. This official count of the six-county metro area in mid-September 2000 was released in 2001 by the Metropolitan Homeless Initiative and the Colorado Department of Human Services.

The 7,689 figure represents a 33 percent increase over the number of homeless counted for the same area in 1999. The average homeless person, according to the survey, is working at least one job, helping to raise children, and living in a motel or motor vehicle.

Colorado Avalanche Ices 2001 Stanley Cup.

Beating the New Jersey Devils took all seven games, but the Colorado Avalanche of the National Hockey League would have waited till hell froze over. The Avs' convincing 3 to 1 victory in the seventh game brought the Stanley Cup, the oldest and most hallowed trophy in professional sports, to the Mile High City.

The party that night in Denver got out of hand as some celebrants lit bonfires, broke windows, rocked cars and threw beer bottles at police. Dozens of arrests were made, and police used tear gas and pepper spray to combat the mobs of mostly young adults in Lower Downtown Denver.

The crowd that showed up a couple of days later for a victory parade was much better-behaved. An estimated 250,000 fans came out in 91-degree heat to honor the new champs. Chants of "We want Joe" drowned out speeches by Gov. Bill Owens and Denver Mayor Wellington Webb at a rally in front of the City and County Building. Finally, team captain Joe Sakic appeared, holding high the silver Stanley Cup.

The applause and cheering for Sakic surpassed even the earlier outburst for Ray Bourque, the stellar defenseman. Bourque had skated for 21 years for the Boston Bruins before asking to be traded to a contender for his final season. Bourque got his wish—and now has his name inscribed on the Stanley Cup.

The Avalanche, a team that previously played as the Quebec Nordiques, has been on the ice in Denver since 1995. The Avs also won the championship and the Stanley Cup in 1996—the first major-league championship in any sport by a Colorado team.

Suggested Reading

Abbott, Carl, Stephen J. Leonard and David McComb. *Colorado: A History of the Centennial State*, 3rd ed. Niwot: University Press of Colorado, 1994. 454 pp.

Benson, Maxine; illus. by Robin Richards. *1001 Colorado Place Names*. Lawrence: University Press of Kansas, 1994. 237 pp.

Cassels, Stephen E. *The Archaeology of Colorado*. Boulder: Johnson Books, 1983. 325 pp.

Caughey, Bruce, and Dean Winstanley. *The Colorado Guide*, rev. ed. Golden: Fulcrum Publishing, 2001. 671 pp.

Colorado Atlas and Gazetteer, 4th ed. Yarmouth, Maine: Delorme, Inc., 1998. 104pp.

Conly, Marc; photos by Nancy Conly. *Waterfalls of Colorado*. Boulder: Pruett Publishing, 1993. 342 pp.

Danilov, Victor J. *Colorado Museums and Historic Sites: A Colorado Guide Book*. Niwot: University Press of Colorado, 2000. 445 pp.

Davidson, Wilma R. *Colorado: The State We're In*. Denver: League of Women Voters of Colorado, 1995. 127 pp.

Gehres, Eleanor M., Sandra Dallas, Maxine Benson and Stanley Cuba, eds. *The Colorado Book*. Golden: Fulcrum Publishing, 1993. 414 pp.

Hafen, LeRoy R., ed. *Colorado and Its People*, 4 vols. New York: Lewis Historical Publishing Co., 1948.

Koch, Don. *An Endless Vista: Colorado's Recreational Lands*. Boulder: Pruett Publishing, 1982. 134 pp.

Koch, Don. *The Colorado Pass Book: A Guide to Colorado's Backroad Mountain Passes*, 3rd ed. Boulder: Pruett Publishing, 2000. 125 pp.

Noel, Thomas J. *Buildings of Colorado*. New York: Oxford University Press, 1997. 688 pp.

Noel, Thomas J. *Colorado: A Liquid History & Tavern Guide to the Highest State*. Golden: Fulcrum Publishing, 1999. 254 pp.

Noel, Thomas J., Paul F. Mahoney and Richard E. Stevens. *Historical Atlas of Colorado*. Norman: University of Oklahoma Press, 1993 (2000 paperback). 160 pp.

Whiteside, James. *Colorado: A Sports History*. Niwot: University Press of Colorado, 1999. 494 pp.

Wolle, Muriel S., *Stampede to Timberline: The Ghost Towns and Mining Camps of Colorado*, 3rd ed. Denver: Sage Books, 1994. 544 pp.

The WPA Guide to 1930s Colorado, new introduction by T. J. Noel. Lawrence: University Press of Kansas, 1987. 511 pp. (This book is a reprint of the best Colorado guide ever written, *Colorado: A Guide to the Highest State*, published in New York by Hastings House in 1941.)

Wynar, Bohdan S. *Colorado Bibliography*. Littleton: Libraries Unlimited, 1980. 565 pp.

Appendix: Colorado State Constitution Preamble, and Declaration of Rights

PREAMBLE

We, the people of Colorado, with profound reverence for the Supreme Ruler of the Universe, in order to form a more independent and perfect government; establish justice; insure tranquility; provide for the common defense; promote the general welfare and secure the blessings of liberty to ourselves and our posterity, do ordain and establish this Constitution for the "State of Colorado."

ARTICLE II, BILL OF RIGHTS

In order to assert our rights, acknowledge our duties, and proclaim the principles upon which our government is founded, we declare:

SECTION I. That all political power is vested in and derived from the people; that all government, of right, originates from the people, is founded upon their will only, and is instituted solely for the good of the whole.

SECTION 2. That the people of this State have the sole and exclusive right of governing themselves, as a free, sovereign and independent State; and to alter and abolish their constitution and form of government whenever they may deem it necessary to their safety and happiness, provided such change be not repugnant to the Constitution of the United States.

SECTION 3. That all persons have certain natural, essential and inalienable rights, among which may be reckoned the right of enjoying and defending their lives and liberties; that of acquiring, possessing and protecting property; and of seeking and obtaining their safety and happiness.

SECTION 4. That the free exercise and enjoyment of religious profession and worship, without discrimination shall forever hereafter be guaranteed; and no person shall be denied any civil or political right, privilege or capacity, on account of his opinions concerning religion; but the liberty of conscience hereby secured shall not be construed to dispense with oaths or affirmations, excuse acts of licentiousness or justify practices inconsistent with the good order, peace, or safety of the State. No person shall be required to attend or support any ministry of place of worship, religious sect, or denomination against his consent. Nor shall any preference be given by law to any religious denomination or mode of worship.

SECTION 5. That all elections shall be free and open; and no power, civil or military, shall at any time interfere to prevent the free exercise of the right of suffrage.

SECTION 6. That courts of justice shall be open to every person, and a speedy remedy afforded for every injury to person, property, or character; and that right and justice should be administered without sale, denial, or delay.

SECTION 7. That the people shall be secure in their persons, papers, homes and effects from unreasonable searches and seizures; and no warrant to search any place or seize any person or thing shall issue without describing the place to be searched, or the person or thing to be seized, as near as may be, nor without probable cause, supported by oath or affirmation, reduced to writing.

SECTION 8. That, until otherwise provided by law, no person shall, for a felony, be proceeded against criminally, otherwise than by indictment, except in cases arising in the land or naval forces, or in the militia when in actual service in time of war or public danger. In all other cases offenses shall be prosecuted criminally by indictment or information.

SECTION 9. That treason against the State can consist only in levying war against it, or in adhering to its enemies, giving them aid and comfort; that no person can be convicted of treason unless on the testimony of two witnesses to the same overt act, or on his confession in open court; that no person can be attainted of treason or felony by the General Assembly; that no conviction can work corruption of blood or forfeiture of estate; that the estates of such persons as may destroy their own lives shall descend or vest as in cases of natural death.

SECTION 10. That no law shall be passed impairing the freedom of speech; that every person shall be free to speak, write, or publish whatever he will on any subject, being responsible for all abuse of that liberty; and that all suits and prosecutions for libel, the truth thereof may be given in evidence, and the jury, under direction of the court, shall determine the law and the fact.

SECTION 11. That no ex post facto law, nor law impairing the obligation of contracts, or retrospective in its operation, or making any irrevocable grant of special privileges, franchises or immunities, shall be passed by the General Assembly.

SECTION 12. That no person shall be imprisoned for debt, unless upon refusal to deliver up his estate for the benefit of his creditors, in such manner as shall be prescribed by law, or in cases of tort or where there is a strong presumption of fraud.

SECTION 13. That the right of no person to keep and bear arms in defense of his home,

person and property, or in aid of the civil power when thereto legally summoned, shall be called into question; but nothing herein contained shall be construed to justify the practice of carrying concealed weapons.

SECTION 14. That private property shall not be taken for private use unless by consent of the owner, except for private ways of necessity, and except for reservoirs, drains, flumes or ditches on or across the lands of others, for agricultural, mining, milling, domestic or sanitary purposes.

SECTION 15. That private property shall not be taken or damaged, for public or private use, without just compensation. Such compensation shall be ascertained by a board of commissioners, of not less than three freeholders, or by a jury, when required by the owner of the property, in such manner as may be prescribed by law, and until the same shall be paid to the owner, or into court for the owner. The property shall not be needlessly disturbed, or the proprietary rights of the owner therein divested; and whenever an attempt is made to take private property for a use alleged to be public, the question whether the contemplated use be really public shall be a judicial question, and determined as such without regard to any legislative assertion that the use is public.

SECTION 16. That in criminal prosecutions the accused shall have the right to appear and defend in person and by counsel; to demand the nature and cause of the accusation; to meet the witnesses against him face to face; to have process to compel the attendance of witnesses in his behalf, and a speedy public trial by an impartial jury of the county or district in which the offense is alleged to have been committed.

SECTION 17. That no person shall be imprisoned for the purpose of securing his testimony in any case longer than may be necessary in order to take his deposition. If he can give security, he shall be discharged; if he cannot give security, his deposition shall be taken by some Judge of the Supreme, District, or County Court, at the earliest time he can attend, at some convenient place by him appointed for that purpose, of which time and place the accused and the attorney prosecuting for the people, shall have reasonable notice. The accused shall have the right to appear in person and by counsel. If he have no counsel, the Judge shall assign him one in that behalf only. On the completion of such examination the witness shall be discharged on his own recognizance, entered in before said Judge, but such deposition shall not be used if, in the opinion of the Court, the personal attendance of the witness might be procured by the prosecution, or is procured by the accused. No exception shall be taken to such deposition as to matters of form.

SECTION 18. That no person shall be compelled to testify against himself in a criminal case, nor shall any person be twice put in jeopardy for the same offense. If the jury disagree, or if the judgment be arrested after verdict, or if the judgment be reversed for error in law, the accused shall not be deemed to have been in jeopardy.

SECTION 19. That all persons shall be bailable by sufficient sureties, except for capital offenses, when the proof is evident or the presumption great.

SECTION 20. That excessive bail shall not be required, nor excessive fine imposed, nor cruel and unusual punishments inflicted.

SECTION 21. That the privilege of the writ of habeus corpus shall never be suspended, unless when, in case of rebellion or invasion, the public safety may require it.

SECTION 22. That the military shall always be in strict subordination to the civil power; that no soldier shall, in time of peace, be quartered in any house without the consent of the owner, nor in time of war except in the manner prescribed by law.

SECTION 23. The right of trial by jury shall remain inviolate in criminal cases; but a jury in civil cases in all courts, or in criminal cases in courts not of record, may consist of less than twelve men, as may be prescribed by law. Hereafter a Grand Jury shall consist of twelve men, any nine of whom concurring may find an indictment; provided, the General Assembly my change, regulate or abolish the grand jury system.

SECTION 24. That the people have the right peaceably to assemble for the common good, and to apply to those invested with the powers of government for redress of grievances, by petition or remonstrance.

SECTION 25. That no person shall be deprived of life, liberty, or property, without due process of law.

SECTION 26. That there shall never be in this State either slavery or involuntary servitude, except as a punishment for crime, whereof the party shall have been duly convicted.

SECTION 27. Aliens, who are or who may hereafter become bona fide residents of the State, may acquire, inherit, possess, enjoy and dispose of property, real and personal, as native born citizens.

SECTION 28. The enumeration in this Constitution of certain rights shall not be construed to deny, impair or disparage others retained by the people.

Index

National Historic Sites; National Register of Historic Places; Native Americans; individual entries

Hmong Americans, 21

hockey, 191–92

holidays, 104

hospitals, 104–6

hotels, 106–7

hot springs, 107

House of Representatives: Congressional district map, 57, 117; state, 116, 118–19; state district map, 117; U.S., 57–58

Hovenweep National Monument, 140

hypothermia, 107–8. *See also* mountain sickness

imports. *See* exports and imports

income per capita: counties with highest, 71; counties with lowest, 71; state, 7

information, tourist, 200–201

insect, state, 197

Irish Americans, 108–9

Italian Americans, 109–10

jackalopes, 110

jackrabbits, 110

Jacobs, Frances Wisebart, 110–11, 127

Japanese Americans, 21

judicial system, 111–12. *See also* Lindsey, Benjamin Barr

kayaking, 208–9

Ku Klux Klan, 112

labor, 112–13

lakes and reservoirs, 113–14, 115. *See also* rivers; sailing; water sports

Laotian Americans, 21

largest: counties by area, 7, 61; counties by population, 60; city, 7

lark bunting, 114–15

latest snowfall, 190

Leadville, 115–16

legislature, 116; districts, 117. *See also* elected officials; House of Representatives; Senate; voting

lesbians, 90

libraries, 116, 120–22

Lindsey, Benjamin Barr, 122

literature, 22. *See also* bookstores; libraries; writers

Little Raven, 122–23, 127, 130. *See also* Native Americans

livestock, 11–12

Longs Peak, 123

lost treasure, 124

Loveland, 124–25

lowest: per capita income for counties, 71; point, 7; precipitation in Denver, 7; temperatures, 7, 51

lynx, 45–46

magpies, 125

main streets, 125

mammal, state, 29, 197

maps, Colorado, 8–9; Congressional districts, 57; Native American territory, 147; rivers, 176; Scenic and Historic Byways, 184–85; ski areas, 188; state legislative districts, 117; state parks, 194–95

marmots, 126

Matchless Mine, 198

Mesa Verde National Park, 78, 141–42

mileage chart, 126, 128–29

military, 126–27. *See also* Air Force Academy

Millennial Heroes, 127, 130

mining, 130–31; coal, 52–53; gold, 77, 93–95; lost treasure, 124; Matchless Mine, 198; museums, 95, 135; silver, 186–87. *See also* labor; Leadville

Mint, U.S., 205–6

motor vehicles, 131–32

motto, state, 7, 197

Mount Evans, 132–33

Mount of the Holy Cross, 133

mountain lions, 45

mountain sheep, 29

mountains: 14,000-foot peaks, 85–86; Front Range, 87; Longs Peak, 123; Mount Evans, 132–33; Mount of the Holy Cross, 133; Pikes Peak, 159–60. *See also* glaciers; Grand Mesa; passes; place names; waterfalls

mountain sickness, 132. *See also* hypothermia

mule deer, 133–34

About the Author

Thomas Jacob "Dr. Colorado" Noel earned a B.A. in history and an M.A. in library science from the University of Denver, and an M.A. and Ph.D. in history from the University of Colorado. He is a professor of history at the University of Colorado at Denver, where he directs the Center for Public History and Preservation and Colorado Studies.

Tom has authored more than 90 articles and 25 books, including *Colorado: A Liquid History*; *Buildings of Colorado*; *Denver: Mining Camp to Metropolis*, with S. Leonard; *The City & The Saloon*; and *The Historical Atlas of Colorado*, with Richard Stevens and Paul Mahoney.

Tom writes the weekend "Dr. Colorado" column for a combined edition of the *Rocky Mountain News* and *The Denver Post*. Since 1976 he has conducted the Smithsonian Institution's annual grand tour of Colorado, "Railroading the Rockies," and he also leads saloon, cemetery, city and other tours.

Tom has received national recognition from the American Society of State and Local History and Who's Who in America. A former chairman of the Denver Landmark Preservation Commission, he currently serves on the National Register Review Board for Colorado and on the board of the Colorado Historical Society.

Dr. Colorado welcomes your comments, corrections and suggestions for the next edition of *The Colorado Almanac*™. His web sites are:

www.coloradowebsites.com/dr-colorado
www.denvergov.org/aboutdenver
www.coloradohistory.org